Studies in International Relations

(Second edition)

George Clarke
Frank Cooney
Irene Morrison
Graeme Pont

Pulse Publications

CONTENTS

The Politics of Development in Africa

The United States of America

The Republic of South Africa

The People's Republic of China

ACKNOWLEDGEMENTS

The authors and publishers would like to thank the following for permission to reproduce copyright material: Empics for photographs on pages 27, 28, 50, 55, 71, 100, 112, 113, 116, 125, 136, 139, 141, 144, 148, 152; Reuters/Finbar O'Reilly 16.

Published and typeset by
Pulse Publications
Braehead, Stewarton Road,
by Kilmaurs, Ayrshire
KA3 2NH

Printed and bound by
Thomson Colour Printers

British Library Cataloguing-in-Publication Data
A Catalogue record for this book is available from the British Library

ISBN 0 948 766 97 2
© Clarke, Cooney, Morrison & Pont 2006

CHAPTER 1

Economic, political and social factors affecting development

Africa is a continent of approximately 690 million people made up of fifty three independent countries, amongst which are fifteen of the least developed nations in the world. Seventy percent of Africa's population subsist on less than $2 a day, yet Africa abounds with natural resources, minerals, land and sea-ports. How can this be?

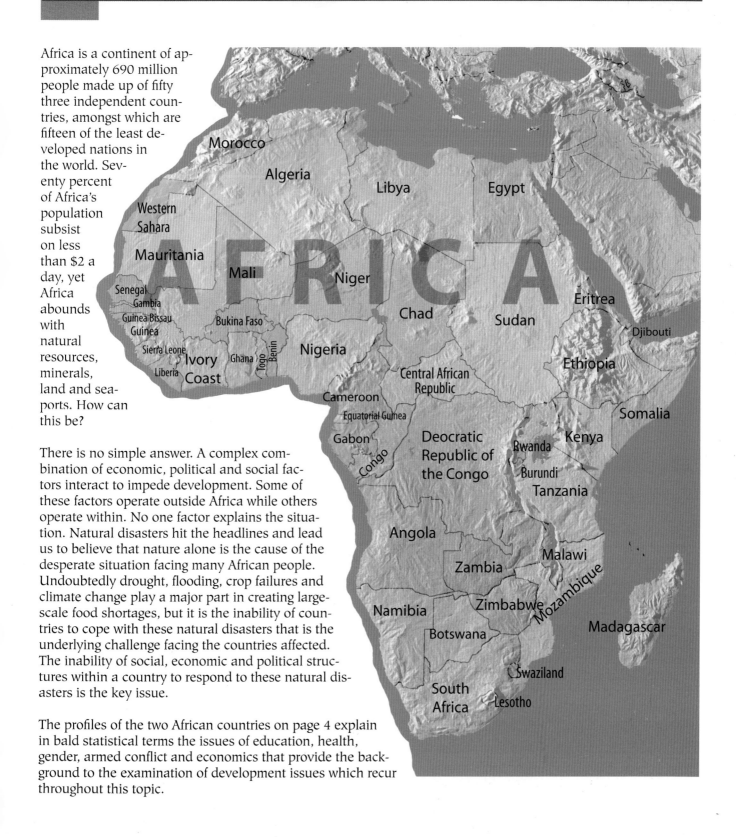

There is no simple answer. A complex combination of economic, political and social factors interact to impede development. Some of these factors operate outside Africa while others operate within. No one factor explains the situation. Natural disasters hit the headlines and lead us to believe that nature alone is the cause of the desperate situation facing many African people. Undoubtedly drought, flooding, crop failures and climate change play a major part in creating large-scale food shortages, but it is the inability of countries to cope with these natural disasters that is the underlying challenge facing the countries affected. The inability of social, economic and political structures within a country to respond to these natural disasters is the key issue.

The profiles of the two African countries on page 4 explain in bald statistical terms the issues of education, health, gender, armed conflict and economics that provide the background to the examination of development issues which recur throughout this topic.

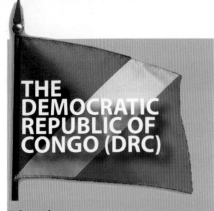

THE DEMOCRATIC REPUBLIC OF CONGO (DRC)

Education
Male literacy	73%
Female literacy	50%
Primary school enrolment:	
Boys	53%
Girls	47%
Secondary school enrolment:	
Boys	24%
Girls	13%

Health
Life expectancy	42 years
People with HIV/AIDS	4.2%
Immunisation levels:	
TB	68%
Polio	55%
Measles	54%
Children protected by a malaria net	12%

Economy
*GNI per capita	$100
*GDP growth	-6.4% per annum
Defence spending (percentage of GDP)	18%

Women
at risk of death in childbirth	1 in 3
with a skilled birth worker present at childbirth	61%
with HIV education	45%

Comments

There has been a history of armed conflict in DRC which only ended recently. Over 3.3 million people were killed in less than five years. The infrastructure, medical and educational services have been devastated and largely remain so. In 2002 there was a major cholera epidemic, which recurred in 2005. Only 46% of the population has access to safe drinking water and in rural areas, where 68% of the population live, only 23% have access to adequate sanitation.

ZAMBIA

Education
Male literacy	79%
Female literacy	72%
Primary school enrolment	
Boys	66%
Girls	66%
Secondary enrolment	
Boys	27%
Girls	21%

Health
Life expectancy	33 years
People with HIV/AIDS	16.5%
Immunisation levels	
TB	94%
Polio	80%
Measles	84%
Children protected by a malaria net	7%

Economy
GNI per capita	$380
GDP growth	-0.9% per annum
Defence spending (percentage of GDP)	9.5%

Women
at risk of death in childbirth	1 in 19
with a skilled birth worker present at childbirth	43%
with HIV education	67%

Comments

Zambia's economy is based primarily on agriculture and mining. The country has recently experienced prolonged dry spells which have affected half of Zambia's provinces, resulting in approximately 2.3 million people in need of emergency food aid. The government has recently launched an appeal for help and is currently in receipt of emergency aid from the United Nations and Non-Governmental Organisations.

THE UNITED KINGDOM

To give a perspective of what the profiles of The Democratic Republic of Congo and Zambia mean it is useful to contrast them with that of the United Kingdom.

Education
Male literacy	99%
Female literacy	99%
Primary school enrolment:	
Boys	100%
Girls	100%
Secondary school enrolment:	
Boys	100%
Girls	100%

Health
Life expectancy	78 years
People with HIV/AIDS	0.1%
Immunisation levels	
TB	100%
Polio	91%
Measles	80%

Economy
GNI per capita	$28,350
GDP growth	2.4% per annum
Defence spending (percentage of GDP)	7%

Women
at risk of death in childbirth	1 in 3800
with a skilled birth worker present at childbirth	99%
with HIV education	100%

Comments

The UK is the fourth most successful economy in the world. Wages and prices are amongst the highest in Europe. The UK suffers from a shortage of skilled labour and key professionals such as doctors, teachers, nurses and dentists, many of whom are now recruited from overseas, attracted by the high wages on offer.

---

*GNI This is the average value of goods produced by a worker in a year for a country.

*GDP This is the average value of goods and services produced in a year by a worker.

ECONOMIC FACTORS AFFECTING DEVELOPMENT

THE EFFECTS OF DEBT

Each year Africa faces demands of over $14.5 billion in debt repayments. Many African governments have borrowed money from the International Monetary Fund (IMF) or the World Bank to finance development. Changes in interest rates, fluctuating market prices for goods sold abroad and the dependency on a limited range of cash crops has meant it has been difficult, if not impossible, to repay these debts.

The IMF attaches conditions when lending money, which can lead to extreme hardship for the countries involved. For example, the IMF has demanded the end to subsidised state marketing boards in Africa which guaranteed countrywide stable prices throughout the year. Furthermore, the IMF can insist that education programmes and health programmes are cut to reduce government spending. If such conditions are not followed, then finance can be stopped. Ghana faces this dilemma because education and health are no longer free in order to help to repay the national debt.

Drop The Debt

There is a worldwide campaign to cancel the debts of poor countries. The British government has cancelled 100% of the debt owed directly to it by agreeing to cover its share of the debts these countries owe to the World Bank and the African Development Bank. In 2005 there were massive demonstrations and campaigns to get the G8 countries to cancel world debt.

Campaigners draw attention to countries where debt was cancelled and the positive effects it has had:

£ In Benin, 54% of the money saved has been spent on health.

£ In Tanzania the government was able to abolish primary school fees leading to a 66% increase in attendance.

£ In Mozambique all children received free immunisation.

£ In Uganda, 2.2 million people gained access to clean water.

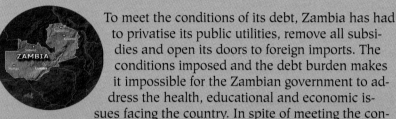

An example of how debt can cripple a country is to be found in Zambia which was once one of Africa's richest countries. Now it is lower placed on the Human Development Index (HDI) than it was in 1975. Along with Zimbabwe, it has the lowest life expectancy in the world at just 33 years; it is expected that half the population will die of AIDS. In 2004 Zambia used 7.35% of its GDP to repay its debt—twice as much as it spent on education. Schools now have average class sizes of seventy pupils and 40% of rural women are illiterate.

case study **ZAMBIA**

To meet the conditions of its debt, Zambia has had to privatise its public utilities, remove all subsidies and open its doors to foreign imports. The conditions imposed and the debt burden makes it impossible for the Zambian government to address the health, educational and economic issues facing the country. In spite of meeting the conditions imposed by lenders, by 2003 Zambia's debt had been reduced by only 5%.

The scale of the debt problem is huge as can be seen from Figures 1.1 and 1.2 below.

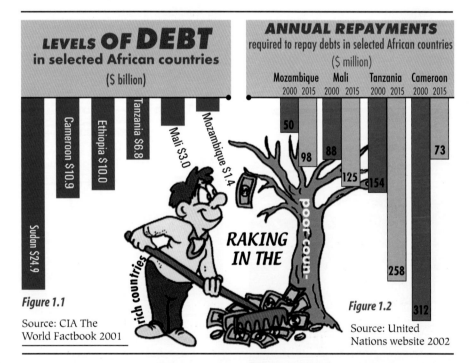

LEVELS OF DEBT in selected African countries ($ billion)

Cameroon $10.9 — Ethiopia $10.0 — Tanzania $6.8 — Mali $3.0 — Mozambique $1.4 — Sudan $24.9

RAKING IN THE poor countries — rich countries

Figure 1.1
Source: CIA The World Factbook 2001

ANNUAL REPAYMENTS required to repay debts in selected African countries ($ million)

	Mozambique		Mali		Tanzania		Cameroon	
	2000	2015	2000	2015	2000	2015	2000	2015
	50	98	88	125	154		73	258

312

Figure 1.2
Source: United Nations website 2002

In August 2004, American demonstrators linked the need to drop the debt with the need to fight AIDS.

The Heavily Indebted Poor Countries (HIPC) Initiative

The World Bank and IMF launched the HIPC Initiative in 1996 to provide relief from debt to HIPC countries. This initiative prompted the British government to ask the G8 countries to further cancel debt and by July 2004, twenty seven countries had already agreed to begin providing relief from debt. However, for HIPC countries to qualify they had to demonstrate that for the previous three years they had been following sound economic policies and poverty reduction programmes. Relief of more then $70 billion was agreed, but as Make Poverty History pointed out, in 2005 little more than 10% of the debt owed by HIPCs had been cancelled.

THE EFFECTS OF CASH CROPS AND TERMS OF TRADE

A condition of receiving a loan from the World Bank or IMF is usually the requirement of growing crops to sell on the open market for profit. On the surface this seems an eminently sensible way for a country to generate income. However, there are associated drawbacks.

In Sudan a condition of receiving a loan was the growing of cotton for export and importing cheaper American grain for food. The bottom fell out of the cotton market so there was not enough money to buy grain to eat. So from being a self-sufficient country that actually had a food surplus, Sudan faced famine.

Mozambique was once the world's leading producer of raw cashew nuts. In the 1970s its government banned the export of raw cashews in favour of selling the processed

THE EFFECTS OF CURRENCY SPECULATION AND INTEREST RATES

In the global market in which we live, decisions or actions taken thousands of miles away can have profound and unexpected consequences for African countries. The finance market is one such example. It is estimated that over $1.85 trillion changes hands every day in the finance markets. Speculators buy and sell currency for profit. For example, one morning the UK pound might be worth 1.47 euros but by afternoon it might have gone down to 1.40. A person who bought £100 worth of euros in the morning and sold them for pounds in afternoon when the rate was 1.40 euros would make a profit of £5. Imagine the profits that can be made when millions of dollars are traded.

Unfortunately, such speculation can have disastrous effects on the economies of African countries. If dealers fear a currency is losing value, a herd instinct can take over with everyone trying to offload that particular currency. Consequently, the value of the currency drops, resulting in imports being more expensive for the African country involved with the value of vital exports being worth less. In 1997–98 a currency crisis hit Asia, Latin America and Africa. The net result was 10 million lost jobs in eastern Asia, and in Brazil in 1999 $30 billion left the country as a consequence of currency dealing.

The Tobin Tax—A Possible Solution?

Nobel prize–winning economist James Tobin proposed a Currency Transactions Tax (CTT) which would put a tax on currency transactions of around 0.1%. This small charge could calm down damaging currency speculation while at the same time raising substantial sums of money to assist with development. The tax could fund a huge anti-poverty programme, for it is estimated that the tax would raise between $50 billion and $300 billion each year. To put this sum into perspective, aid currently given to Africa by rich countries amounts to $23 billion a year.

The tax has not yet been introduced, but the UN and EU are seriously considering the proposal as are a number of national governments. Chancellor Gordon Brown has stated that he has an "open mind" about the idea.

In Kenya during 1997–98 high interest rates on treasury bills (30%) attracted many investors. This inflow of foreign currency boosted the Kenyan economy, but when the interest rates fell the money left the country virtually overnight, leaving Kenya with considerable financial problems. This is a typical example of the problems faced by many African countries.

case study
Interest rates

variety. However, in the 1990s the World Bank abolished restrictions in the cashew market and Mozambique could not compete in the world market. The cashew nut industry collapsed and 90% of those employed in the industry lost their jobs.

The case of Mozambique highlights the precarious situation of relying too heavily on one or a few cash crops. In times of overproduction prices drop as the law of supply and demand comes into play. The production of cash crops is a controversial issue. It is true that income is generated but smaller farmers can lose out to larger concerns and the land available to grow food for domestic consumption becomes ever more limited.

Terms of Trade

Africa's share of world trade dropped from 6% in 1985 to 2% in 2005. Half of all food produced has rotted by the time it reaches the marketplace as a result of inadequate infrastructures. African producers do not compete on equal terms in world markets. The World Trade Organisation (WTO) insists on free markets, therefore subsidies by African governments to their producers are not permitted nor are import taxes that would inhibit free and equal trade.

In reality, African producers are significantly disadvantaged. For example, US cotton farmers receive $4 billion in subsidies while European farmers are subsidised through the Common Agricultural

Policy (CAP). This can produce surpluses which are dumped cheaply in African countries, undercutting local producers and putting them out of business.

If we take the example of sugar, the issues involved become apparent. In Africa it costs approximately £75 to produce a tonne of sugar but in Europe the cost is around £300. This on the surface would seem to work to the benefit of African farmers. However, two factors work against this: the CAP subsidises European sugar producers annually with £550 million; secondly, the EU applies huge tariffs on imported African sugar making it impossible for producers in Malawi or Mozambique to compete and sell their sugar in Europe.

POLITICAL FACTORS AFFECTING DEVELOPMENT

THE EFFECTS OF ARMED CONFLICT

Along with HIV/AIDS and malaria, armed conflicts are now a leading cause of world hunger. The number and the scale of conflict-related food shortages is increasing. The Food and Agriculture Organisation (FAO) reported in 2004 that in 15% of cases during 1986–1993, conflict was cited as the main cause of food emergencies while during the period 1992–2003 it accounted for a massive 35%.

Armed conflict leads to food shortages on a large scale and for long periods of time destroys any prospect of economic and social development. In recent years there have been major armed conflicts in Sudan, Rwanda, Mozambique, Somalia and the Democratic Republic of Congo, to name but a few. The effects of armed conflict are catastrophic for the countries involved and it can take decades to reconstruct after the conflict has ceased.

The scale of the problem was identified in the Commission for Africa Report (published in 2005) which said, " Wars are expensive not only in the cost to human life but also in damage to buildings, roads, homes and land. Rebuilding costs for the Democratic Republic of Congo are estimated at $20 billion. The genocide ten years ago in Rwanda cost $1 billion in terms of damage to property alone." The report goes on to say that after the fighting stops, "Women who have been caught up in the war have to be helped since rape and sexual violence is widespread." Furthermore, the authors of the report go on to say, "It is not only roads and buildings which need rebuilding. Trust needs to be built up between sections of the community."

THE EFFECT OF BAD GOVERNANCE AND KLEPTOCRACY

The Commission for Africa Report is unambiguous in identifying bad governance as a key issue in explaining lack of development in many African countries: "A key difficulty for Africa in the past forty years has been the weakness of governance." Bad governance means that

➡ the police cannot be trusted,

➡ taxes are not efficiently collected,

➡ the government cannot be trusted to deliver key services,

➡ there is corruption,

➡ human rights are abused,

➡ and the legal system is not independent.

A young person from Ethiopia sums up the situation in the Commission for Africa Report: "We know some officials … who became well-off immediately after they took up a position in aid distribution."

Kleptocracy can go hand in hand with bad governance. Kleptocracy describes a situation where an elite group, and/ or a dictator, exercise their power to the benefit of themselves at the expense of the population at large. Funds or aid are diverted to equip the military who will ensure the government remains in power. Corruption is ignored because this keeps officials content with the present ruling elite since their well-being is linked to those in power. Those who support the regime are rewarded while those who do not suffer. Essential services are denied the money needed because funds are used to maintain the corrupt political system. In Nigeria, the late dictator General Sani Abacha succeeded in stealing between $1 billion and $3 billion in five years.

In Sudan the Christian south was persecuted by the Muslim government in the north until the civil war ended in 2005 and in Zimbabwe today those who do not support President Robert Mugabe suffer mercilessly as the case study on page 9

The Results of Armed Conflict

An enormous number of major issues confront countries which are involved in armed conflict, including the following:

✳ Millions of people can be uprooted from their homes and land, destroying any prospect of being self-sufficient, as has happened in Sudan.

✳ Vast numbers of refugees are created who are without food, water, shelter and medical support e.g. Rwanda.

✳ Emergency aid can be severely disrupted or temporarily stopped because of the dangers caused by shooting, fighting, attacks and the high-jacking of aid trucks. This was a problem in Sudan.

✳ Food becomes a weapon with soldiers destroying food and livestock, adopting a scorched earth policy whereby they burn to the ground any crops or food supplies they have not plundered. Wells are often contaminated or mined which forces farmers off the land.

✳ Governments will block food supplies in order to starve enemies. In 1998 in Sudan, thousands died in the south of the country because the government in the north acted in this way; overall, 1.2 million people became at risk of starvation.

✳ Essential money for social services is diverted to the war effort, so hospitals and schools suffer badly. During the Civil War in Sudan, the government was spending $550 million on the military, while the annual average GDP was only $1000.

✳ Disease and illness increase while the future economic development of the country is devastated because few children are being educated. The Democratic Republic of Congo (DRC) is still suffering in this way.

✳ Thousands of orphans are created while others are separated from their families.

✳ Many children are forced to become child soldiers, returning severely traumatised and unable to function normally and require long-term help. This is a serious issue facing DRC.

shows. However, there are African leaders who preside over democratic governments such as President John Kufuor of Ghana and President Festus Mogae of Botswana.

Harare, capital of Zimbabwe

Zimbabwe was once the economic leader in Africa and an exporter of food, but as a consequence of government mismanagement the country has experienced a series of economic disasters. Since 2000, the country has been unable to feed itself adequately. President Mugabe introduced a land distribution programme that resulted in most white farmers being driven off their land, crippling commercial farming. Vast areas of farmland remain unused.

Zimbabwe faces staggering economic problems which result largely from the actions of the government. The IMF has suspended financial assistance because of the government's failure to meet budgetary goals. The exchange rate has fallen dramatically and in 2005 inflation stood at 80%. In 2002 it was widely acknowledged that President Mugabe had rigged the election to ensure his re-election. In May 2004 Mugabe refused food aid claiming that Zimbabwe had enough food to feed its people. Independent analysts estimated that more than 5 million people faced famine. Political opposition has been crushed with thugs terrorising those who oppose Mugabe. There are severe restrictions on the press and foreign journalists are effectively banned from entering the country.

In July 2005 police and troops, under the direction of Mugabe, bulldozed 200,000 homes to "crack down on crime and illegal housing". (See the photo below.) Thousands of people were forced to sleep in the open without food or shelter. Opposition representatives dismiss Mugabe's claim saying that his goal was to scatter opponents and lessen the chances of a popular uprising. In the event almost 30,000 were arrested.

The Economic and Social Decline of Zimbabwe

factfile!

- Between 1999 and 2003 the economy declined by over 30%.

- In 2004 the unemployment rate was 80%.

- Per capita income was lower in 2004 than in 1980.

- Life expectancy fell from 56 years in 1985 to 33 years in 2003.

- 70% of the population live below the poverty line.

- Debt in 2004 stood at 52% of GDP.

- Child mortality rose more than 50% between 1990 and 2003. Currently, Zimbabwe has the fastest rise in infant mortality in the world.

- The rate of HIV infection is one of the highest in the world with 25% of the population being infected.

- Almost 1 in 5 children are orphans as a consequence of the HIV problem.

- In 1999 primary school completion rates were 83%. However, by 2003 this had declined to 63%.

- Inflation rose to 500% in 2004 and stood at 133% at the beginning of 2005.

- Foreign investment and tourism have collapsed.

- In January 2005, 50% of the population needed emergency food aid.

- Out of a population of 12 million, almost 4 million have emigrated abroad, many of whom are the skilled and educated people Zimbabwe needs.

SOCIAL FACTORS AFFECTING DEVELOPMENT

HEALTH ISSUES

HIV/AIDS

There is an HIV/AIDS epidemic in Africa. HIV/AIDS is one of the three major killers in Africa accounting for 2.3 million deaths in 2004. Approximately 25.4 million African people are living with HIV and over 12 million children in the continent have been orphaned as a result of AIDS. The statistical data relating to HIV/AIDS listed in the Factfile demonstrates in horrific detail the scale of the problem. Without doubt, HIV/AIDS is one of the biggest challenges confronting African countries.

HIV/AIDS places huge burdens on societies in Africa. Medical services cannot cope with demand with 50% of beds in some countries being given over to AIDS sufferers. The economy suffers and the social problems created are immense. As an example, a study undertaken by the Zimbabwe Farmers Union showed that the death of a breadwinner due to AIDS will cut the market output of maize on a small-scale farm by 61%. Similar results were obtained in further studies involving different crops.

Countries in Africa have lost, on average, ten to twenty years of life expectancy and the epidemic is worsening. Botswana, which has the world's second highest incidence of HIV, with 37.3% of its population affected, faces a rapid increase in extreme poverty amongst its poorest households. The poorest households could face a decline in their income of at least 13%. Life expectancy is only 39 years; it would have been 72 had it not been for AIDS. In 2001 at the UN General Assembly, the President of Botswana, Festus Mogae said, "we are threatened with extinction. People are dying in chillingly high numbers. It is a crisis of the first magnitude."

The vast majority of Africans living with HIV/AIDS are between the ages of 15 and 49, which is the

factfile!

HIV/ AIDS in Africa

- AIDS could slash the wealth of some African countries by as much as 20% according to an International AIDS Conference in Durban.
- If an African country has 20% or more of its population infected then GDP can decline by up to 2% each year.
- 75% of all people in the world infected by AIDS live in Africa.
- In some African countries, AIDS is the major cause of children being orphaned.
- Half of all people with HIV become infected before they are aged 25.
- HIV/AIDS undermines the caring capacity of families and communities by deepening poverty as a result of a loss of labour and the high costs of medical treatment and funerals.
- Food is often the main need of poor families living with HIV/AIDS. Malnutrition increases as HIV progresses.
- Without good food, the anti-retroviral drugs used to treat the condition are not as effective as they could be.
- Seven million of Africa's farmers have died of AIDS.
- TB is the main cause of death amongst AIDS sufferers.
- By 2020 it is estimated that HIV/AIDS will have killed 20% of southern Africa's farm workers.

Graves are dug in anticipation of the people who will die from AIDS-related illnesses in South Africa. 40% of all deaths in Zimbabwe are AIDS-related.

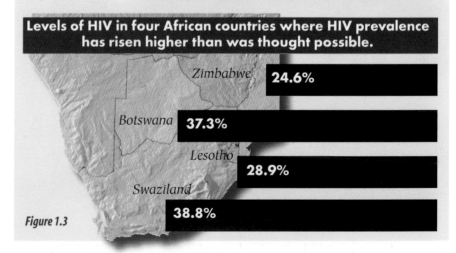

Levels of HIV in four African countries where HIV prevalence has risen higher than was thought possible.

Zimbabwe **24.6%**

Botswana **37.3%**

Lesotho **28.9%**

Swaziland **38.8%**

Figure 1.3

Reduction in market output due to AIDS deaths in Zimbabwe	
Crops	Reduction in Marketed Output
Maize	61%
Cotton	47%
Vegetables	49%
Groundnuts	47%
Cattle owned	29%

Table 1.1

Cost of HIV/AIDS on a tea estate in Malawi			
Description	Total Cost (£)	Related to HIV(%)	Cost of HIV (£)
Provision of medical services	22,275	25	5,569
Funeral costs	928	75	696
Death in service benefits	4691	100	4,691
Absence	14,875	25	3,719
Total	42,769		14,675

Table 1.2

prime of their working lives. The effects on the labour supply and on the economy in general are dramatic with employers, schools, factories and hospitals constantly having to find and train staff to replace those who have become too ill to work. This reality, coupled with a decline in school enrolment, sets in motion a set of circumstances with long-term implications. All areas of the public sector and the economy have been weakened with the prospects for future development looking bleak.

A concerning analysis comes from UN economists. In a report they stated, "A country whose growth rate is 2% a year in the absence of AIDS will increase its GNI per capita by 81% in one generation. Now suppose that AIDS reduces growth to just 1.5% per year. The same country will increase GNI by only 56% in the same period."

FARMING METHODS

Poor farming practices such as deforestation, overcropping and overgrazing are exhausting the land in many African countries. Increasingly, fertile farmland is under threat from erosion, salination or desertification. Added to these problems is poor irrigation and water management. These combined factors result in limited agricultural yields.

According to the FAO in its 2004 Food Insecurity Report, countries which were on track to meet the first Millennium Development Goal (see page 18) had one thing in common: they had significantly better than average agricultural growth. This emphasises the importance of appropriate farming methods and

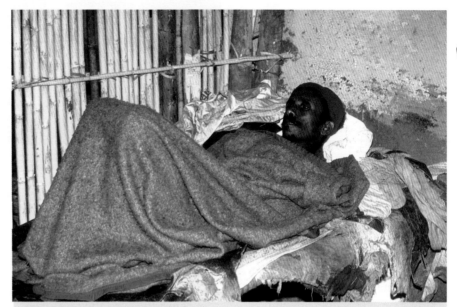

A bedridden malaria victim in Ethiopia

MALARIA

Malaria is Africa's biggest killer and the consequences for development are similar to those caused by HIV/AIDS. It is estimated that malaria accounts for economic losses amongst African countries totalling $12 billion per year. Malaria is also responsible for slowing economic growth by around 1.3% per annum.

Every year one million people die of malaria in the world—90% of them are in Africa. Every thirty seconds an African child dies as a result of malaria. 95% of all malaria cases are to be found in Africa.

The illness means that millions of people cannot work to their full potential with many others being unable to work at all. Malaria causes fever, chills, muscle ache and a range of flu-like symptoms. Kidney failure can develop and also brain disease and severe anaemia. Babies born to women infected with malaria have low birth weights which decreases their chances of survival.

good management of agricultural land.

Wood is the major fuel for many rural Africans and large numbers of trees are cut down to provide fuel and shelter every year. Land is also cleared to replace agricultural land which has failed due to overuse.

Trees are not replanted which results in deforestation which leads in turn to desertification with soil being blown away or washed away during the rainy season. Deforestation has hit Ethiopia hard with only 4% of its land covered by forest, down from a proportion of 40% in 1900.

LAND TENURE AND THE POSITION OF WOMEN

Custom and law have combined in many African countries to exclude women from the right to own or inherit land. Land is an important source of food, cash crops, water and fuel, and is critical for providing shelter. Those who control land and its resources have economic power.

In situations of marital conflict or divorce, the insecurity of a wife's position with regard to land is heightened. When such women return to their family villages they lose out on the land they have farmed and developed during the marriage because the land belongs to the husband.

Women play a key role in agriculture in Africa, producing up to 80% of food in addition to undertaking 90% of all household work. They play the major role in looking after animals and growing crops, not to mention fetching water for the needs of the family. In most African countries where school attendance is low, it is even lower for girls—less than 50% in many cases. As a consequence, women are excluded from agricultural training and information, despite the fact that they bear the biggest burden of agricultural work.

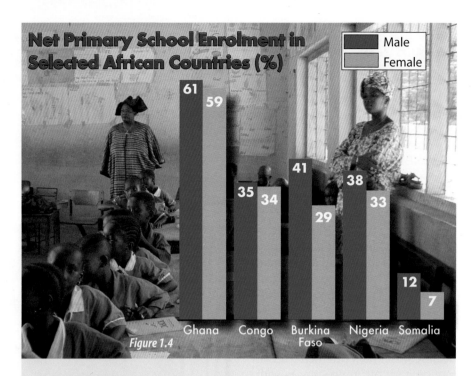

Net Primary School Enrolment in Selected African Countries (%)

Male
Female

	Ghana	Congo	Burkina Faso	Nigeria	Somalia
Male	61	35	41	38	12
Female	59	34	29	33	7

Figure 1.4

EDUCATION

As can be seen from the figures above, in many African countries enrolment levels at primary school are low for boys as well as for girls. Without adequate education a country's ability to prosper is severely limited. For many African children the prospect of undertaking any work other than unskilled labour is very slim. As we have seen, debt owed by countries has meant that free education has ended for thousands of children, further adding to the problem of achieving even the most basic level of education.

Without education, where do the doctors, teachers, engineers, scientists, skilled workers and others needed to assist development come from?

case study
GHANA

Women lack full land rights but constitute 52% of the agricultural labour force and produce 70% of subsistence crops. They represent 90% of the labour force involved in the marketing of farm produce. There is a growing scarcity of land which further affects their limited rights to land.

Women are often given poor or marginal land. Land clearing is done by men which gives them the control over how the land is used. In marriage a wife's duty is to work her husband's farm. She has no opportunity to farm for herself, or to decide what should be grown. If there is a divorce, the woman loses the land she has farmed because customary law does not recognise marital property. There is, therefore, little incentive in many cases for the woman to develop the land to its full potential because she could easily lose it all.

CHAPTER 2

Responses to development issues in Africa

International organisations, Non-governmental Organisations, individual countries and groupings of countries all have a part to play in addressing the issues faced by many African countries. There is no single silver bullet that can solve the complicated problems facing African people. Aid and support can come in many forms and what might be appropriate in one situation may not be suitable in another. At times, immediate short-term emergency aid is essential, while at other times a prolonged programme of long-term support and aid is required.

MULTILATERAL AID

This is aid provided by multi-national organisations such as the United Nations, the European Union or the African Union. The advantage of multilateral aid is that it is not usually tied and these organisations can operate on a large scale because of their economic power.

BILATERAL AID

This is government-to-government assistance where one country gives aid directly to another. The aid is usually long-term and part of a programme of development. At other times it can take the form of emergency assistance when disaster strikes. Increasingly, aid comes without strings attached, though much assistance still comes in the form of Tied Aid. (See page 14.)

NON-GOVERNMENTAL ORGANISATION (NGO) AID

This is provided by voluntary organisations such as Save the Children, Action Aid, Oxfam, Christian Aid etc. Often NGOs will target particular groups, such as children, or will provide specialist services. They are motivated by humanitarian concern and have no political ties.

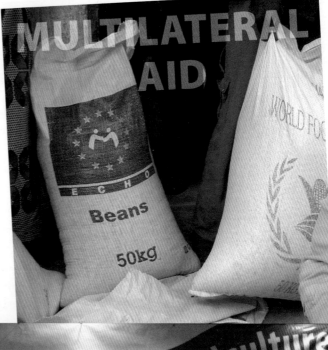

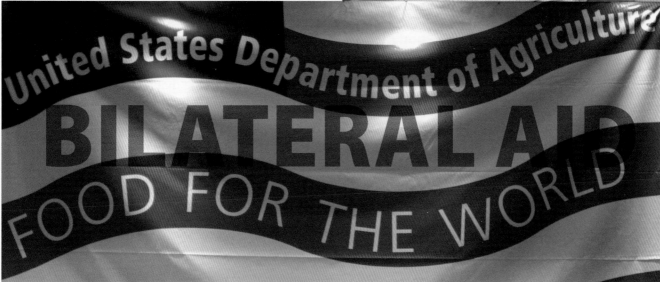

TIED AID

Tied Aid refers to aid given to a country but with conditions attached. Aid is conditional on the recipient purchasing goods and services from the donor country. Tied Aid has been a target of fierce criticism. It is estimated that tying aid can increase the prices of goods and services by up to 25%.

The Non-governmental Organisation, Actionaid, has summarised the main criticisms of tied aid as perceived by the organisation.

- Spending on goods and services takes place in the donor country not in the recipient country.

- It favours companies in the donor country rather than in the recipient country.

- It can increase the costs of aid programmes because the best price is ignored in favour of buying from the donor country.

- It excludes and discourages companies and businesses in the recipient country from participating so local people do not benefit.

- It results in an over-reliance on knowledge, technology and spare parts from the donor country. Self-reliance is discouraged, leading to aid dependency.

The United Nations (UN) has identified that a large majority of its members continue to tie aid. For example, approximately 75% of Canada's aid is tied which is the highest proportion in the world. The USA, Germany, Japan and France are also identified as being major givers of tied aid. Njoki Njoroge, director of a coalition of over 200 NGOs explained, "The USA makes sure that 80 cents in every dollar is returned to the home country (USA)." She cites an example of the USA insisting that expensive American tractors and other moving equipment had to be bought as part of a deal to improve the infrastructure in African countries.

FOOD AID

Food aid is essential when a disaster strikes such as the famines in Ethiopia, Sudan or in southern Africa. It offers an immediate solution, providing unparalleled short-term relief. Starving people are fed and tens of thousands of lives are saved. However, if food aid continues beyond an immediate crisis there can be a host of negative effects. Therefore it is essential to balance short-term and long-term needs.

Some Problems associated with Food Aid

- If it is not tightly controlled by the donor it can be misdirected by corrupt governments for their own uses, as happened recently in Sudan. It can be a cheap way of developed countries dumping surpluses. Speed of delivery can be slow, so food can fail to reach starving people in time. This is what prompted the Band Aid appeal in 1980. Governments were simply not acting quickly enough.

- If food aid continues after the crisis has past, local farmers are forced to compete with free food supplies. Farming collapses or recipient governments are less motivated to invest in developing agriculture.

- Food aid is a short-term solution only, otherwise recipients can become aid dependent and the long-term causes of food shortages go unaddressed.

AN EXAMPLE OF TIED AID—ERITREA

It was discovered that it would be significantly cheaper to rebuild Eritrea's network of railways using local experts and resources, rather than being forced to pay for foreign consultants, experts and materials. This could not be done because the donor had imposed the condition that all expertise and equipment had to be purchased from its organisations and companies.

Changing Perspectives Towards Tied Aid

In 2004, four nations provided more than 90% of their aid untied. Norway, Denmark and The Netherlands have untied most of their aid, while the UK untied all of its aid as of April 2001. The UK government is also working to encourage other governments to do likewise.

The Organisation for Economic Cooperation and Development (OECD), which is made up of twenty two developed countries, reached an agreement in 2001 to eliminate tied aid. The policy would result in half of the $8,000 billion given each year by its members being free from conditions.

Also in 2001 the European Union (EU) announced that it would support the OECD agreement, but only in relation to the world's forty eight least developed countries.

The Benefits of Untying Aid

● Competitive tendering would be encouraged, attracting bids from local companies.

● It would assist the development of the private sector in recipient countries, thereby creating more jobs.

● Local ownership would be encouraged.

● The value of aid would be worth more to the recipient.

● Dependency on outside support would be reduced, so self-sufficiency would be more likely.

Good Aid

Good Aid is targeted at the people most in need and is not tied. It involves local people who are consulted about possible solutions. It is monitored to ensure that it is delivering what was intended and goes hand in hand with improving good governance in the recipient country. Ultimately, good aid should address the issues that hamper development so that in the future, the recipient country will become self-sufficient and capable of dealing with the social and economic hurdles that get in the way of development.

MULTI-LATERAL RESPONSES TO DEVELOPMENT ISSUES

THE AFRICAN UNION (AU)

In 1999 the Heads of State and the governments of the Organisation of African Unity issued the Sirte Declaration, seeking the establishment of an African Union (AU). The purpose of the AU was

- to address the social, economic and political problems faced by many African countries,
- to accelerate economic development and
- to confront the problems created by globalisation.

In July 2002 the African Union was formally created.

The AU has become the most important African institution promoting one African voice to represent the whole continent. The AU seeks to create a strong and united Africa, with particular attention being paid to the needs of women and young people. Peace and security

Aims of the AU

● Eliminate the remaining problems left by colonialism.
● Seek to unite African states in a common cause creating solidarity amongst African countries.
● To accelerate economic development by coordinating and intensifying cooperation.
● Protect individual African states and their right to run their own affairs.
● To promote and encourage international cooperation, especially within the United Nations.
● To promote and defend African concerns on a variety of issues relevant to African people.

are viewed as essential elements in creating development and a united Africa. A number of initiatives have been adopted to realise these goals.

To what extent has the AU made progress?

There have been a number of initiatives in the short life of the AU. A common position was taken on addressing the debt crisis. In 2000 the Solemn Declaration laid down the principles for the promotion of democracy and good governance. The AU has also responded to challenges such as HIV/AIDS, malaria, refugees, landmines and controlling the spread of weapons in Africa.

Perhaps the most significant development has been the creation of the Peace and Security Council, designed to address regional conflicts in Africa which are the cause of so much poverty and suffering. Africa is therefore taking responsibility for addressing its own security problems and not relying on outside intervention which has often been inadequate or unsuccessful. For example, the outside world stood by as millions were killed during the Rwandan civil war. Now, the AU has declared that within ten days an African Standby Force can be sent to intervene in a crisis which has emerged.

Can the AU Meet its Aims?

Presently, the AU faces major hurdles. It is a very new organisation which is still finding its way. An AU official summed up this problem to a journalist in 2005 when he compared the AU to a house under construction with no roof yet. "People are asking us for protection from the rain and we are not ready yet."

Perhaps a more fundamental problem is finance. Will the AU ever be able to finance the initiatives it seeks to realise? So far, the record is not encouraging. (See Case Study Darfur.) In addition, the AU has proved reluctant to become involved in one of the major challenges to its aims in the shape of Robert Mugabe's violent oppression and economic destruction of Zimbabwe. (See Case Study on page 17.)

There have also been complaints that the administration of the AU is over-complex and does not allow for speedy decision making. Moreover, it is not yet clear where the AU will find the resources, both human and financial, to address the issues facing Africa. Without significant support and finance from the international community, a question mark must hang over the ability of the AU to realise its aims.

Darfur is an area of Sudan which in 2005 saw continuing massacres of civilians, wholesale destruction of communities, widespread raping of women and girls and appalling devastation at the hands of government-backed troops. These massive abuses of civil rights had been part of a campaign going back two years. The West had stood back and done nothing to stop the situation. Even in 2005 the international community had not sanctioned the Sudanese government or intervened. Instead, it called on the AU to send 3,320 observers and police to deter further outrages—but at that time no such AU force existed.

During February 2005 the AU had sent 1,400 troops to Darfur and had reached the target requested by the UN a month later.

case study
The AU & Darfur

An aerial view of an abandoned village in the desert of North Darfur in November 2004. Attacks by government-backed Arab militias forced more than 1.5 million Sudanese to flee their villages creating what the UN calls the world's worst humanitarian crisis.

However, by May, the AU was requesting foreign assistance to support its initiatives in Darfur. A huge equipment request was made including armoured vehicles, aircraft, trucks, cars and communication equipment. A European diplomat summed up the situation: "The principle is that the AU will furnish the soldiers and the command as long as its partners take charge of logistics and finance."

Clearly, the AU in this situation demonstrated its lack of finance and, importantly, its lack of equipment to undertake the task in Darfur. These problems were highlighted in January 2005 in a meeting of African leaders in Gabon where it was stated that the AU was trying to be more assertive in ending African wars but African states lacked the funds and equipment to carry out the actions necessary.

However, it must be said that in 2005 the AU force was bringing some stability to the region by heading off attacks, negotiating the release of hostages and providing enough security for some villagers to return to their homes. These are optimistic signs, but without more support and finance, the AU will be limited in what it can achieve.

ZIMBABWE

Zimbabwe was, until recently, one of the most successful countries in Africa. Today, over five million people face hunger. President Mugabe has refused food aid claiming there is no problem. His policies have directly led to the economic catastrophe that is Zimbabwe today. He does not allow effective political opposition and the press is severely censored. Most foreign journalists are banned because they report on the violence, intimidation, abuses of human rights and the economic disaster that Mugabe presides over. The EU and the USA maintain that Mugabe held on to power illegally by intimidation and poll-rigging and consequently they will not deal with the Zimbabwean government. However, AU observers at the elections endorsed the results despite huge opposition in Zimbabwe. As a result,

President Robert Mugabe addressing a UN meeting. He is accused of impoverishing many ordinary Zimbabweans.

the EU has been unable to hold meetings to discuss development assistance to Africa because AU leaders insisted that the EU could not be allowed to dictate that Zimbabwe could not attend.

The AU has been criticised heavily for its failure to act on Zimbabwe. The South African Catholic Bishops' Conference in August 2004 expressed the views of many when it issued the following statement: "The Zimbabwe-

an situation of starvation and malnutrition, wilful political violence and intimidation, and the immoral use of food aid by the Zimbabwean government demands stronger and transparent intervention by African governments through the AU." In July 2004 civil rights groups in Zimbabwe expressed deep disappointment that the AU had decided not to make public a report by the AU Commission on Human and People's Rights that was

highly critical of human rights in Zimbabwe. Reports of torture, illegal arrests of opposition MPs, and severe restrictions on civil liberties were highlighted.

Brian Kagoro, chief executive of the Crisis in Zimbabwe Coalition, a group of pro-democracy supporters, was quoted as saying, "The lack of action on the part of the AU is likely to dent its credibility. The body now runs the risk of not being taken seriously like its predecessor, the Organisation of African Unity."

THE UNITED NATIONS (UN)

The United Nations plays a significant role in attempting to deal with development issues in Africa. One of the main aims of the UN is co-operation in order to promote economic and social progress throughout the world and it is this aim that guides the work of the Specialised Agencies through which aid and assistance is channelled. The UN Declaration of Human Rights describes the rights that the citizens of all member countries should enjoy. Many of these rights are denied to African people as a result of social, economic and political factors and the UN Specialised Agencies work to create conditions whereby more men, women and children can share these rights such as equality, freedom, a decent standard of liv-

ing, access to education and health care and many others.

Millennium Development Goals

In September 2000 at the United Nations Millennium Summit, nearly 190 countries signed up to a range of goals and targets designed to reduce world poverty and hunger and improve life for people in developing countries. The goals were practical in nature and designed to encourage the international community to stop talking about making a difference and join together to start taking action.

Eighteen precise targets were also drawn up which the countries involved had to aim to meet in a specified time. Almost all the tar-

gets are to be achieved by 2015. While some progress is being made, in some of the affected developing countries progress is too slow, inconsistent and in some cases non-existent. In 2005, there were still more people living in poverty in sub-Saharan Africa than in 1990.

The Millennium Goals are undoubtedly designed to address the major problems facing many African countries and the setting of a time limit to achieve the goals means that those involved and those benefiting from assistance have a clear target to be reached. However, when we examine the targets designed to achieve the goals, some people say that the objectives set are too modest and will certainly not solve the problems of countries in Africa, though they

hunger will be halved. Undoubtedly this would mean progress, but what kind of progress? However, other targets are more ambitious such as ensuring that by 2015 all children will be able to complete a full course in primary education. Likewise, by 2015 the target is to reduce the under-five mortality rate by two-thirds.

Some of the targets indicate the huge problem of addressing the issues facing developing countries and acknowledge that it will take decades to eradicate them. For instance, by 2015 it is aimed to halt the spread of HIV/AIDS and malaria and then begin to reverse the number of cases. Clearly these are extremely long-term goals and for the foreseeable future, the situation will remain grim for millions of African people. It will take many years to judge the effectiveness of the Millennium Development Goals.

The United Kingdom government has adopted the Millennium Development goals and through the Department for International Devel-

opment (see below) has made the goals the main focus of its work.

A Critical View of the Millennium Goals

MAKE POVERTY HISTORY is the largest coalition ever assembled in the UK to fight against global poverty. In its campaign literature published in June 2005 it was critical of the progress made since 2000 in achieving the Millennium Goals. It argued that five years after the Millennium Goals were agreed, "The world is failing dismally to reach those targets."

It claims that at the current rate of progress:

☞ The pledge to halve the number of people living in absolute poverty will not be met until 2147.

☞ Primary education for all will not be achieved until 2130.

☞ The pledge of cutting infant mortality by two-thirds will not be reached until 2165.

will without question improve the situation. The targets to address extreme poverty and hunger state that by 2015 the number of people living on less than $1 a day and the proportion of people suffering from

DFID Department for International Development

THE WORK OF THE DEPARTMENT FOR INTERNATIONAL DEVELOPMENT

DFID (The Department for International Aid and Development) organises, plans and delivers all development assistance managed by the British government. The department is led by a Cabinet Minister who in 2005 was Hilary Benn. Mr Benn stated that the objective for his department was "To contribute to the achievement of the Millennium Development Goals and the elimination of world poverty." DFID is committed to long-term projects to assist development and tackle the underlying causes of poverty. In addition, DFID responds to short-term emergencies and food shortages. All DFID's development work is linked to the United Nations' eight Millennium Goals

which have a 2015 deadline. (See page 17.) DFID aid is not tied.

DFID works bilaterally and also multilaterally in partnership with other governments, the private sector, the World Bank, the United Nations and the EU. The department had a budget of almost $4 billion in 2004 and the Labour government is committed to continuing to increase this figure. However, it must be noted that the British government, along with other UN members, has signed up to allocate 0.70% of GNI to overseas aid but as can be seen from Figure 2.2 the UK allocates less than 0.40%. Also note that Figures 2.1 and 2.2 show that although the USA gives the largest amount in overseas aid in cash terms, as a

percentage of GNI the USA comes out bottom of the twenty two countries in Figure 2.2.

The DFID in Action

DFID works in over 150 countries, with 43% of the department's budget going to African countries. The country in Africa which received most aid in 2003–2004 was Tanzania which received $80 million in aid. 50% of the DFID budget of £3,965 billion was spent on bilateral assistance. Thirteen of the top twenty recipients of bilateral aid were African countries which indicates the nature of the problems facing Africa. (See Table 2.1)

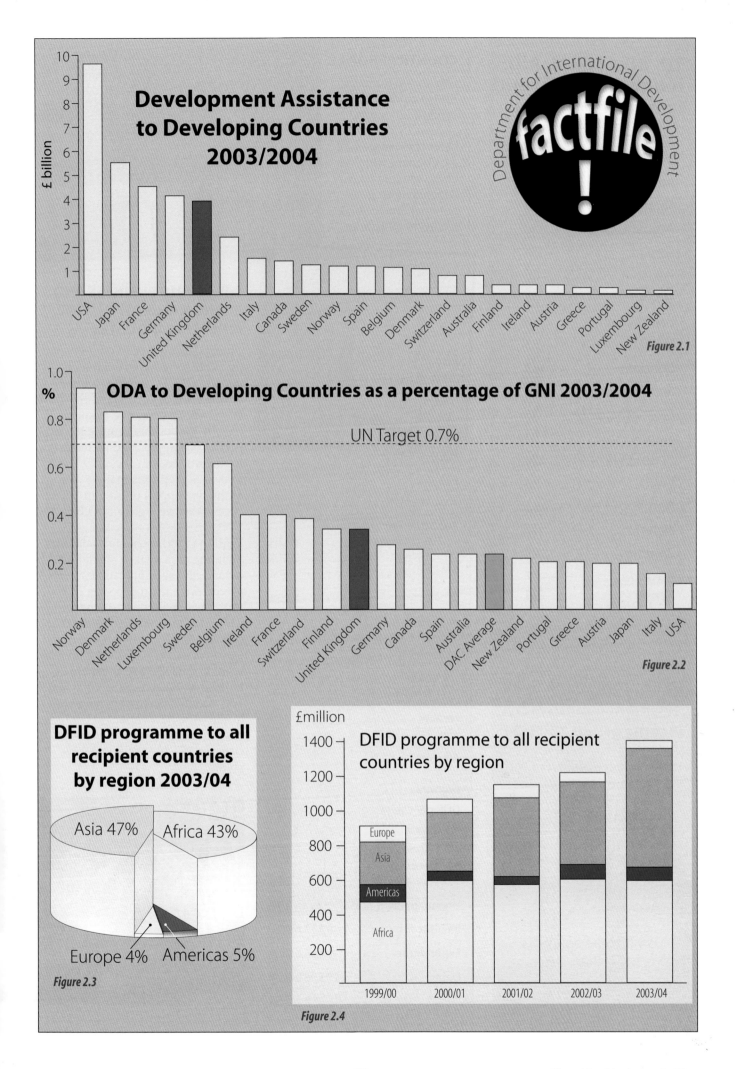

Development Assistance to Developing Countries 2003/2004

Department for International Development

factfile!

£ billion — USA, Japan, France, Germany, United Kingdom, Netherlands, Italy, Canada, Sweden, Norway, Spain, Belgium, Denmark, Switzerland, Australia, Finland, Ireland, Austria, Greece, Portugal, Luxembourg, New Zealand

Figure 2.1

ODA to Developing Countries as a percentage of GNI 2003/2004

%

UN Target 0.7%

Norway, Denmark, Netherlands, Luxembourg, Sweden, Belgium, Ireland, France, Switzerland, Finland, United Kingdom, Germany, Canada, Spain, Australia, DAC Average, New Zealand, Portugal, Greece, Austria, Japan, Italy, USA

Figure 2.2

DFID programme to all recipient countries by region 2003/04

Asia 47% Africa 43%

Europe 4% Americas 5%

Figure 2.3

DFID programme to all recipient countries by region

£million

Europe
Asia
Americas
Africa

1999/00   2000/01   2001/02   2002/03   2003/04

Figure 2.4

The politics of development in Africa

UK BILATERAL AID: top twenty recipient countries (2003/4)

Country	£m
Iraq	209
India	200
Tanzania	80
Afghanistan	80
Ghana	68
Pakistan	66
Uganda	56
Bangladesh	56
Malawi	55
Ethiopia	43
South Africa	42
Mozambique	36
Sierra Leone	34
Zimbabwe	34
China	32
Nepal	32
Nigeria	31
Zambia	28
Rwanda	27
Kenya	26

Table 2.1 (African countries)

DFID programme to all recipient countries by income group 2003/04

Upper Middle Income Countries 4%

Lower Middle Income Countries 22%

Low Income Countries 74%

Figure 2.5

COUNTRY PROFILE

Ghana is a former British colony which achieved independence in 1957. It has a democratic system of government with free elections. It is heavily dependent on international finance and technical assistance.

case study
GHANA

People

Population	21,029,853
Age Structure:	
0–14 years	37.1%
15–64	59.1%
65 years+	3.7%
Growth rate	1.25%
Infant mortality (deaths per 1000 live births)	51.43
Life expectancy (years):	
male	55.04
female	56.99
Fertility (children per woman)	3.02
Affected by AIDS	3.1%

Economy

GDP per capita	$2,300
Employed in:	
Agriculture	60%
Industry	15%
Services	25%
Unemployment rate	20%
Income	$2.17 billion
Expenditure	$2.56 billion
Debt	$7.396 billion

IMPROVING BUSINESS AND ECONOMIC GROWTH – THE PINEAPPLE INDUSTRY

Pineapples are one of Ghana's major exports. To assist Ghanaian people, DFID is working with the government of Ghana and other agencies to improve business growth. Under this venture the export of pineapples had increased from 2,000 tons in the early 1980s to over 50,000 tons in 2005. Many of the pineapples on sale in UK supermarkets were grown in Ghana.

With the DFID scheme each family in the area owns a small plot of land and sells pineapples at an agreed price to an exporter. In return, the exporter assists the farmer with finance, training, fertilisers and even materials for building a home. However, supermarkets are now favouring a new, sweeter variety of pineapple instead of the Ghanaian one. Attempts are being made to introduce the new variety to Ghana but farmers are worried about the cost of replacing their pineapple plants.

BRINGING WATER TO GHANA'S COCOA WORKERS

A well brings clean water to a village and reduces the risk of water-borne diseases. It also means that less time is spent on fetching water and so leaves more time for other activities.

Tens of thousands of cocoa farmers have been given access to fresh water by a DFID joint scheme involving Cadbury Schweppes, the NGO WaterAid and the Ghanaian cooperative Kuapo Kokoo which markets its cocoa under the fair trade banner. Up to March 2005, 260 wells had been drilled in villages to give year-round access to clean drinking water.

Fresh drinking water has brought a number of benefits: people now no longer have to queue for hours for water; people no long-er suffer from water-borne diseases; village children have more time to attend school because they no longer have to spend a quarter of their waking hours fetching water for their families. However, this is only a small-scale project and much needs to be done.

Fresh drinking water is a key need for many African people. DFID funding to improve water and sanitation in Africa will double between 2005 and 2008 from £47.5 million to £95 million.

MALARIA PREVENTION

Malaria is a major killer in Africa with at least 24 million pregnancies threatened by malaria each year. It also accounts for 30% of outpatient visits to hospitals and up to 50% of all hospital admissions. In south-eastern Ghana a $215,000 DFID pilot project helps pregnant women attending ante-natal clinics to protect themselves and their newborn children against malaria. Midwives issue pregnant women with vouchers towards the cost of nets treated with insecticide. This means a discount of up to half the cost of a net. Two-thirds of pregnant women bought a net. However, even at $4 this proved too expensive for the poorest women. In addition to the nets, expert advice is given by the midwives on preventing malaria.

Malaria Knowledge Programme

In Africa, malaria is the major killer of children under the age of five. Mothers are responsible for ensuring the condition is treated and for paying for such treatment. Howev-

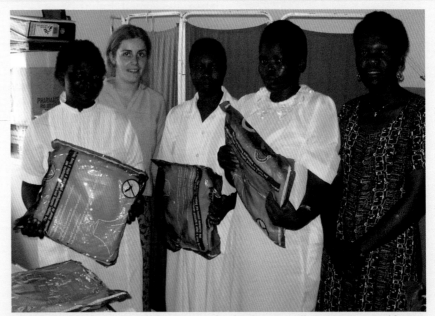

Nets treated with insecticide have proved to be the most effective way to tackle malaria in the home.

er, many women cannot access the treatment required or cannot pay for the treatment because in families with little money the priority of the husband is to buy seeds to grow crops. There is a general lack of awareness amongst men of the importance of treating malaria.

DFID has been involved in funding a £30,000 training scheme for twenty local health care workers in three districts of Ghana to find ways to solve the problems identified earlier. In addition to using role play, discussions, and community education, they provide access to credit and health insurance and there are signs that the scheme is working. Local health care insurance schemes have been set up; husbands have been made aware of the problems faced by their wives.

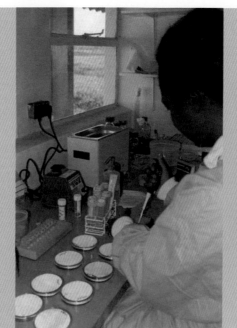

The ProTEST project in Zambia was funded by a DFID grant of £197,043 during the years 1999 – 2001 and DFID has pledged a further £259 million to similar projects between 2002 and 2008. The trial project in Zambia encouraged people to go for voluntary HIV testing and TB screening. TB is becoming one of Africa's biggest killer diseases for people with HIV/AIDS.

The ProTEST project refers people with TB for treatment and others get preventive drug treatment. Those with HIV are offered counselling and support. People were also shown how to reduce the risk of contracting HIV and TB. The project was also introduced to two other African countries and in total 140,000 people were tested. The World Health Organisation (WHO) estimated the project helped prevent thousands of new HIV and TB infections. So successful were the projects that they are to be extended to other countries in Africa.

A lab in Nigeria tests samples for TB infection

case study **The ProTEST Project**

---

case study **Wetlands Project**

Farmers in Northern Nigeria have benefited from a DFID-funded water management project. Local people were involved in clearing 15km of the Burum Gana channel, which was blocked and dried up. Crops can now be grown and communities thrive once more.

In Sabon Gari in Nigeria, villagers face the opposite problem from the one above. The swollen Marma channel experiences annual flooding which destroys farmland and communities. Many people lose their homes and farms and have to migrate. The government is planning to introduce flood prevention measures and increase water flow. DFID has committed £2.9 million over 2002–2007 to the Wetlands Project. It is estimated that around 1.5 million people will directly benefit from the project.

HOW SUCCESSFUL IS DFID?

The UN recommends, and its members have agreed that, 0.7% of GNI should be allocated to overseas aid. Britain, however, allocated less than 0.5% in 2005. Britain therefore could, and some say should, be giving more. Tony Blair has committed Britain to reaching the goal of 0.7% in the future, but at the moment amongst the top richest countries in the world, Britain is around the middle in the contributions it gives. Denmark, for example, devotes almost 1.2% of GNI to overseas aid.

Although Britain has dropped all tied aid, there are still concerns that British interests are sometimes linked to projects. For example, in 2002 DFID awarded $10 million to Ghana for a water project on the condition that two foreign water companies would sign leases to run water supplies for ten years. Christian Aid estimates that this could result in the cost of drinking water increasing by 300%. Likewise, in Tanzania it was claimed that a British radar system, which was purchased by Tanzania, was more expensive than it needed to be and was out of date. This is not tied aid but concerns were expressed about the issue at the time.

There have been concerns expressed that former colonies are given preference when it comes to deciding which countries in Africa should receive aid. In addition it is claimed that aid is used to control the internal affairs of African countries. Necessarily, any government has to be selective when deciding which countries will receive aid, meaning that however good the intentions are, many countries will not be helped.

CHAPTER 3

The work of the UN, the EU and NGOs

UN SPECIALISED AGENCIES

 United Nations Childrens Fund

 Food and Agriculture Organisation

 World Food Programme

 International Labour Organisation

 World Health Organisation

 United Nations Education, Scientific and Cultural Organisation

To meet its goals of promoting economic and social progress and of promoting human rights, the UN works in Africa through its Specialised Agencies. In this section the work of three of these agencies will be examined in depth.

The United Nations Children's Fund

UNICEF focuses on the needs of children and their mothers. Emergency aid, medical programmes, educational programmes and promoting children's rights are all areas UNICEF is involved with.

The World Food Programme

WFP focuses on combatting hunger and encouraging long-term food security.

The Food and Agriculture Organisation

FAO focuses on developing agriculture, raising levels of nutrition and improving conditions for rural dwellers.

UNICEF

The Priorities and Work Factfile outlines in broad terms what UNICEF does in countries in which it is involved. A combination of some or all of this work will be evident in any African country which has been targeted. UNICEF is involved in helping women and children in forty five sub-Saharan African countries and the assistance and aid offered is acknowledged to be of a high quality. Millions of children and their mothers in Africa have benefited directly from the work of UNICEF. However, the massive scale of the problems encountered, such as in Angola (see page 24), can confound even the best efforts of those involved.

UNICEF'S PRIORITIES AND WORK

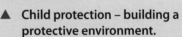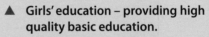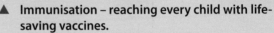

▲ Child protection – building a protective environment.

▲ Girls' education – providing high quality basic education.

▲ Immunisation – reaching every child with life-saving vaccines.

▲ HIV/AIDS – preventing parent to child transmission; helping those orphaned.

▲ Helping communities and families.

▲ Emergency assistance for countries in crisis.

▲ Providing good quality lessons in schools.

▲ Gender equality.

▲ Preventive health care.

▲ Promoting breastfeeding, a healthy diet and addressing nutritional deficiencies.

▲ Working for children's rights.

▲ Improving sanitation, water supplies and hygiene.

factfile!

Angola suffered forty years of almost continuous war until 4 April 2002 when a peace accord was signed. The country's health and education services were devastated and even today Angola has one of the world's worst infant mortality rates. 25% of children die before their fifth birthday. 45% of Angola's children suffer chronic malnutrition, almost half of all children do not have access to school and under half of the population does not have access to safe water. Added to these factors is a huge landmine problem. It is estimated that there are more landmines than children in Angola. There is clearly a colossal challenge facing the Angolan government, UNICEF and other agencies working in the country, made worse by the fact that 60% of Angola's population are children. Despite its best efforts, in 2005 UNICEF

Victims of landmines wait to be fitted with tailor-made leg prostheses at a hospital in Angola.

described the situation of children as "dire." A rising HIV/AIDS rate seriously threatens Angola's recovery and the country's future.

UNICEF has launched Angola's biggest ever health and education

campaigns including mass immunisations. Half of the 4.5 million children who were previously unregistered now have birth certificates. Former child soldiers have been supported and reunited with their families. UNICEF has plans to reduce child mortality and to provide education for all. A further goal is to restore health systems across the country and assist the government to reconstruct the country. The tasks are massive and will only be accomplished over many years. If war erupts again, no one can tell what might happen.

In January 2005 a peace agreement was signed ending twenty one years of civil war in Sudan. However, in the western Darfur region, where a conflict exploded in 2003, fighting is still ongoing with 2.4 million people affected. The situation in Darfur and the results of the civil war caused huge problems for the ordinary people of Sudan.

In 2005, four million people were still displaced from their homes and UNICEF reported "social and economic underdevelopment" across the country. UNICEF also reported that there were "significant inequalities regarding access to services

between children living in different areas of the country." A set of recommendations was prepared by UNICEF including more money to be spent on health care, more money to be spent on education, more attention to be given to the education of girls, action on HIV/AIDS and a range of child protection measures.

There is considerable abuse of children's rights in Sudan. Slavery, discrimination against illegitimate children, the recruitment of child soldiers, child abuse and the criminalising of destitute street children are a few of the long-standing problems UNICEF is attempting to address. UNICEF has highlighted the need for legislation in Sudan to conform to the UN's Declaration of the Rights of the Child. These prob-

lems and abuses relating to Sudanese children are embedded in the culture of the country. Consequently, much work is needed over time to rectify the situation.

However, UNICEF successfully introduced an immunisation programme, Immunisation Plus, which covered 60% of children under one year and 90% of children aged from under one year to five years. Sanitation programmes, better nutrition, health programmes and education programmes have all been introduced. Some indication of the long road ahead is to be found when analysing, for example, UNICEF's intervention to promote girls' education. The percentage of girls enrolling in school increased from 45.3% in 2000–2001 to a mere 45.6% in 2001–2002.

FAO

The FAO works to raise awareness amongst rural communities as to how best to manage land and water supplies, and to increase food production. It undertakes many research projects and puts the results of these within the reach of those who most need them. For example, the FAO Internet site receives a million hits a month from individuals and organisations wishing to access reports and technical documents. By spreading knowledge, sharing expertise and becoming involved in a variety of projects, the FAO has become a leading force in the war against hunger.

Satellite image of South Africa provides data to assess such variables as future crop yields and weather problems.

FAO'S PRIORITIES AND WORK

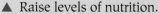

▲ Achieve food security for all.
▲ Raise levels of nutrition.
▲ Improve agricultural productivity.
▲ Improve the lives of rural populations.
▲ Provide research and advice.
▲ Mobilise action to meet the needs of specific countries.
▲ Supply tools, legal advice, and information.
▲ Act as a neutral forum where representatives from developing countries can meet to discuss issues of common concern and attempt to find solutions to the problems of food insecurity.

Between 1997 and 2001, the FAO created a huge database containing information on roads, climate, drought, natural resources and a host of other indicators. By using a high-resolution satellite, Africa is continuously scanned, reporting on weather patterns, projected crop yields and so forth allowing comparisons with previous years to be made. The gathered data allows African governments, NGOs, the UN Specialised Agencies and other aid providers the opportunity to forward plan and take account of potential disasters such as drought or famine. All these interested groups are alerted on a daily basis and they, in turn, confer with the African countries' governments on what action might be needed.

The Africover project has developed a combined approach to addressing the problems of food insecurity in Africa. The FAO has worked in partnership with African governments to provide training in the use of the technology associated with the Africover project in addition to training in the methodologies required to interpret and develop the databases created by the satellite monitoring of Africa.

PILOT PROJECT IN CHAD

A village in Chad where FAO works with poor farmers.

The FAO is involved in pilot projects which, if successful, are adopted on a larger scale. One such project was the Livestock Diversification Project in Chad. In 2004 the pilot was concluded and the potential of livestock diversification as a means of improving food security and increasing the incomes of poor farmers was demonstrated.

Local breeds of small animals were bred by poor local farmers including poultry, sheep, goats and pigs. Aqua culture was also developed whereby indigenous fish were farmed in greater numbers than traditional methods allowed. This diversity of food supply ensured that families were not reliant on one main food resource which, if it failed, could lead to famine. Poultry were vaccinated to halt the spread

of a virus which hitherto had killed up to 80% of stocks. Hand in hand with this came training for the farmers in preventing illnesses in their animals and promoting knowledge of animal health care. Credit facilities for the farmers were also provided.

When the project concluded in 2004, the FAO reported that household food security had improved greatly, living conditions had improved and farmers had wider access to markets for their animals. An additional

benefit of farming chickens, ducks and guinea fowl was that income was generated for women and young people in the villages. The project is being extended to Mali, Burkina Faso, Niger, Togo and Cameroon. In each of these countries the FAO is taking into account that country's particular circumstances, including the types of animals specific to each country.

As is always the case with such projects, there is no one size fits all solution. The FAO analysis of this project identi-

fied a number of issues that remain unresolved. For example, producers in more remote rural areas face considerable problems in achieving the successes outlined above. Many people in these remote areas have poor access to the goods and services needed to thrive. Crucially, they have poor access to markets where they can sell the animals they have bred. So, while their food supply has improved, their ability to develop economically from the project is limited.

From 1999 until the present time, The Gambia has been the recipient of a wide variety of assistance from the FAO. Listing all of the projects and aid The Gambia has received can give a fuller picture of the nature and scope of the work undertaken by the FAO (see opposite).

Such projects undertaken by the FAO are often long-term in nature and do not seek to provide a quick solution to an immediate problem. Instead, they focus on long-term solutions to food insecurity by taking into account the particular circumstances of each country. Such aid allows African people to become involved and responsible for their own development, rather than passively relying on handouts. Empowering people to take responsibility for their food production and economic development allows them to become less reliant on outside assistance and to have a framework from which they can progress.

FAO PROJECTS

- Technical support for farmers.
- Emergency eradication of African Swine Fever.
- Undertaking an agricultural census.
- Strengthening the National Food Control system.
- Developing fisheries in communities.
- Promoting vegetable and fruit tree production.
- Rabbit breeding.
- Supporting pig breeders.
- Developing bee keeping.
- Developing technologies to establish a fish smoking industry.
- Providing life jackets for fishermen to ensure continued fishing during the heavy rain season.
- Forestry improvement.
- Controlling the use of pesticides to the benefit of farmers.
- Advice, guidance and evaluation of projects.

WFP

The WFP is the UN Specialised Agency most involved in combatting hunger in the world. It is the largest food aid organisation in the world, but importantly it works to eradicate hunger by helping those most at risk of hunger to become self-reliant. The WFP spent $2,900 billion in a year according to its most recently published figures in 2005. By attacking the causes of food shortages and by feeding those facing famine who are caught up in emergencies or disasters, the WFP is at the forefront of tackling hunger in sub-Saharan Africa where 203.5 million people suffer the effects of not having enough to eat.

THE WFP'S EMERGENCY FOOD AID

In 2004 the WFP reached 89 million people caught up in food emergencies. Some disasters were man-made while others were natural. In all cases the WFP is first contacted by the government of the country involved and using a combination of ships, trucks, aircraft, and animals, (ranging from elephants to donkeys) supplies of food are delivered to those in need. The money for such operations comes from a WFP appeal to the international community. Sixty countries support the work of the WFP.

The WFP will act alone or in tandem with NGOs. Food rations are distributed, with account being taken of what a local population eats. However, great care is taken to ensure that the right combination of food types is included. Working with the local community, the WFP ensures that food reaches those in most need, particularly focusing on women, pregnant mothers, children and the elderly.

THE SCALE OF THE PROBLEM OF HUNGER

- ▲ Ten million people a year die of hunger and hunger-related diseases.
- ▲ One in three of the world's hungry lives in sub-Saharan Africa.
- ▲ During the period 1970–1997 the number of hungry people in the world dropped from 959 million to 791 million. However, by 2002 the number had risen to 852 million and is increasing at a rate of almost 4 million each year.
- ▲ In the 1990s global poverty dropped by 20%, but world hunger increased by 18 million people.
- ▲ Hunger kills more people in Africa than AIDS, malaria, and TB combined.
- ▲ Undernourished mothers have children with low birth weights.
- ▲ Three-quarters of all hungry people live in rural areas. About 167 million children in the world are underweight as a result of acute hunger.
- ▲ Acute hunger stops physical and mental growth.
- ▲ Children suffering from hunger are much more likely to die if they contract common diseases.
- ▲ Undernourished children lose their curiosity and motivation and millions do not carry on with their education as a consequence.
- ▲ Every five seconds a child dies of hunger.
- ▲ For a cost of 19 cents, a child can be fed in school for a day in Africa.
- ▲ Women are much more affected by hunger than men. Seven out of ten of the world's hungry are women and girls.
- ▲ Drought is the main cause of food shortages in poor countries.

factfile!

Djibouti has suffered civil war and increasing poverty over recent years. It faces a multitude of economic difficulties with the government falling significantly into arrears with its debt repayments. The WFP has a logistics base in Djibouti from which it organises food aid for the area and transportation of the food to the people of Djibouti and Ethiopia.

There are huge warehouses at the port which are capable of holding 7,000 tons of food supplies. Throughout the country are other smaller warehouses which are kept secure. A network of trucks and trains distributes the food to where it is most needed. All areas under threat of hunger in the region are linked by radio and email to the logistics base. This example is characteristic of the organisation

A labourer works at a grain store inside a WFP warehouse. The food is donated to fight malnutrition and hunger.

and planning that typifies the work of the WFP.

Problems Faced By the WFP

War and armed conflict can cause major problems for the WFP when attempting to deliver food supplies to those in need. In Sudan for example, trucks have been hijacked resulting in 20–30% of food aid being diverted to the army for its own use. Aid workers have come under attack and in 2000 during the civil war, Operation Lifeline Sudan had to be suspended because of the risks posed by constant bombing in the area. As a result, tens of thousands of hungry Sudanese people died from lack of food.

In July 2002 a major crisis developed in Angola prompting the United Nations to appeal to international donors to fund emergency programmes there. The humanitarian crisis was described by the UN as "one of the worst in the world". A war in Angola had left half a million people living in appalling conditions. In addition, a quarter of a million displaced people were located in thirty-five camps around the country. The UN estimated that, overall, at least three million people would require emergency assistance.

However, despite this clearly desperate situation, the WFP found itself with a major problem when trying to help the hungry of Angola. Only a third of the money needed was forthcoming by July 2002 and the WFP had only received 41% of its requirements. The appeal target of $232,768,666 was not being met and even after further appeals the WFP had a shortfall of $88,160,808 at the end of the year. Interestingly, perhaps in response to internal UN pressures, or in acknowledgement of the difficulties of funding appeals generally, the WFP revised its appeal for 2003 downwards to only $71,092,743, despite the huge shortfall the previous year. This occurred despite the announcement by the UN that "at least four million people are highly vulnerable, of whom nearly two million currently depend on some kind of international assistance to survive". The UN went on to state, " a larger percentage of people are displaced in Angola than virtually any other country."

Providing Free School Meals

The WFP is the largest provider of free school meals. In many African countries the WFP promotes education for girls and part of this initiative involves giving a month's free food rations to the parents of girls enrolled in school. This has resulted in an increase in enrolment of girls of up to 300% in some areas. It has been demonstrated that where African women have been educated in school there is a 50% drop in child malnutrition.

A UNESCO survey has shown that in countries with an adult literacy rate of 40%, per capita GNI averaged $210 while in countries with at least an 80% rate, GNI was $1000, thus illustrating the importance of education as part of any development programme.

Girls who attend school marry later in life and have 50% fewer children than those girls who do not attend school. Girls who do not attend school often marry as young as eleven and have, on average, six or seven children.

The United Nations has an excellent track record of providing assistance to developing countries in Africa as highlighted by the case studies on pages 24–28.

However, much more could be done. The UN and all its agencies spends about $10 billion each year, which seems a large sum until one considers that this works out at $1.70 for each of the world's inhabitants—a tiny fraction of what governments spend on military budgets. For over a decade, the UN has been forced to cut back on key programmes to developing countries because of financial crises, caused largely by member states not paying their contributions to the UN. In addition, many members have cut contributions to voluntary funds.

The UN can be overly bureaucratic in its decision making and also undemocratic which can result in the UN being slow to act in times of crisis. The UN was criticised for being too slow to act in Ethiopia and Sudan when millions were facing famine there. Moreover,

THE UNITED NATIONS – AN ASSESSMENT

during the famine in Sudan in the 1990s, aid was delayed until the Islamic government admitted that there was famine in the country.

The USA Plays Politics

On 31 December 2004, members' arrears to the UN budget stood at over $357 million, of which the USA owed $241 million. The USA was referred to by a UN report on late payers as the "major delinquent country", owing $1.2 billion as of December 1999. Other major countries had outstanding payments of $0.6 billion. In November 1999 the US Congress passed legislation making repayment of US arrears contingent on a number of conditions which aimed to force the UN to adopt policies which were contrary to the views of the majority of members, thereby threatening to wreck the process of multilateral decision making.

When the USA settled its 1999 outstanding payments, it set a number of conditions, the most important of which was a reduction in its share of contributions to specialised agencies from 25% of the budget to 22%. In February 2003, the USA still owed $1.327 billion in payments.

The UN has considered proposals to reform the way it is funded but important contributors, led by the USA, have blocked such moves, fearing they will lose political power in the UN.

THE EUROPEAN UNION (EU)

Aid provided by the EU is multilateral and financed through the European Development Fund. Up until 2000, aid to African, Caribbean and Pacific (ACP) states was delivered through the mechanism of the Lomé Convention. Today the Cotonou Agreement, signed in June 2000 in Cotonou, the capital city of the African country Benin, has replaced the Lomé Convention.

What is the Cotonou Agreement?

The Cotonou agreement is a twenty-year programme for delivering aid to ACP countries. It reformed many of the shortcomings of the Lomé Convention which had operated since 1975. For the first five-year period, 13.5 billion euros was allocated for aid. There will be reviews every five years until the

twenty-year period is up, but annual reviews can be undertaken if necessary. During this first five years the EU has supported ACP governments to create a balanced economy, expand the private sector and improve social services in the countries covered by the agreement. Another objective is to integrate ACP states into the global economy.

The EU will work with governments and encourage greater participation of people at grass roots level. Sanctions will be applied to countries which abuse human rights. Overall, the aim is to make ACP countries more democratic and answerable for their actions.

It is further aimed to encourage equality between men and women, manage the environment in a sus-

tainable way and work in partnership with countries, eventually removing trade barriers between the EU and ACP states. This will be reciprocal with both sides taking down trade barriers.

The Cotonou Agreement is based on five interlinked pillars:

The Five Pillars

- a comprehensive political dimension
- participatory approaches
- a strengthened focus on poverty reduction
- a new framework for economic and trade cooperation
- a reform of financial cooperation

Why The Need For Reform?

The Lomé convention had been criticised on a number of fronts. The ACP countries were given privileged access to EU markets and aid, but little was required of the recipients. Evaluations of aid given to ACP countries often showed that little account had been taken of the policies and administration of the countries involved. ACP countries' share of the EU market declined from 6.7% in 1976 to only 3% in 1998 and of this small share, 60% of total exports were concentrated on only ten products.

The rise of globalisation and the technological revolution has, in many respects, excluded ACP countries. A new approach was needed to include these countries. Lomé had fundamentally failed to improve the economic positions of most of the ACP countries and a culture of dependency had been fostered. Martin Holland, writing in *The Brown Journal of World Affairs* sums the situation up:

> "Few, if any, of the Lomé countries saw a radical transformation in their economic well-being; dependency continued to define their relationship with Europe."

case study
Eritrea & EU aid

Education is a priority for investment under the Cotonou Agreement

The Commission for Eritrea signed a strategy and cooperation agreement over five years worth 96.8 million euros. The aid, which will end in 2007, is aimed at political, social and economic development. In the short-term the aid focused on dealing with the aftermath of years of armed conflict. Rehabilitation programmes, assistance in demobilisation of armed forces, and reintegration of soldiers back into civilian life all featured in the package. In addition, improving transport and education were given priority status.

The EU made clear that under the terms of the Cotonou agreement assistance would only continue if issues such as holding free elections, freeing political prisoners and moving towards good governance took place. Under Article 96 of the Cotonou Agreement, aid can be withheld if the EU considers that a recipient country has "failed to fulfil its obligations stemming from rights and democratic principles and the rule of law."

Criticisms of the Cotonou Agreement

A number of NGOs and even the British government have concerns about aspects of the Cotonou agreement. The issue of 'reciprocity' is the cause of much criticism. Simply stated, reciprocity means that, for example, if the EU undertakes to remove import tariffs on goods coming from an ACP country, then that country should respond in kind by cutting a tariff on EU goods being exported to that country. In other words, the EU expects a level playing field in matters of trade.

Critics point out that this will force open the markets of some of the poorest countries in the world, allowing EU companies to flood these countries with their goods at the expense of local producers. Some have said that the agreement is a way for Europe to further its commercial interests. The United Nations Commission for Africa has expressed its concern by warning that sub-Saharan Africa's low and medium technology industries may have to cut half of their unskilled labour if existing protections are cut.

Academics at the Institute for Development Studies at Sussex University have concluded that three-quarters of ACP countries could lose at least 40% of the revenues they currently receive from applying trade tariffs to EU imports. The British government urged the EU not to "pursue any offensive interests" in ACP countries and asked that they should be left to make their own decisions about opening their markets. In response, Mogens Peter Carl, a senior trade official at the European Commission, commented that Britain's statement was "an unwelcome shift".

case study
Ethiopia & EU aid

Above is the road to Korem in Ethiopia. Improving transport like this road is one of the priorities of the Cotonou Agreement in Ethiopia.

A programme to develop the infrastructure is being undertaken in Ethiopia, which has suffered from wars, famine and extreme poverty for many years. The EU is currently supporting the construction of the 132 km Kombolcha-Mille road. Another construction project, the 514 km Addis-Dessie-Wodiya road, which will link the north to Addis and Djibouti, is expected to be completed in December 2009. A 336 km road was completed in 2005. A hydroelectric power plant and an airport are also part of the assistance agreed.

These are clearly long-term projects whose benefit will not be realised for some time. Whether or not this is what the people of Ethiopia want at this time is unknown, for it was the government of Ethiopia with whom negotiations took place.

THE WORK OF NON-GOVERNMENTAL ORGANISATIONS (NGOs)

NGOs raise money from voluntary and private sources to fund projects in developing countries. They are free from government interference and determine for themselves what their aims and policies are. They provide emergency relief at times of crisis and are most obviously in the public eye at these times when they are involved in high profile fund-raising, for example during the famines in Ethiopia and Sudan.

NGOs work in partnership with other bodies providing short-term and long-term aid. There are literally hundreds of NGOs some of which provide specifically targeted aid to certain groups, for instance Save the Children. Others act on a broader scale, for example Oxfam. By focusing on the work of three NGOs, a fuller picture of the role and work of NGOs generally will unfold.

CHRISTIAN AID

Christian Aid was established in 1945, celebrating its 60th anniversary in 2005. It channels its funds into local community groups to help people directly. No money is given to governments. It does not send goods overseas, preferring to give directly to communities who can purchase local commodities, thus benefiting the economy of the country involved. Volunteers are not sent overseas, but instead local people are employed.

Where Does the Money Go?

Every pound received is spent as follows:

2p on administration

19p on fund-raising

52p on long-term development projects

16p on campaigning and education

11p in response to emergencies

Southern Africa Emergency Appeal

case study
Christian Aid in action
1

This is an example of a large-scale Christian Aid project. The Appeal was launched in 2002 after severe drought left more than 12 million people in southern Africa at risk of starvation. Christian Aid raised more than £3.5 million, and with contributions from organisations such as DFID, Ireland Aid and the European Union, eventually managed to raise £10.5 million. Most of the money was spent on emergency projects including dam building, replacing livestock, training people in farming techniques and distributing seeds for drought-resistant crops. Most of the aid went to Zimbabwe, Angola and Malawi.

In addition to this immediate help, Christian Aid also raised awareness about HIV/AIDS and supported vulnerable groups such as widows, orphans, elderly people and those suffering from HIV. Longer term projects have also been undertaken including: preparing people to cope with future emergencies, developing lasting skills such as harvesting rainwater and providing education about crops resistant to drought.

In the short-term the Appeal meant that the worst of the food crisis was averted. However, the cause of the food crisis had its roots in long-term problems. Harvests today are still poor with many people in the affected areas continuing to live in extreme poverty, barely able to grow enough to eat. Hungry families are forced to sell off vital assets to buy food. It is important to remember that even before the Appeal was launched, in a normal year half of all households in southern Africa ran out of food for between four and five months. Millions of people in the affected areas are still reliant on food aid.

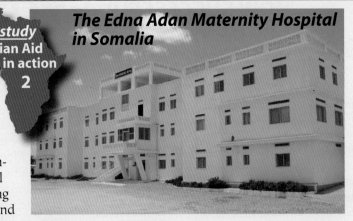

case study
Christian Aid
in action
2

The Edna Adan Maternity Hospital in Somalia

This is a good example of a small-scale Christian Aid project. Christian Aid began supporting this maternity hospital in 2002 with a grant to establish a six-month midwife training course. The hospital is the only nurse training institution in Somalia and prior to its establishment there had been no training for nurses and midwives since 1987.

The goal of the project is to improve health for mothers and children after years of civil war. In 2003 the infant mortality rate was very high at 175 deaths per one thousand live births. For every one thousand births, sixteen mothers died in childbirth. Female Genital Mutilation (FGM) is also a huge problem which causes complications during childbirth. The hospital teaches women about the problems relating to FGM and how it causes infections and other complications which result in most women requiring an episiotomy in order to give birth.

The project has resulted in many babies being delivered safely and fewer deaths occuring during childbirth. It is significantly contributing to improving the general health of women and children in Somalia. However, most women still say they will practice FGM on their daughters when they reach the age of 6–8 years because they say the culture of the country means that no man would marry a woman who had not had the process.

SAVE THE CHILDREN

Save the Children is an NGO which focuses on the needs of children, working in a practical way to address these needs. Save the Children is involved in helping children in twenty one African countries. The organisation is involved in delivering emergency relief in addition to working on long-term projects. It works collaboratively with other organisations and African governments and when a famine occurs it undertakes an analysis to ensure that it is are not duplicating the work already being done by other organisations and agencies.

Save the Children targets the most vulnerable groups, such as families whose head is female, and assists with growing food and accessing safe water. It also supplies seeds and tools, helps improve crop yields, and trains local people in soil conservation and irrigation techniques.

Save the Children in Mozambique

Two-thirds of the population lives in absolute poverty and under-five death rates are amongst the worst in the world. HIV/AIDS has led to the destruction of families and to a growth in street children. Up to 1 million children are in need of protection from abuse and exploitation. Save the Children is working to protect children's rights and is addressing the problem of HIV/AIDS.

RWANDA

MOZAMBIQUE

Save the Children in Rwanda

Rwanda is one of the world's poorest countries and is recovering from the aftermath of the 1994 genocide in which over a million people were slaughtered. Children suffer extreme poverty as a result of so many adults being killed by massacres or HIV/AIDS. Many suffer chronic malnutrition and have no access to health or social services. Save the Children is providing emergency relief and is working on long-term projects including improving health, food security, social services and child-focused HIV/AIDS protection policies.

These case studies are typical of the projects that Save the Children is involved with in the twenty one African countries to which it supplies aid and assistance. The problems that this NGO tries to address are huge and while it makes a difference to the lives of children in the countries in which it operates, the scale of the task facing Save the Children is massive. HIV/AIDS, as we have seen, is an enormous issue confronting the people of Africa, with the situation becoming worse in many areas.

The politics of development in Africa

ACTIONAID INTERNATIONAL

ActionAid was formed in 1972 and it targets the world's poorest and most disadvantaged people. It works with local partners in the forty two countries in which it operates. These partners range from small community groups to national organisations. ActionAid claims to have a unique vision which involves working with communities over many years and not imposing solutions on these communities. ActionAid focuses on food rights, education, HIV/AIDS, emergencies and womens' and girls' issues.

Marta, who is HIV positive, with her daughter Martica. Tell a poor person they could die of AIDS in ten years and they say "I shall probably be dead before that of something else".

In Nigeria ActionAid is targeting HIV/AIDs and is working with the government there to build peace in the country and to promote good governance. In Tanzania this NGO worked to persuade the government to abolish school fees and as a result 500,000 more children are now in education.

ActionAid's response to the disaster in Mozambique, after massive floods, gives an insight into how it operates when involved in emergency aid. After the floods it worked with local farmers to introduce a new vitamin-rich sweet potato. A programme of long-term recovery was addressed which attempted to ensure that the victims of the disaster could earn a living in the future. In addition, measures were taken to involve the people in the political process and to consider how they could cope with any future emergencies.

HOW SUCCESSFUL ARE NGOS?

How does one define success? The scale of the issues affecting Africa's development are immense and dwarf the resources of all, let alone one particular, NGO. What is true, however, is that at their best, NGOs can make a striking and important contribution to improving the lives and futures of those they are involved with. The examples given in the case studies show how lives have been changed for the better.

Needless to say, NGOs have their shortcomings. A growing concern focuses on the increasing numbers of NGOs which compete for money from a generous public who increasingly experience compassion fatigue when so many heartfelt pleas compete with one another. Some NGOs are accused of spending too much on administration, which can have the effect of the public at large choosing to ignore fund-raising appeals. Some NGOs are well meaning, but lack expertise and fall short of the standards expected of an aid organisation. In comparison to the UN and international governments, individual NGOs operate on a small scale and consequently their impact is necessarily limited.

There are numerous examples of superb work being done by various organisations, but their impact in addressing the multiple causes that impede development is on a small scale. In addition, many NGOs, such as Save the Children, target particular groups, so their success can only be measured within the narrow framework which they have set themselves. NGOs are one part in the jigsaw that is the possible solution to addressing the issues surrounding Africa's development. It is a matter of judgement as to how effective they are as part of the larger picture.

THE AID DEBATE

Surprisingly, both within and outwith Africa there is informed debate questioning whether or not aid should be given to African governments. Moeletsi Mbeki, (brother of South Africa's President) is Deputy Chairman of the South African Institute of International Affairs based in Johannesburg. In the *Mail On Sunday* on 3 July 2005 he wrote a long open letter to Bob Geldof in which he applauded the intentions of Live 8 but said that Geldof did not understand the "core problem" in Africa. He identified bad governance as the "core problem" and went on to explain that much aid goes to prop up corrupt governments. He went on to say "African governments must be more accountable ... to the citizens of Africa. Only then can African people do anything effective about poverty and AIDS. Without that, they are never going to find a solution."

IS AID THE WAY FORWARD TO ASSIST AFRICA'S DEVELOPMENT?

No one agency or government can solve the problems confronting many African countries. The social, economic and political factors which explain Africa's development issues are complicated and cannot be addressed satisfactorily by short-term solutions.

Huge levels of international debt, corrupt or inefficient governments, trade that favours developed nations, the power of international corporations, the devastation caused by HIV/AIDS and desperate poverty must all be tackled. This will require from governments an effort of will and commitment unparalleled in scope and dedication. Currently, admirable work is being undertaken by a variety of providers, but each has its limits and shortcomings.

Aid is Not the Answer

Richard Dowden, Director of the Royal African Society, argues a radical view, claiming that aid is not the answer to Africa's problems. While he concedes that humanitarian relief will always be needed when a disaster hits a country, he questions the view that aid can transform societies. At best, he argues, aid can only accelerate a process that is already under way. He explains that nearly a trillion dollars has been spent on aid to Africa since the 1960s but the situation now for African people is worse than ever. Much aid was spent without consultation with local people and what is left is abandoned and useless projects.

Africa is a continent in which countries were created artificially by colonial powers and have, therefore, not produced effective governments. This means that aid providers have had to work along-side bad governance, making it impossible to deliver the development needed. He highlights the fact that South Africa and Botswana have well-run governments and do not need aid. On the other hand, where governments have collapsed, as in Somalia, it is impossible to put development aid into action effectively. Those in the middle, he explains, such as Mozambique, have become aid-dependent and have had their self-reliance undermined. Dowden maintains that only Africans can bring change to Africa.

Good governance is the essential component which will facilitate development he argues. Only by African governments raising appropriate taxes and spending them wisely can development take place. Short-term aid to assist countries moving in this direction may be appropriate, but otherwise aid will be wasted. The people themselves must undertake development and hold African governments accountable for their actions.

The role of international governments is a vital one. They can create fairer trade systems, end unfair subsidies to their farmers, and lower tariffs and trade barriers to allow Africa to trade more processed goods. Furthermore, the developed world should stop the brain drain from Africa by ceasing to lure talented and highly educated Africans to lucrative work in Europe and America. The British government in particular should take action to stop arms trading with African countries, thus creating more stability. Finally, action needs to be taken to stop money laundering by corrupt African leaders who frequently use British banks for their purposes.

Aid Needs to be Doubled

Max Lawson is Policy Adviser for the internationally known and respected NGO, Oxfam. He argues that aid to Africa "must be doubled." If aid were to be stopped, he argues, the millions of Africans caught up in conflict or natural disasters would suffer unimaginably. He maintains that aid is like a life support system which if cut off would result in widespread deaths.

He makes a strong case that long-term development aid can play a crucial role in assisting developing countries work their way out of poverty. Education gives children a chance of a better life which they otherwise would not have and in many African countries children are attending schools thanks to international aid projects. Road building projects have allowed Ethiopian farmers, for example, to reach markets to sell their crops more easily. Children can get to school and more people can travel to receive medical assistance. Many African countries have been devastated by war and international aid is helping to rebuild these countries. Assistance has been given to help with reconciliation and building peaceful societies.

Aid is not the only answer to Africa's problems, argues Max Lawson. He wants to see unfair terms of trade with African countries ending. However, he maintains that it is not the 'either or' situation that Richard Dowden's analysis claims. Aid has a part to play and must be improved where it is not achieving its aims. More needs to be done to empower ordinary people and fight government corruption. Democracy is spreading in Africa and aid can strengthen this process. Max Lawson states that we provide too little aid to Africa and the current £13 billion a year given by rich countries needs to be doubled along with ending debt and changing the rules of world trade.

MAKE POVERTY HISTORY

In July 2005 the G8 summit was held in Gleneagles in Scotland. G8 is a group of the world's eight most powerful industrialised countries comprising the UK, the USA, France, Germany, Italy, Russia, Canada and Japan. In 2005, the UK held the presidency of G8. Poverty in Africa was the main topic of discussion and Make Poverty History, a coalition of over 400 development agencies concerned with fighting global poverty, used this opportunity to get its message across to the world.

Not only did Make Poverty History raise awareness of development issues in Africa, it also campaigned on a massive scale to get the G8 countries to agree to a number of demands.

It demanded the following:

◆ All unpayable debts of the world's poorest countries to be cancelled in full without harming aid budgets to meet any costs.

◆ Stop forcing poor countries to follow particular policies in return for debt cancellation.

◆ Agree to a just and transparent system for handling debt problems which will take account of the needs and views of countries, and not just those of creditors.

◆ Set a binding deadline for spending 0.7% of GNI on aid.

◆ Ensure that aid supports poor communities' own plans for fighting poverty.

◆ Ensure that 70% of aid goes to the poorest countries by 2010.

◆ Commit to giving a certain amount of aid over a set period of time, so that countries can make long-term plans.

◆ Stop tying aid to purchases of goods and services from donor countries.

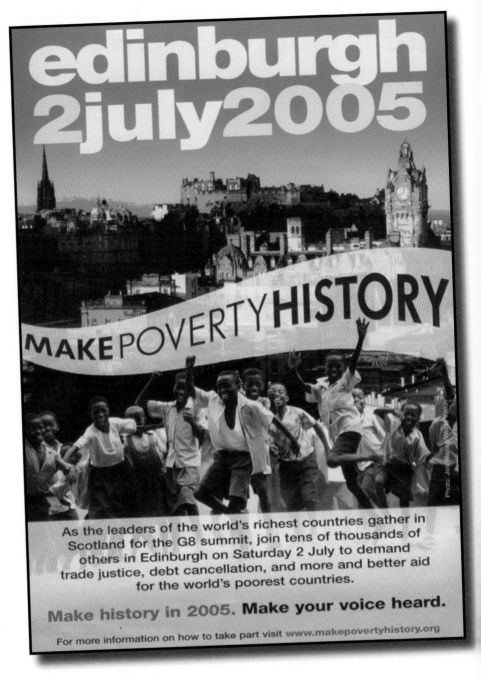

This campaign differs from the work usually associated with NGOs because the purpose was not to be involved with supplying aid but to effect change, influence decision making, and raise public awareness. It mobilised tens of thousands of people to protest in Edinburgh on 2 July to show solidarity and send a message to G8 that ending world poverty was a major concern of numerous ordinary people. This message was echoed at Live 8 concerts around the world on the same day. Both events indicated that ordinary people could and would play a part in working to end the poverty and desperation that is faced by millions in the world.

The United States of America

CHAPTER 4

The land and the people

BACKGROUND

The power and influence of the USA in the twenty first century is based on its land, its industrial strength and the ingenuity and size of its population. The land area of the USA is 9,809,390 square kilometres and stretches from the arctic regions of Alaska to the sub-tropical climates of Florida and Louisiana and to the desert area around the Mexican border. It is the fourth largest country in the world in area.

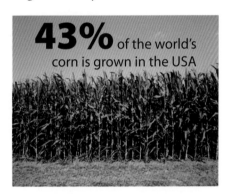

43% of the world's corn is grown in the USA

The land and the climate enable the USA to have the largest agricultural output of any country. The USA produces 10% of the world's wheat and 43% of the world's corn, yet agriculture accounts for a mere 1% of US economic output. However, US companies dominate the world's agricultural markets and are powerful enough to decide world prices for a number of important crops.

The USA is also rich in minerals. This has enabled US industry to become the world's dominant economy. It is among the world's leading producers of aluminium, copper, gold and lead as well as many other minerals. The USA is the second largest coal producer after China

and second only to Russia in the production of liquid natural gas. It is the third largest producer of crude petroleum after Saudi Arabia and Russia.

26% of the world's primary energy is produced in the USA

However, such is the demand in the USA from industry and consumers, it is one of the world's largest importers of energy. The USA accounts for 26% of the world's primary energy production but consumes 30% of the world's energy output. In 2005, the USA was responsible for 24% of the world's carbon dioxide emissions from burning fossil fuels.

20% of the world's estimated total production comes from the USA

In 2000, the industrial strength of the USA was such that its GDP was $9,077 billion or about 33% of the industrial world's production. In 2002, the USA produced over $10 trillion worth of goods and services which is over 20% the world's estimated total production of $47 trillion. This industrial and trading capacity gives the USA an overwhelmingly dominant position in the world. It means that the USA can use its industrial muscle as a political weapon over most other countries.

American ingenuity ensures that the USA benefits from technological developments

The ingenuity of its people has enabled the USA to be at the forefront of most significant economic developments over the past century or more. In 2000, the US government issued over 70,000 patents to US corporations and over 22,000 to individual citizens. Although challenged from time to time, the USA has usually managed to overcome competition by buying it out. In 1998, US companies bought 746 foreign companies with a total value of $127,760 million. These were mainly companies that provide power and electronic equipment which will become increasingly important in the energy-hungry world of the twenty first century.

The US population is the third largest in the world behind China and India. It holds a strong belief in capitalism which has enabled it to exploit the land, the climate and the mineral wealth of the USA to make it dominant in the world.

Capitalism has enabled US business and commerce to extend its influence to all parts of the world. Household names such as Esso, Boeing, McDonald's and Microsoft are examples of how influential US capitalism is in our lives. The products that US capitalism has exported clean our clothes and our homes, fill our larders, fridges and freezers, provide us with entertainment on our TV screens, at the cinema, on our computers and on our iPods. US capitalism provides us with many of our shopping experiences as well as our transport, our medical techniques and drugs to cure a multitude of ailments.

In short the USA dominates our lives in many obvious ways but also in many ways that we do not realise.

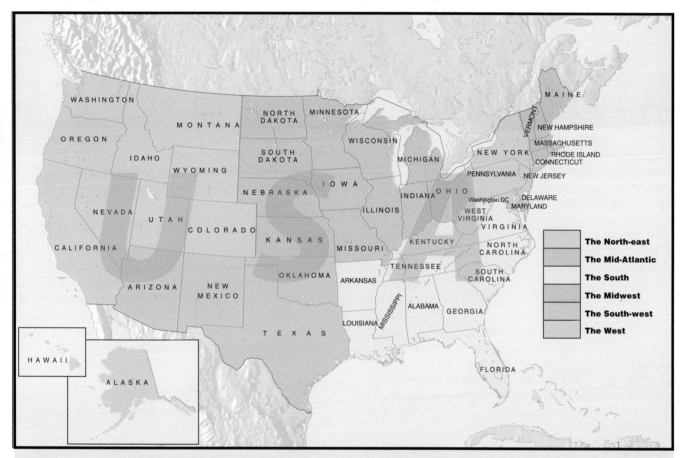

Figure 4.1

US GEOGRAPHY

In order to understand the distribution of the various population groups it is important to have a working knowledge of the regions of the USA.

There are six main geographical areas in the USA.

The North-east (Maine, New Hampshire, Vermont, Massachusetts, Connecticut, and Rhode Island)

The Mid-Atlantic (New York, New Jersey, Pennsylvania, Delaware, Washington, DC, and Maryland)

The South (Virginia, West Virginia, Kentucky, Tennessee, North Carolina, South Carolina, Georgia, Florida, Alabama, Mississippi, Arkansas, Louisiana)

The Midwest (Ohio, Michigan, Indiana, Wisconsin, Illinois, Minnesota, Iowa, Missouri, North Dakota, South Dakota, Kansas and Nebraska)

The South-west (Texas, Oklahoma, New Mexico, Arizona)

The West (Colorado, Wyoming, Montana, Utah, California, Nevada, Idaho, Oregon, Washington, Alaska, and Hawaii)

WHAT IS CAPITALISM?

An ideology is a set of ideas which describe how a society should operate. Capitalism is an economic ideology. Most Americans believe that capitalism is the ideology that is best for the US economy.

The principles that underpin capitalism are private ownership, the profit motive, the market, competition and choice as well as limited government intervention.

The principle of private ownership is that most organisations involved in the primary, manufacturing and service sectors should be privately owned by individuals who invest their capital. Capital is money that is saved or borrowed and can be owned by individuals or organisations. Some services may be provided by the government, such as the armed forces, the postal service or the issue of currency, but most should be provided privately.

Linked to this is the profit motive. Individuals are willing to invest their capital in business ventures because they intend to make a profit from their investments. The greater the profit they think they will make the greater their willingness to invest. Of course they may incur losses if they invest in the wrong business and this will drive those individuals out of the market.

The market is the hub of the capitalist economic system. The operation of the market determines the supply, the demand and the price of goods. The price of a commodity is determined by the demand—how many people want it, and the supply—how much is available. Private entrepreneurs are encouraged to set up businesses if the demand is high and prices are high. People are forced to leave if there is over-supply and prices are low.

With several suppliers there is competition and the consumer has choice. Competition leads to efficient production and the creation of products that consumers want. Therefore consumers' needs are met in the most efficient ways possible and their standards of living are improved.

Finally, the government should remain out of the market as much as possible. It is necessary to regulate for reasons of safety and to protect those involved from unscrupulous people who would produce goods that are not fit for the purpose intended or who would cheat the unwary of their capital. Nevertheless, as far as possible the government should apply a light touch and let the market create its own economic conditions.

Problems with capitalism

In theory, capitalism is the most efficient way for the economy to work. However, in practice capitalism has to have a great deal of regulation in order to control it. Through the years the US government has had to pass laws to protect consumers, investors, employers and workers.

The market is often dominated and therefore controlled by large organisations which can manipulate it in their own interest. At the start of the twentieth century the US government had to act to break up powerful organisations in steel, oil and the railroads. At the end of the twentieth century it had to act to stop the overwhelming power of the Microsoft organisation and it had to take action against the managers of the Enron organisation who had defrauded thousands of people.

Although in theory the market will find its own level if left to itself, in practice people and governments have to remain vigilant to its imperfections and be aware that it will be manipulated in the interests of powerful players.

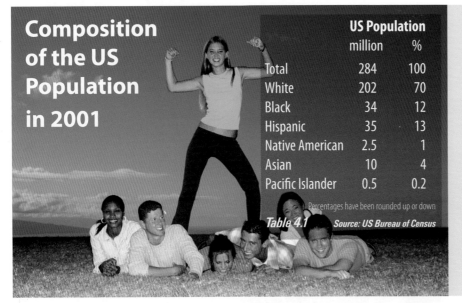

Composition of the US Population in 2001

US Population		
	million	%
Total	284	100
White	202	70
Black	34	12
Hispanic	35	13
Native American	2.5	1
Asian	10	4
Pacific Islander	0.5	0.2

Percentages have been rounded up or down

Table 4.1   *Source: US Bureau of Census*

The US Bureau of Census categorises the population by race and ethnicity. Race categorises people by physical characteristics whereas ethnicity categorises people by language and culture. The main racial groups identified by the Bureau of Census are the Pacific Islanders, Native Americans (which comprises Eskimo, Aleut and American Indian), Asians, Blacks and finally Whites. (See Table 4.1.) The ethnic category recognised by the Bureau of Census is Hispanic. Hispanics accounted for 13% of the US population in 2001.

HISPANICS

Size of the main Hispanic subgroups in 2000

Mexican American	66%
Puerto Rican	9%
Cuban	4%
Central and South American	15%
Other Hispanic	6%

Table 4.2   Source: US Census Bureau

Distribution of Mexican Americans (2000)

West 57%

Other 10%

South-west 33%

Figure 4.2

A significant number of this group are illegal aliens. These people are often called wetbacks, which is a term of abuse. In 2002, the US government estimated that there were 8 million illegal aliens in the US—mainly Mexican Americans.

There are so many illegal aliens from Mexico in particular because it is easy to enter the US from there. There is a long border, unfenced in many places and it is easy to cross over or under the fence where it exists. The border patrol, with 10,000 personnel in 2000, has highly sophisticated equipment but is undermanned for the size of the task.

Organised gangs led by 'coyotes' transport people over to work in the US. US farmers pay to have illegal workers brought over to work for them because they are cheap and not unionised. People in towns employ illegal workers as maids, nannies, pool attendants etc. and businessmen employ them in sweat shops. Therefore those people who

Mexican Americans

The Hispanics can be sub-divided into distinct groups. The largest sub-group are the Mexican Americans who make up 66% of the Hispanic population. They are concentrated in the western and southern border states such as Texas, Arizona, Colorado, New Mexico and California. 90% of the Mexican Americans are to be found in this area. These states are just over the border from Mexico which is why most live there.

They are attracted to the USA by its high living standards and they are able to afford much more than in their own home countries despite taking low paid work. Many do agricultural work, following planting and harvesting throughout the South and West. However, most work in cities as maids, gardeners, pool cleaners or in sweat shops making things such as clothes. Many maintain their families in Mexico by sending them money.

might otherwise object to the presence of illegal workers in the USA are the very people who are encouraging the influx by actively seeking to employ them.

Entering the USA to work is very attractive to illegal aliens. Despite working for very small wages and enduring harsh conditions they are able to enjoy living standards that are far better than in their country of origin and can find opportunities to work and feed their families.

However, the treatment of illegal aliens can be harsh. There have been well-documented and videoed incidents of beatings and murder by police and border guards. Employers exploit them with low wages, unsafe working conditions, long hours and being sacked with no warning or pay because they cannot complain to anyone. Organised gangs often take their money then dump them in the middle of nowhere or sometimes kill them.

Puerto Ricans

In 2000, 64% of Puerto Ricans lived in the Mid-Atlantic, mainly in New York. Puerto Rico is a Free Associated State of the USA which entitles Puerto Ricans to enter mainland USA to work and live. Many move to New York to subsidise their families at home and intend to return. They are trying to escape island poverty and work in low paid jobs such as taxi driving or as caretakers.

Cubans

80% of the Cubans in the USA live in the South—mainly in Florida and particularly in Miami. Florida is ninety miles from Cuba and it was to there that political refugees initially fled when Cuba was taken over by Fidel Castro and his fellow revolutionaries. However, many people who fled from Cuba subsequently were economic refugees who were chasing the American Dream.

Many Cubans call themselves exiles, not immigrants, because they

say they intend to return to Cuba when they can. Today the US turns back many fleeing Cubans. 46% live in city centres while 42.5% live in the suburbs and only 8.5% live in non-metropolitan areas.

ASIAN AND PACIFIC ISLANDERS

Asians are immigrants, or are descended from immigrants, who have arrived on the west coast of America from Far Eastern countries such as China, Japan and Korea, over the past 150 years. Consequently, the majority have settled in the cities of the West and South because these states face the Far East. Pacific Islanders mainly live in Hawaii.

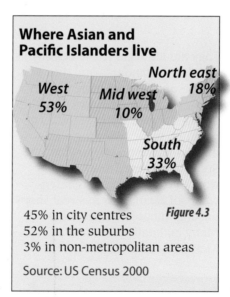

Where Asian and Pacific Islanders live

West 53%
Mid west 10%
North east 18%
South 33%

45% in city centres
52% in the suburbs
3% in non-metropolitan areas

Source: US Census 2000

Figure 4.3

For the first time the 2000 US Census counted Asians and Pacific Islanders separately.

The Asian population is clearly concentrated in the West—particularly California—and in the cities of the North-east and the South.

NATIVE AMERICANS

In the 2000 census, Native American was the group name given to American Indian, Eskimo (Innuit) and Aleut. The Eskimo and the Aleut inhabit Alaska, mainly within the Arctic Circle. The American Indians are concentrated in several western states mainly on reservations.

In the 1960s and 1970s the average income on reservations was 25% of the US average. There was widespread poverty and alcoholism due to unemployment and there was malnutrition, ill health and low educational attainment.

The 1980 Indian Gaming Act made gaming legal on reservations but they did not have to pay Federal or State taxes. Reservations are recognised in US law as foreign territories and they are not subject to all the laws of the USA. As a result, the incomes on many reservations soared. The revenues provided jobs and improvements in health, education and welfare facilities. There was a dramatic increase in the number of US citizens claiming to be Indian. Over 50% of American Indians live in non-metropolitan areas.

BLACKS

Distribution of Blacks in the USA

West 10%

Mid-west 19%

North-east 18%

South 54%

Figure 4.4

Source: US Census Bureau

Concentration in the cities

	Metropolitan areas	Non-metropolitan areas
South	78%	22%
North and West	97%	3%

Table 4.3

Distribution in the Cities of the North and West

City centres	69%
Suburbs	28%

Table 4.4

In the USA the majority of Blacks live in the South. Most live in the South for historical reasons as it was the centre of slavery in the nineteenth century. From the 1940s to the 1970s, Blacks migrated from the South to the cities of the North and West but since the 1970s this movement has reversed and increasing numbers of Blacks are moving to the South from the cities of the North.

They are moving back to escape the poverty and segregation that exists in the cities of the North. The South offers an improved lifestyle where their dollars can buy more, the pace of life is easier and the weather is better. In the South they experience greater equality both socially and economically and many middle-class Blacks are moving into Black-dominated areas through choice. In a sense segregation is becoming a lifestyle choice for middle-class Blacks.

Outside the South, Blacks overwhelmingly live in the metropolitan areas of the North and West. (See Table 4.3.)

Within these cities more than two-thirds of black city residents are concentrated in the city centres— mainly in the ghettos. Fewer than 30% live in the suburbs and then mainly in segregated suburbs. So, middle-class Blacks in the northern cities who have escaped the ghetto find themselves in middle-class black ghettos.

When Blacks moved from the South they moved to the poorer sections of the inner city. This led to white flight as Whites who were becoming wealthier in the post-war economic boom moved out to the newly created suburbs.

A Black middle class soon developed as they improved their education and secured better jobs and Blacks began to move out to the

suburbs. However, Whites moved out as Blacks moved in or else took steps such as making it difficult for Blacks to get mortgages or forming management groups to prevent Blacks from moving in.

This process led to the development of the ghettos in the cities of the North and West. Those Blacks who were trapped in the inner cities experienced high levels of unemployment, widespread poverty, single parent families, poor education and health, and high levels of crime. The general social breakdown in the ghetto created a cycle of poverty which trapped the majority in its grip. The poor and excluded had few role models except the pimps and the drug dealers and there were few black businesses or businessmen for the next generation to try to copy. So the majority of Blacks born in the ghetto remained trapped in the ghetto and many became the victims of drugs, violence or AIDS.

THE IMPACT OF POPULATION GROWTH

The relationship between the birth rate and the death rate is the first factor that affects population growth. If the birth rate is greater than the death rate then the population will grow, and if the death rate is higher than the birth rate then the population will fall. The second factor is migration. If more people enter the country than leave then the population will rise and vice versa.

The fastest growing group in the USA is the Hispanics, and in particular the Mexican Americans. In 2003 the Hispanics had overtaken Blacks as the largest minority group in the US. At this rate, by mid-century Whites will cease to be over 50% of the population and will become the largest minority group. By the end of the twenty first century Hispanics will be one-third of the US population with Whites only just ahead with 40%.

The Hispanic population is growing rapidly because it is a relatively young population and large numbers cross the border from Mexico each year. During the 1990s there were 4.2 million immigrants to the USA from Mexico and Central and South America. The next largest area of immigration was Asia with 2.8 million immigrants.

Secondly, Hispanic women have relatively more children than other women in the USA. There are more women in the childbearing age group—15 to 44—because they are, on average, a younger population. Also, they have a higher fertility rate than any other group because of custom and religion. (They are mostly Catholic.) In 2000, the fertility rate for Hispanic women was significantly higher than for other groups.

In 2001, Hispanic births reached 50.2% of all births in California. The Hispanic population is poised to become the majority population in California by the middle of the century.

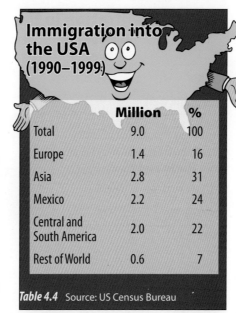

Immigration into the USA (1990–1999)

	Million	%
Total	9.0	100
Europe	1.4	16
Asia	2.8	31
Mexico	2.2	24
Central and South America	2.0	22
Rest of World	0.6	7

Table 4.4   Source: US Census Bureau

Fertility rates

(per thousand) 2000

White	60.0
Black	63.2
Asian	54.6
Hispanic	95.1

Table 4.5

Source: US Census Bureau

THE ISSUE OF IMMIGRATION

Immigration has been an issue in US politics for many years. From 1924 to 1968, the quota system favoured migrants from northern Europe and excluded Asian migrants. During this period one debate centred around the unfairness of this policy towards Asians and Latin Americans. A second issue was about the economic impact of immigration. Many employers supported the continuation of immigration because of the benefits of cheap labour and larger markets. However, employees who suffered from low wages and unemployment because they were in competition with the immigrants objected to immigration.

In 1968, this quota system was abolished. The number of Asian and Latin American migrants increased rapidly. The arguments continued over the economic impact of increasing numbers of new arrivals but now also included the impact of Hispanics and Asians on the culture of the USA which developed some racist themes.

There were those who argued that immigrants were net contributors to the economy. They started small businesses to achieve the American Dream. They were a relatively young population and economically active so were net contributors, through taxation, to the budgets of both state and Federal governments in the USA. On the other side, the opponents of immigration complained that a young and relatively poor population cost US taxpayers large amounts in welfare payments, education, medical provision and other social services.

Furthermore, there was a debate between those in the USA who claimed that US society would be strengthened by multiculturalism and those who claimed the essence of the American way of life was under threat.

OPPOSITION TO CONTINUED IMMIGRATION–1990s

In the first half of the 1990s there was a growing mood of anti-immigration due in part to the downturn in the US economy. With unemployment rising and wage rates falling, blue-collar workers, both white and minority, faced competition from migrants. White-collar workers faced competition from second generation Asians who were increasingly successful due to the the value they placed on education.

'Angry White Males' blamed immigration for their problems. The 1990 *Immigration Act* had increased the number of immigrants allowed to enter the US annually from 270,000 to 700,000 plus unlimited numbers of spouses, parents and children.

Many Whites and Blacks, particularly in California, felt their way of life was under threat. They felt overwhelmed by the growth of Hispanic culture—Spanish spoken in business, shops, entertainment and schools, Spanish radio and TV channels, Spanish cuisine and Spanish festivals. As Hispanic numbers grew in certain areas Whites and Blacks left.

There was also the cost to the taxpayer. In the 1990s, estimates put costs at over $30 billion each year to pay for illegal immigrants to receive things such as education, health and welfare. However, during the same period the Urban Institute calculated that throughout the USA, immigrants contributed between $25 and $30 billion more in taxes than they received in services.

Blacks also felt threatened by the Koreans in parts of California. Koreans opened successful small businesses, particularly shops, in black neighbourhoods. Blacks accused them of taking money out of poor black neighbourhoods. Korean-owned businesses provided amenities for Blacks that otherwise would not have existed. This resentment led Blacks to target Korean shops during riots in Los Angeles.

Illegal immigrants were seen by other workers as causing low wages and making excessive demands on the welfare system.

Proposition 187

Apparent government inaction over immigration led California to vote for Proposition 187 in 1994. A Proposition is a question put to the electorate of a state at the time of an election. If a majority vote in favour the state legislature must pass it into law. The aim of Proposition 187 was to discourage illegal immigration to California by denying illegal aliens and their children access to education, health and welfare benefits. Furthermore teachers, social workers and health workers were required to report anyone they thought suspicious. There were an estimated 1.6 million illegal immigrants in California in 1994.

The effect of Proposition 187 was felt mainly by Hispanics who thought it was racist. They argued that officials were likely to be

In October 1994, more than 70,000 people converged to protest the impending passage of California's Proposition 187. Many observers believe that the defiant display of Mexican flags by protesters inflamed anti-immigrant sentiment and contributed to the initiative's subsequent passage.

suspicious of Spanish-sounding names rather than English-sounding names. Others argued it would increase prejudice against brown-skinned people whether they were illegal, legal, visitors or tourists.

Proposition 187 was immediately challenged in the courts and the government of California was prevented from putting it into law until the courts decided if it was constitutional or not. In 1997, a federal judge ruled that most of Proposition 187 was unconstitutional because the Constitution gives responsibility for immigration matters to the Federal government. It is therefore unconstitutional for California— a state government—to pass laws on immigration matters. However, Proposition 187 became a symbol of the mood of opposition to immigration in the US.

Between 1996 and 2001, the mood of anti-immigration softened in the US. The economy improved and reduced unemployment led to less opposition to immigration. Political parties also realised that certain anti-immigration policies were a vote loser in the Hispanic areas of the US. As the Hispanic population is the fastest growing community, both Democrats and Republicans saw that if they lost the support of large numbers of Hispanic voters they would face defeat in election after election.

Despite this mood change there were two laws introduced to tighten up on immigration. The 1996 Immigration Reform Law doubled the Border Patrol from 5,175 in 1996 to 10,000 in 2000. This was an attempt to reduce the flow of illegal immigrants across the US – Mexican border.

The 1996 Welfare Reform Law stopped access to welfare for legal immigrants until they had lived in the USA for five years and stopped welfare access for illegal immigrants altogether. It was intended to make the US less of a soft touch and to deter immigration. However, as the mood softened both the Federal government and individual states restored some welfare payments.

IMMIGRATION AFTER SEPTEMBER 11, 2001

Following the destruction of the World Trade Centre, attitudes hardened and there was a public outcry demanding the reform of immigration laws. Both the public and politicians were incensed by the news that the pilots who flew the planes into the World Trade Centre had been able to change their visas from 'tourist' to 'student' without adequate security checks.

In this climate of opinion, the US Congress rushed to pass two Acts, the USA PATRIOT Act and the Border Security Act. These were intended to restrict and control the entry of aliens to the USA. The Executive issued several Orders which gave it a massive increase in powers, for which it was answerable to itself, and indeed could overrule court decisions. The judges also increased the power of the US government.

In 2003, the Immigration and Naturalisation Service (INS) was switched from the jurisdiction of the Department of Justice to become an agency of the newly created Department of Homeland Security. It became part of the Department's new US Citizenship and Immigration Services (USCIS). This radically changed the emphasis of the INS. Where, previously, a visa could be applied for and granted on a turnaround basis, it suddenly took months with extensive background checks before being granted—and only then if there was not the merest hint of any suspicion. If any question should arise about whether a case should be approved or denied, it will be denied. "No immigration official wants to be the one who lets in the next terrorist."

A lawyer who specialised in immigration matters, observed, "What we used to have in dealing with the INS was a culture of service. What we have now is a culture of 'no'."

The USA PATRIOT Act 2001

(Uniting and Strengthening America by Providing Appropriate Tools Required to Intercept and Obstruct Terrorism)

The intention of the USA PATRIOT Act was, in its own words, "to further close our borders to foreign terrorists and to detain and remove those within our borders." It introduced new criteria for denying en-

The USA PATRIOT Act trebled the number of border patrols on the US –Canadian border

try and gave the Attorney General (the chief law officer of the Federal government) exclusive power to certify an alien as a terrorist if he/she had "reasonable grounds to believe" that an alien is a terrorist or has committed an act of terrorism.

Once a person is certified by the Attorney General as a terrorist he or she must be detained. The law does say that an alien detained under the Act must be released within seven days if not charged with a violation. However, the charge need not be for an act of terrorism. It may be for a minor infraction of the immigration laws, and not even one related to the alleged terrorist act. If a violation is found, the suspect may be held for an unspecified length of time.

The Act also trebled the number of the border patrols on the US – Canadian border and gave the INS access to the FBI's criminal records. It introduced new grounds for denying or deporting people who were "deemed to be representatives of foreign terrorist organisations or of any group that publicly endorses terrorist acts".

Border Security Act (November 2001)

The *Border Security Act* provided a bigger budget to increase the number of INS and Customs Service staff and to upgrade their technology. It also allowed the sharing of information among federal agencies to resolve deportation issues. It introduced new rules for informing the authorities about immigrants. For example, the Act required airlines and passenger ships to transmit lists of arriving passengers on their way to the United States and colleges had to certify that foreign students did in fact enrol and were continuing to attend.

Executive regulation
(issued 29 October 2001)

The government took the power to detain an alien even if an immigration judge had ordered the alien's release. This allowed the government to continue to detain for long periods aliens held for the most minor immigration violations.

Judicial Change

On 21 September, 2001, Chief Immigration Judge Michael Creppy issued a memo which gave the Attorney General the right "to require Immigration Judges to close the hearing to the public." Therefore the Attorney General has the power to decide if proceedings are to be held in secret or in public.

These changes have extended the power of the US Executive not only over immigration but also over US citizens. (See Chapter 5.)

Impact on Immigration

In the aftermath of September 11 2001, there was an immediate reduction in the number of migrants to the USA as well as a significant impact on those seeking asylum.

IMMIGRATION to the USA

2000	849,807
2001	1,064,318
2002	1,063,732
2003	705,827
2004	946,142

Table 4.7

Source: Us Census Bureau

Refugees and Asylum Seekers

2001	188,500
2002	126,084
2003	44,230
2004	71,230

Table 4.8

Source: Us Census Bureau

CHAPTER 5

The system of government in the USA

The US system of government developed out of the American Revolution. When the thirteen colonies gained their independence from Britain in 1787, their leaders realised they would have to work together or their rivalries would eventually lead to wars as had happened in the nation states of Europe. The founding fathers, as taxpayers, wanted a system of government that would cost them as little as possible, and as independently minded people they wanted a government that would interfere in their lives as little as possible. They had rid themselves of British rule because it had passed laws that interfered in their lives and taxed them handsomely for the privilege. Furthermore they wanted to design a system of government that would deny any one person or small group too much power. They had just thrown out a dictatorship and did not want to fashion a new one. Finally, they had to create a system of government where none now existed.

It was against this background that the US Constitution was created.

Unlike Britain which had evolved its constitution over centuries, they had to invent a constitution very quickly. Thus it had to be a written constitution detailing what the new government could and could not do so that everyone had a clear reference point.

The basis of the new constitution was to be the people of the United States and the individual states as the colonies had become. Anything not specified in the US Constitution as being a power of the new Federal government was reserved for the states or the people.

A single Federal government was introduced in order to maintain peace between rival states. It would be the referee in any disputes between the states and thus prevent them from going to war with each other. Moreover, it would help to keep taxes down. Instead of thirteen armies there would be one army to which they could all contribute. There would be only one ambassador to each of the foreign capitals. Avoiding duplication would keep down taxes. Creating one currency and one postal service under the control of the Federal government should also lead to harmony.

However, the framers of this new Constitution were mainly rich gentlemen, lawyers and landowners. They did not want to see an individual or a small group assuming dictatorial power. Neither did they want to see the general public, through their voting power, electing people who would challenge their privileged positions in society. Therefore they built two ideas into the US Constitution—the separation of powers and checks and balances.

To avoid the dictatorship of the electorate they introduced the electoral college for the election of the President. Thus the electors in each state would elect reliable representatives from that state to sit on an electoral college which would be trusted to chose a President of the right calibre.

THE SEPARATION OF POWERS

"The concentration of [all the powers of government] in the same hands is precisely the definition of despotic government ... The government we fought for was one not only founded on free principles but in which the powers of government should be so divided and balanced among several bodies of magistracy ... that no one could transcend their legal limits without being effectively checked and restrained by the others ... For this reason ... the legislative, executive, and judicial departments should be separate and distinct, so that no person should exercise the powers of more than one of them at the same time."

Thomas Jefferson

Thomas Jefferson became the third President of the United States in 1801

Any government has to be able to fulfil three functions.

- It must be able to make laws—the legislative function.
- It must be able to carry out those laws—the executive function.
- It must be able to make judgements according to those laws—the judicial function.

If it is unable to carry out any of these functions effectively then it cannot govern.

If these functions are concentrated into too few hands then the government can easily become dictatorial. Therefore a strict 'separation of powers' was built into the US Constitution.

The Legislative function is the work of Congress. For a law to be made it has to be passed by both the Senate and the House of Representatives and finally be signed by the President.

The Executive function of government is the work of the President. The President is in charge of carrying out the laws enacted by Congress through the various Departments of State which are responsible to their respective Secretaries of State who are appointed by the President and who, along with the President, form the White House Cabinet.

The Judicial function is the work of the Supreme Court. It is the nine Justices of the Supreme Court who ultimately decide whether laws enacted by Congress and executed by the President are acceptable according to the Constitution. If they declare a law to be unconstitutional then it cannot be applied in the USA. Also, they can change the way existing laws are applied by redefining what they mean.

Therefore the three functions necessary for government to operate are clearly separated in the USA by the provisions of the Constitution.

CHECKS AND BALANCES

In order to ensure further that no group could gain too much power the separation of powers was reinforced by a series of checks and balances.

The power of the Federal government is balanced against the rights of the state governments and the people. All powers not assigned by the Constitution to the Federal government are, in the text of the Constitution itself, *"reserved to the states respectively, or to the people."* This is the important principle of subsidiarity which means any task a government has to perform is assigned to the lowest level of government able to perform it.

Should the Federal government wish to extend the range of its authority it must amend the Constitution. To do this two-thirds of the Senate and two-thirds of the House of Representatives must agree as well as the President. In addition, three-quarters of the state governments must also agree to ratify the changes. This makes any extension of Federal power very difficult to achieve.

The power of the President is checked by both Congress and the Supreme Court. If either of these institutions believes that the President is not acting in the best interests of the people of the United

States it has the power to check his actions.

The Office of the President proposes most laws during each session of Congress. However, it is Congress that must pass the laws. For example, the President draws up the budget each year to allow the government to function but Congress has to vote through the money. So this is a check on the power of the President.

On the other hand, Congress may pass new legislation, but if the President uses his veto and refuses to sign it, it does not become law. This is a check upon the power of Congress. Congress can overturn a veto if it has a two-thirds majority in both Houses but in practice this would be very difficult to achieve.

Another balancing item which can check the growing power of the Federal government is the system of election. The President is elected for a fixed term of four years and for a maximum of two terms. Therefore there is a time limit on the power a President can build up. The President has to face election after four years and so must remain aware of the wishes of the electorate.

Members of the House of Representatives are elected every two years so must always be aware of the will of the electorate. An unpopular President might find a hostile House of Representatives elected midway through his term of office which will check his ability to pass unpopular legislation. Senators are elected for six years but one-third come up for election every two years. So again the electorate can put a check on the power of the Senate and also on the President in the midterm of the Presidency.

The Supreme Court Justices are appointed for life by the President. Once they are appointed a President cannot get rid of them. Many Presidents have had to live with a Supreme Court which had an alternative view on the law of the USA. These Presidents have had to soften their policies in the face of a hostile Supreme Court.

A few Presidents have been able to appoint more than one Supreme Court Justice because of death or retiral and so have influenced decisions many years into the future. Nevertheless, they personally have not been able to benefit to any great extent from their nominees.

Many Presidential appointments to Cabinet, to ambassadorships, to NATO and the United Nations are open to scrutiny by Congress which can call the nominees to testify before its committees and can turn down the nominations.

It is clear that the US Constitution has a significant number of checks and balances built in to prevent any one individual or group managing to gain dictatorial power over the people.

THE POWERS OF THE PRESIDENT

The powers of the President of the United States are set out in Article II of the Constitution. It defines the role of the President as head of the executive branch of the US government. It describes the powers of the President and defines those powers which can be exercised without legislative approval and which require the consent of the Senate or Congress.

The President's powers lie in a number of areas. Firstly, he has the most important role in national security. Secondly, he has an important part to play in the legislative function, both in the formation of legislation and in passing laws. Finally, he is the head of the administration for the US government.

National security

In the area of national security, the President is the Commander-in-Chief of the armed forces and is charged with the defence of the USA. He can order the use of troops overseas without declaring war. However, in order to declare war officially, he must get the approval of Congress. The President can also make treaties with other

nations but the Senate must approve any treaty before it becomes official.

The President is also responsible for the internal security of the USA. Following the attack on the World Trade Centre in 2001, the President used an Executive Order to create The Department for Homeland Security. This was later reinforced by the *Homeland Security Act* in 2002. This has significantly increased the ability of the administration to monitor its citizens.

The President nominates US ambassadors to other countries with the agreement of a majority of the Senate. He also receives ambassadors from other nations, which gives official US recognition to these countries.

The President and legislation

The President has a number of important functions in the legislative process. At the start of each session of Congress in January, the President addresses both Houses with his State of the Union Address. He outlines some of the important issues which have affected the USA in the previous twelve months and gives an indication of the actions his administration intends to take in the next year. These will state briefly the main themes of his budget and some of the legislation he wishes to see enacted. However, the President cannot introduce bills directly. He can propose a bill, but a member of Congress must submit it for him.

It is also a function of the President to approve any bill passed by Congress. When both Houses have passed a bill, they send it to the President for his approval. If he agrees with the bill, he signs it and the law takes effect, but if the President does not agree with a bill, he can veto it.

There are two ways the President can exercise his veto. He can send the bill back to Congress unsigned, usually with a list of reasons explaining why he has rejected it. This usually stops a bill becoming law because it requires a two-thirds majority in both Houses to overturn the veto. Secondly, he can use his 'pocket' veto. A pocket veto is when the President fails to sign a bill within the ten days allowed by the Constitution. If Congress is in session and the President fails to sign the bill, it becomes law without his signature. However, if Congress is adjourned then the law is not enacted and the President has exercised his pocket veto.

The President can bypass Congress in certain circumstances by issuing an Executive Order. This has the power of law but does not need Congress to sanction it. Therefore the President can make laws in the USA with no check from Congress. In his first administration, President Bush issued 168 Executive Orders.

Patronage

The President is responsible for the executive function of the US government, namely to carry out the laws passed by the legislative branch of government. In Article 3 Section 2 the Constitution states that the President has to "Take care that the laws be faithfully executed". In order to do this he appoints the heads of each Executive Branch department such as the Secretary of Education. President Bush appointed fifteen Secretaries, each of whom runs a department of government whose officials carry out the work of government. Currently these are the Secretaries of Agriculture, Commerce, Defence, Education, Energy, Health and Human Services, Homeland Security, Housing and Urban Development, Interior, Labour, State, Transportation, Treasury, and Veterans Affairs, and the Attorney General wh heads the Department of Justice. Along with six other members, including the Vice President of the USA, these people form the Cabinet, which advises the President on policy.

He also appoints ambassadors, Supreme Court Justices, and other officials, with the agreement of a majority of the Senate.

The President is the single most powerful person in the USA and due to the power and influence of the USA the single most powerful person in the world. The President is the only person elected by all the people of the USA and consequently a popular President will increase the influence of the presidency for the period he is in power. A popular President will have greater influence over Congress which will allow him to pass much of the legislation he wants and thus power will shift towards his Office.

Throughout the history of the USA, power has shifted from the people and the states towards the Federal authority and while there have

President Bush named his top economic adviser, Ben Bernanke, right, as the new chairman of the Federal Reserve Board, replacing Alan Greenspan, left, in the Oval Office at the White House in October 2005. Bush's appointment of a Fed chairman and the filling of two Supreme Court vacancies carry the potential to affect people's lives more directly than most of the heated policy debates in Congress.

been shifts of influence between Congress and the President from time to time, the power of the US President is far greater today than the Founding Fathers of the USA either envisaged or intended.

Presidential Power since 2001

The Department of Homeland Security brought together twenty two agencies (departments of government) into one agency dedicated to protecting America from terrorism. The reorganisation radically changed the approach these agencies took to carrying out their functions. By bringing these departments together and requiring them to join up their intelligence and surveillance, The Department of Homeland Security has become an organisation that is capable of providing the government with information not only about those suspected of terrorism, but also about every American citizen. The danger is that the White House could use this considerable power for its own political ends against its own citizens as it did at the time of 'Watergate'.

Several laws passed since 2001 have shifted power to a significant extent from the individual in the USA to the government, and in particular the Office of the President. The *USA PATRIOT Act* gives the Attorney General the power to order the detention of anyone he has "reasonable grounds" to suspect is 'a terrorist' or is linked to 'terrorism'. No proof is necessary. With an Executive Order issued in 2001, the President gave the Attorney General the power to overrule the courts if they order the release of someone deemed to be a terrorist.

These Executive Orders were designed to give the President powers at the time of an emergency. However, the administration of President Bush says it will retain these powers as long as there is a threat of terrorism and the USA is engaged in its War on Terrorism. By its nature that could continue indefinitely. The fallout from the events of September 11th 2001 could be the extension of Presidential power and control over the people of the USA.

This constitutional danger is identified in this extract.

"The current order is unlimited, in a fight against terrorism that could go on for years. And the Bush order could easily be extended to citizens, under this administration's legal theory. Because the 6th Amendment makes no distinction between citizens and aliens, the claim of war exigency could sweep its protections aside for anyone in this country who might fit the vague definitions of aiding terrorism … Necessity—as it has done throughout our history—supersedes the law of the Constitution … Given the vagueness of the order, and the equally vague USA PATRIOT Act, the potential to abuse both the presidential order and the congressional enactment does not seem so far-fetched … That is the greatest danger of the Bush order. It is an act of executive fiat, imposed without even consulting the Congress. And it seeks to exclude the courts entirely from a process that may fundamentally affect life and liberty.
(Martin S Sheffer *White House Studies* 22 September 2003)

CHAPTER 6

Political parties and their support

Political parties in the USA are not the same as political parties in the UK. In the US there is no national party structure with a central party headquarters and constituency parties full of activists and supporters around the country. The only time a political party exists as a national entity in the US is for the few days of the National Convention every four years. At this gathering state delegates from their respective parties meet to choose their candidates for President and Vice President. The election in the US is a series of individual state campaigns which combine to create a national campaign.

Most candidates organise their own campaigns by raising funds from wealthy backers and interested parties. They will decide their own issues and put them forward. Individual candidates may be 'Republican' or 'Democrat' but there is no party line that they have to support. A Democrat candidate for Congress may be against gun control while the Democrat candidate for President may be for gun control. A Republican candidate for Congress may oppose controls on abortion while the rest of the party may favour more control. Candidates decide the issues for themselves. Indeed, it is not necessarily important to know whether a candidate is a Democrat or a Republican, it is more important to discover whether he or she is liberal or conservative towards the important issues of the day.

Nevertheless, each party will have a national strategy to identify key swing states and key groups within these states. It will spend millions of dollars on advertising, based on an analysis of what its strategists believe the electorate wants to hear. Today it will take several million dollars to elect a Member of Congress, even more to elect a Senator and over $250 million to elect a President. In 2004, Kerry spent over $250 million and lost handsomely.

The two major political parties in the USA over the past 150 years have been the Republican Party and the Democratic Party. In the last few national elections support for these two parties has been divided by geography, wealth, gender, race / ethnicity and certain specific issues.

The Democratic Party has most of its support in the coastal areas of the USA and the major cities. The Republican support is concentrated in the Midwest and the South and is more rural. The Democratic Party has majority support among poorer people, whereas more middle and higher income earners support the Republicans. Women have been more likely to vote Democrat whereas men tend to be more Republican. The Democrats have relied on the support of Blacks and Hispanics to win elections in the past few decades. Those people who are described as liberal on many of the issues tend to favour the Democrats while those with conservative views in the USA have cast their ballots for the Republican Party.

GEOGRAPHICAL SUPPORT

Between the end of the Civil War and the 1960s, the Democrats dominated the South because white voters blamed the Republican Party for the emancipation of the slaves. The Blacks supported the Republicans.

However, in the 1950s and 1960s the Democratic Party came to be identified with the Black Civil Rights movement. The Whites in the South switched their loyalty to the Republican Party while Black support shifted from the Republi-

Regional Vote

	Percentage of voters	Republican Party	Democratic Party
North-east	22	43	56
Midwest	26	51	48
South	32	58	42
West	20	49	50

Table 6.1 Source: CNN Exit Poll 2004

Urban – Rural Divide

	Percentage of voters	Republican Party	Democratic Party
Urban	30	45	54
Suburban	46	52	47
Rural	25	57	42

Table 6.2 Source: CNN Exit Poll 2004

Voting by wealth

	Percentage of voters	Republican Party	Democratic Party
Less than $50,000	45	44	55
More than $50,000	55	56	43

Table 6.3 Source: CNN Exit Poll 2004

cans to the Democrats. Blacks had been attracted to the Democratic Party since the 1930s when its New Deal had helped many overcome the problems of the Depression. When a Democratic President forced through the *Civil Rights Act* and the *Voting Rights Act* in the 1960s, the Black vote became firm for the Democrats. Since 1980, the states in the South have solidly supported the Republicans in every Presidential election because the majority population is white.

The Democratic Party has a majority of the support in the large cities of the USA where 30% of the electorate live. This support is mainly from the poor who depend on low paid employment or on welfare for their income.

Republican Party support is stronger in the suburban areas of the cit-

ies and in rural USA. This is where the majority of those who earn more than $50,000 per year live and as long as they feel that the Republicans are better at running the economy and keeping their taxes down than the Democrats, they will continue to vote Republican. Republican support is growing in suburban USA. Nonetheless, this group is not solid in its support for the Republicans and if people believed that the US economy would be safer in the hands of the Democrats then they would readily change their support.

GENDER AND RACE

The female vote is important because there are more women voters than male voters in US elections. In 2004, 54% of voters were women. Women have traditionally been more likely to vote for the Demo-

crats. In 1996, 54% of women voters supported the Democrats. However, the Republicans have been making inroads into this vote and in 2004 the Democrats enjoyed a narrow majority of 51% compared to 48% for the Republicans.

It is also important to know the race or ethnicity of the voter as well as their gender. In 2004 white men, who accounted for 36% of all voters, voted 62% to 37% in favour of the Republicans and white women voted 55% to 44% in favour. However, among non-white voters, who accounted for 22% of the electorate, men voted 67% to 30% in favour of the Democratic Party and women were supporters by 75% to 24%. (See Table 6.4.) Therefore race and ethnicity is an important factor in party support in the USA.

Gender and Race

	Percentage of voters	Republican Party	Democratic Party
White men	36	62	37
White women	41	55	44
Non-white men	10	30	67
Non-white women	12	24	75

Table 6.4 Source: CNN Exit Poll 2004

CHANGING POLITICAL SUPPORT

From 1955 to 1995 the Democrats were the majority party in both Houses of Congress with the exception of the Senate between 1981 and 1987. Although a majority position in either the House of Representatives or the Senate does not mean that members of a party will vote together on any issue, it does indicate that through these years, Democratic Party members had more influence in US political life than their Republican opponents. During these years, though, there were more Republican Presidents than Democrat Presidents. Between 1955 and 2005, Republicans held the Presidential Office for thirty years.

Since 1995, the Republican Party appears to have been in the ascendancy. In fact, if it had not been for the popularity of Bill Clinton, the change in party fortunes might have happened sooner. By the 1990s the Republican Party was more in tune with the issues which concerned white middle America. Its more conservative views on lower taxation and welfare reductions appealed to voters worried about competition from abroad and the effect it was having on employment and incomes in the USA.

The Democratic Party has come to be identified with helping the poor and the minorities. Its more liberal stance on welfare and Affirmative Action has maintained its support from the poor, Blacks and sections of the Hispanic minority. How-

House of Representatives

Year	Majority Party	Minority Party	Other
1991–93	D267	R167	1
1993–95	D258	R176	1
1995–97	R230	D204	1
1997–99	R226	D207	2
1999–01	R223	D210	2
2001–03	R221	D212	2
2003–05	R229	D204	1
2005–07	R231	D202	2

Table 6.5

Senate

Year	Majority Party	Minority Party	Other
1991–93	D56	R44	0
1993–95	D57	R43	0
1995–97	R52	D48	0
1997–99	R55	D45	0
1999–01	R55	D45	0
2001–03	R50	D50	0
2003–05	R51	D48	1
2005–07	R55	D44	1

Table 6.6

Sources: Census Bureau & Library of Congress

The McGlade family from Bradenton, Fla., kneels in prayer in front of an abortion clinic in Orlando, Fla., during a protest by people opposed to abortion. The Republicans targeted these groups and they are more influential in elections.

ever this is a shrinking constituency. There are far fewer liberal white Americans willing to support the Democratic Party on these issues than there were twenty to thirty years ago.

The 'religious right'

The 'religious right' has become more influential in US politics in recent years. Originating from the 'Bible belt' that runs through the South, many protestant groups have strong views on the place of religious teaching in schools, are against abortion and homosexual marriage, and see 'the family' as the bedrock of the American way of life. These views struck a cord with many white voters as well as attracting people from the minorities. Many Hispanics are Catholic, are very family-centred and oppose abortion. The Demo-

cratic Party has become identified with an image that is pro-abortion and pro-gay rights.

After the election of 2000, Republican strategists realised that four million evangelical Christians had not voted. The Republicans set out to win that vote. Their strategy was based on a message of traditional cultural values, anti-gay marriage, anti-abortion and a simple style of faith-based leadership. The strategy appealed to other groups. Republican support from Hispanics increased and Catholic support rose from 47% to 52%, despite the fact that the Democrat candidate was a Catholic. The only socially conservative group to reject the Repub-

licans was the middle-class black vote.

The success of this strategy was seen in several states. For example, in Ohio, a state on which the 2004 election hinged, polls suggested that about a quarter of the voters described themselves as evangelical Christians. They voted overwhelmingly for Bush. The Republicans won Ohio by only 130,000 votes. Without this fundamentalist vote the Republicans would have lost Ohio and the Democrats would have won the White House.

Nevertheless, it is easy to overstate the importance of moral issues as the deciding factor which determines how the majority of Americans vote. In an exit poll in 2004, the issue of moral values was given by 22% of voters as having the most influence on them. Although this was the highest percentage of all the issues, 55% of American voters in the same poll said that abortion should be legal.

Since 2001, terrorism and the War in Iraq have had an impact on US voters and could become more influential in the near future. Terrorism was given as the most important issue by 19% of voters in 2004 and 54% felt that the USA was safer than in 2000. This has helped to increase support for the Republicans. However, the War in Iraq was the deciding issue for 15% of voters, and although 51% approved of the US invasion, 52% felt that the war was going badly. With over 1,000 US military personnel dead, with the possibility of more fatalities to follow, and if the USA becomes stuck in a protracted operation in Iraq, many Americans may turn away from the Republicans and the prospects for their future dominance in US politics may be undermined.

BLACKS AND THE POLITICAL PARTIES

There has been an increase in black representation at Federal level in the House of Representatives. In 1993, the number of black Congressmen/ women increased from twenty five to thirty eight and has remained around that level ever since. It would appear that over the past fifteen years there has been progress in black representation.

However in 2003, Blacks made up 9% of the House of Representatives and 0% of the Senate, whereas they were 12% of the population. If Blacks were represented in proportion to their population size there would have been fifty three black Congressmen/ women and twelve black Senators. Although there has been some improvement in the recent past, Blacks do not have equal representation.

Despite this, Black influence is stronger in Congress than the numbers appear to show. Blacks overwhelmingly vote Democrat. In most elections, over 90% of the Blacks who vote, vote Democrat. Democrats tend to be more favourable to Black issues than Republicans. The Democrats are also more likely to support Affirmative Action and

Black Membership of Congress								
	1991	1993	1995	1997	1999	2001	2003	2005
House of Representatives	25	38	40	39	39	36	37	42
Senate	0	1	1	1	0	0	0	1

Table 6.7 Source: US Census Bureau

welfare payments and are more likely to use government power to help the poor. Many white Democrat Congressmen/ women support these issues because they owe their election to the black vote in their District and more than one Democrat President, including Bill Clinton, has owed his Presidency to the black vote. Furthermore, several Blacks have seniority in Congress. They have become chairpersons of powerful Congressional committees which gives them influence.

For a Bill to get through the House of Representatives, 218 members must vote for it. There are forty two black members of the House, which means that they can deliver 20% of the votes needed if they vote together. The Black Caucus consists of all the black members of the

House of Representatives. They discuss the issues and agree a common approach. The Black Caucus is strong in Congress and its united approach gives black members influence beyond their apparent numerical strength. As they can deliver forty two votes on an issue, they can trade off their support for support from others on issues of interest to them.

Majority–minority districts

There was a significant increase in the number black Representatives elected to the House of Representatives in 1993 as a direct result of the *Voting Rights Act* which was passed in 1982. Under this legislation, District boundaries were redrawn to ensure there were Black or Hispanic majorities in some Dis-

The Black Caucus can deliver over 20% of the votes required to pass a Bill through the House of Representatives. This requires Democrat and Republican members to vote together.

tricts so that more black or Hispanic Congressmen/ women were elected. (Congressmen/ women represent Districts.) These were called majority-minority districts.

The process of redrawing electoral boundaries to achieve a particular electoral result is called gerrymandering. An example is District 12 in North Carolina which follows the line of an interstate highway for many miles combining pockets of minority voters who live along its length.

Majority-minority districts were first introduced in the 1992 election and led to a significant jump in the number of black Representatives in Congress. However, it could be argued that this increase led to a reduction in black influence in Congress. There were more Representatives who were black but this meant there were fewer white Democrats elected.

In many Districts the black vote is the swing vote. For example, if 55% of the white voters vote Republican and 45% vote Democrat, but 90% of the black voters vote Democrat, then the black vote swings the contest in favour of the Democrat candidate. Imagine a town where there are three Districts and in each 30% of the voters are black Democrat supporters. That town may send three white Democrat Congressmen/ women to the House of Representatives—each one of whom is interested in black issues because he or she depends on the black voters to elect them. After the District boundaries are redrawn there are two Districts with no black voters and one District with an overwhelming number of black voters. At the next election a black Democrat is elected who is interested in black issues. However, there are two white Republicans elected and they have no interest in black issues because there are no black voters in their area.

Since the mid-1990s, fewer Democrats have been elected. In the 1970s and 1980s the Democrats were the majority party in the House of Representatives at every election—often with huge majorities. However, the Democrats lost ground in 1993 and lost control of the House in 1995. Since then the Republicans have controlled both the House of Representatives and the Senate.

Despite the fact that there has been an increase in the number of Blacks in Congress, the influence of the black vote has been diluted because there are fewer congress members who depend on black voters for their electoral success. Also, Blacks support the Democratic Party but it has been in the minority since 1995.

Motor-Voter Law

Another law that was intended to increase the minority turnout but did not have the expected effect was the Motor-Voter Law. From 1995, voters could register at driver licence centres and public assistance offices. This was an attempt to increase voter registration amongst the poor and ethnic minorities. Democrats thought their support would increase from a larger turnout of these groups.

However, it was the Republican Party that gained most. Its support rose in many more states and districts than did support for the Democrats. The Republican Party has been the majority party in Congress ever since. It is far less interested in black issues. For example, the Bush administration is opposed to Affirmative Action Programmes.

Blacks have less influence on the political parties in the US than they might otherwise have because of their lower levels of voter registration and turnout. In the US it is the voter's responsibility to register to vote before each election. Blacks are less likely to register to vote than the majority white population. Black voter turnout is significantly below that for Whites—usually between 5% and 10% less.

BLACKS AND TURNOUT

There are a number of reasons why fewer black voters turn out. Firstly, they suffer from apathy and feel alienated. Many Blacks have experienced limited social and economic improvement, therefore they believe there is little point in voting. Reasons given for not voting are things like 'my vote does not count' or 'politicians talk down to me, they do not listen to me' or 'candidates don't care about me, just my vote'. The perception of many Blacks is that there is little or no value in turning out to vote.

Secondly, there is education. The higher the level of education, the more likely a person is to vote. A higher proportion of Blacks than Whites drop out of high school, college and university. Many also have problems with basic literacy, which makes it difficult to register and to read the ballot paper.

Next is voter concentration. In the majority-minority districts there are overwhelming numbers of ethnic minorities. Many think their vote is not necessary because their preferred candidate will win without their support, so they do not turn out.

Another issue is lifestyle. Many Blacks do not buy newspapers and do not watch the news so they do not know there is an election. Also, access to the polls is difficult. They may have to travel some distance and have no means of transport, or in the ghetto they may have to pass through areas controlled by gangs who may attack them.

Finally, there is the media. In the last few elections turnout has fallen in western states where it is lower than in the East. Due to the time difference, polling figures are known in the West before the polls open. From early on an election day, TV programmes carry projections of exit polls which show the likely outcome in presidential elections. Indeed, candidates have, on occasion, accepted defeat based on the vote in the eastern states before the polls have even opened in California and other western states. Therefore western voters are discouraged from turning out to vote in an election that is already won and lost.

For all these reasons many Blacks have disenfranchised themselves and therefore do not have the influence they could have on the parties if more of them were to vote. However, in Florida in the 2000 Presidential election, Black voters found themselves disenfranchised for other reasons. (See page 59.)

The Republicans and the Black Vote

The Republican Party is trying to win over sections of the black vote. They are targeting middle-class Christian Blacks who are under 35. This age group was born after the era of the Civil Rights movement and for them it is history with which they have no emotional ties. They did not live through the violence and oppression of the period. Secondly, this group are successful and the Republican values of individualism, self-reliance, home-ownership and minimal government have an appeal. Finally, many young Blacks are attracted to the Christian and family-centred values that the Republican Party has become identified with. They do not identify with the policies of the Democrats on abortion, homosexuality and feminism.

In the 2004 Presidential election, black support for the Democrats fell by 2% while the black Republican vote went up by 2% to 11%. Although this shows continuing overwhelming black support for the Democrats, the problem for them is that the switch is not uniform across the age range. Almost all Blacks who switched are under 50, with the vast majority under 35.

In a Gallup Poll in 2005, only 9% of Blacks described themselves as Republicans but they were almost all under 35. However, the Republicans launched a high profile campaign to win over Blacks.

Voter Registration VOTE and Turnout (%)

	TOTAL		WHITE		BLACK		HISPANIC	
	Registered	Voted	Registered	Voted	Registered	Voted	Registered	Voted
1992	68.2	61.3	70.1	63.6	63.9	54.0	35.0	28.9
1996	65.9	54.2	67.7	56.0	63.5	50.6	35.7	26.7
2000	76.0	51.3	70.4	56.2	67.5	53.5	37.3	27.5
2004	65.9	58.3	67.9	60.3	64.4	56.3	34.3	29.8

Table 6.8 Source: Census Bureau

A half century ago, Adam Hunter's grandfather helped register Blacks living in rural South Carolina to vote. Hunter's father, born on a tobacco farm and taught in segregated schools, was inspired by the civil rights movement to join the Democratic Party. His parents have both headed the local Democratic committee in their New Jersey town, and Hunter himself worked as a campaign volunteer before he was old enough to vote. Hunter, 22, is a first-year law student at Howard University, a historically black campus with a long record of liberal activism. He has political ambitions of his own—but not with the Democrats.

Instead, Hunter, who as an undergraduate headed Howard's chapter of College Republicans, sees himself as part of a younger generation of African Americans. He is ready to cast aside traditional loyalties to the Democratic Party and forge his own political identity.

"My father and I are not that different, ideologically, but if you look at the time period we grew up in, that's where we're different," Hunter said. "My foundation doesn't make me beholden to the Democratic Party. To me there's nothing more undemocratic than the idea that you have to vote for a Democrat or don't vote at all come election day."

Hunter is one of a growing number of young African Americans leaving the party of their parents and grandparents in favour of the GOP—or choosing not to have a political affiliation at all.

Hunter said he's well aware of the Democratic Party's history of helping minorities; he doesn't think that means they deserve his vote forty years after key civil rights battles. Other issues are more important to him, he says: privatising Social Security, lowering taxes, and business development. "I strongly believe that there should be options for Americans—rich, poor, old, young—to invest," he said.

(GOP is 'Grand Old Party', a nickname for the Republican Party)

Extract from: More young Blacks ready to embrace GOP—*Boston Globe* 22 August, 2005

BLACKS AND THE 2000 PRESIDENTIAL ELECTION

The US Presidential election of 2000 was notable for the fact that the winner lost. Al Gore won more of the popular vote across the USA than George W Bush but lost the electoral college vote on the narrowest of margins—five electoral college votes. Bush won Florida by only 537 votes. Had Gore won Florida, he would have become the President.

The Democrats lost many votes, particularly among Blacks, because of felony disenfranchisement and the butterfly ballot. Had all Blacks been allowed to vote then the Democrats would have won, and political power between the

Presidential Race 2000

	Popular Vote	Electoral College Vote	Florida Popular Vote
George Bush	50,456,169	271	2,912,790
Al Gore	50,996,116	266	2,912,253
Majority	539,947	5	537

Table 6.9   Source: Census Bureau

parties would have been altered.

Florida is one of only ten states in the USA which disenfranchise felons for life. Florida permanently disenfranchises more than 400,000 ex-offenders. However, a disproportionate number of ethnic minorities were disenfranchised. 31.2% of black men in Florida, more than 200,000 potential black

voters, were denied the right to vote compared to a national figure of adult felony disenfranchisement of only 2%. Had these Blacks been able to vote then the outcome of the election would have been totally different.

Another problem was the type of ballot paper used in some Florida counties. For example, Palm Beach County uses the 'butter-

fly ballot' on which the names of the candidates are placed on the left and right columns of a page and a series of punch holes are found in a centre column.

An unexpectedly large number of votes in Palm Beach went to third-party candidates and there was a higher than average number of spoiled papers. *The Palm Beach Post* reviewed the spoiled ballots and found that the Democratic Party candidate lost 5,830 votes because voters had voted twice—first for Buchanan then, realizing their mistake, a second time for Gore.

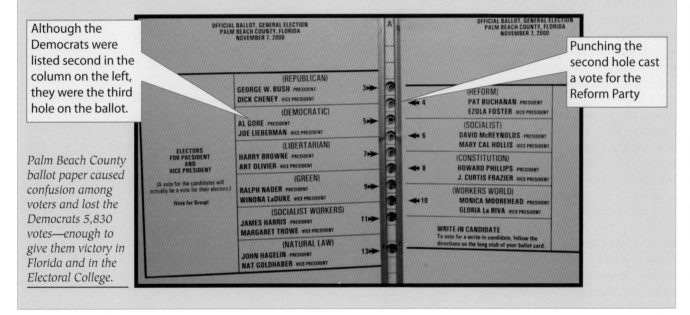

Although the Democrats were listed second in the column on the left, they were the third hole on the ballot.

Punching the second hole cast a vote for the Reform Party

Palm Beach County ballot paper caused confusion among voters and lost the Democrats 5,830 votes—enough to give them victory in Florida and in the Electoral College.

The Chairperson of the Republican National Committee made seventeen appearances in one month to recruit new black voters to the Republican Party in 2005—a non-election year. In this campaign the Republican Party is styling itself as "the party of Lincoln," and is asking potential black voters to decide

which party is best placed to "build on the civil rights movement's success ... closing the wealth gap, closing the health gap, offering people real access to opportunity?"

The Republicans firmly believe that if they can win over a further 10% of the young black vote they can

tilt the balance of power towards themselves in many key states. For example, in Ohio in the 2004 Presidential election, a state they won by only 130,000 votes, the Republicans managed to double their share of the black vote.

HISPANICS AND POLITICS

The introduction of majority-minority Districts increased the number of Hispanic members of the House of Representatives from eleven to seventeen in 1993. Since then Hispanic representation has increased further. This demonstrates a growing awareness of the importance of politics within the Hispanic community and shows that the political parties are increasingly working to win the Hispanic vote.

Most Hispanics migrate to the USA for economic reasons. In the past, few had any interest in the politics of the USA, so turnout rates were low and consequently politicians paid little attention to issues that concerned the Hispanics. However, following the anti-immigration mood which led to Proposition 187 in California in the mid-1990s, many in the Hispanic community realized that politics had a major impact on their lives. This has encouraged more Hispanics to turn out to vote.

Hispanics and turnout

Hispanic turnout is increasing, but quite slowly. In 1996, Hispanic turnout was 26.7%. It rose to 27.5% in 2000 and by the 2004 Presidential election it was 28%. Although this was a small percentage increase the Hispanic population is the fastest growing group in the USA so the actual number voting is rising significantly. The Hispanic population eligible to vote rose from 10.4 million in 1994 to 16.1 million in 2004 and it will continue to rise. In 2000, just over 6 million Hispanics voted but in 2004, 9.3 million turned out— an increase of 50% in four years.

It appears that Hispanic turnout is approximately half that of the other main groups in the USA. This is because the statistics include those who are resi-dent in the USA but who are not US citizens. Hispanics have more non-citizens than any other group. In 2004, of the 27 million Hispanics in the US, 11 million were non-citizens and therefore not eligible to vote. If we only look at those who are US citizens then 57.8% of Hispanics registered to vote and the 9.3 million Hispanics who actually voted represent a turnout of 47%. While this figure still lags behind the 56% of Blacks who voted and the 68% turnout rate for Whites, it is far more respectable.

Another important factor is that the Hispanic vote is heavily concentrated. In 2004, the Hispanics were 8% of all US voters but in New Mexico they were 30% of the voters. The biggest concentration of Hispanic voters is in California, Florida, Texas, and New York. These are the key electoral states that virtually determine who will sit in the White House.

This made the politicians realise that the Hispanic vote was an important vote to win. Candidates and parties now design policies to meet Hispanic issues and spend millions of dollars on advertising in Spanish on Spanish TV channels and in the Spanish press in order to woo the Hispanic vote.

Despite increasing awareness of the political process by Hispanics, and increasing numbers of Hispanics being elected, they are still proportionately under-represented as a group in the House of Representatives and the Senate. In 2005, Hispanics were 12.5% of the population of the USA but there were only two Hispanic Senators and twenty four members of the House of Representatives. If Hispanics were to be represented proportionately there should be thirteen Hispanic Senators and fifty six Congressmen/ women in the House of Representatives.

Hispanics and the Political Parties

Traditionally the Democrats, more than the Republicans, were identified with issues that appealed to the majority of Hispanics, especially poor Mexican Americans and Puerto Ricans—issues such as better welfare provision, funding

Hispanic Representation 1991–2005

	1991	1993	1995	1997	1999	2001	2003	2005
The House of Representatives	11	17	17	21	19	19	22	24
Senate	0	0	0	0	0	0	0	2

	Number of Hispanics in Congress in 2005	Number required to reflect Hispanic population
House of Representatives	24	56
Senate	2	13

Table 6.10   Source: Census Bureau

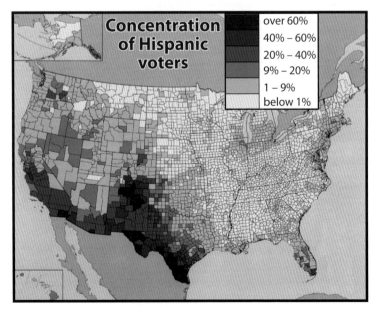

Concentration of Hispanic voters

- over 60%
- 40% – 60%
- 20% – 40%
- 9% – 20%
- 1 – 9%
- below 1%

A Republican politician is supported by prominent Hispanics in a campaign in New York city in 2005. This reflects the increase in support Hispanics gave Republicans.

public education and health care. The Democratic Party is also associated with the Catholic vote and Hispanics are predominantly Catholic. The Republicans came to be identified with anti-immigration and associated policies which many Hispanics did not like.

However, wealthy Hispanics identified with the Republican policies that were for the entrepreneur and the businessman, such as low taxation and minimum government. The Cubans are strongly Republican, partly because many are successful businessmen but also because the Republican party has strong anti-Marxist identification.

In the 1996 Presidential election, 70% of Hispanics voted for the Democratic candidate and only 20% for the Republican (the oth-er 10% voted for candidates from other parties). This was nearly four to one in favour of the Democrats. Hispanics were punishing the Republican Party for its tough stance on welfare benefits for legal immigrants and in particular the party's support for Proposition 187.

This posed major problems for the Republican Party. If Hispanics continued to vote against it in these proportions in some of the key states then the Republican Party faced being out of power indefinitely. By the 2000 election, the Republicans had dropped or softened many of their policies and took more interest in Hispanic issues. The result was that the Hispanic vote split sixty two to thirty five in favour of the Democrats or under two to one.

The Hispanic vote was not as solid as the Democrats thought. It had to be won. As a result both Democrats and Republicans put more effort into winning the Hispanic vote after years of ignoring it. Both parties now identify Hispanic issues and campaign aggressively on these issues in Spanish in Hispanic areas. They also try to find Hispanic candidates to win votes in certain states.

Between 2000 and 2004, the Republicans worked very hard to win the Hispanic vote. The party reversed its traditional policies which were against the interests of Hispanics. It reversed its support for English-only education in favour of bilingual education. It opposed benefit cuts for legal aliens and rejected the proposal that the children of undocumented workers should be denied public education. It even proposed an amnesty to allow illegal immigrants to gain lawful status and eventual citizenship.

In 2004, the Republicans' strategy paid off. They won 45% of the Hispanic vote and reduced the Democrats' share to 55%. This enabled the Republicans to win all the states in the South-west whereas four years earlier these states had been shared between the parties. Republican strategists believe that if they can increase their total of the Hispanic vote by just 5% they will defeat the Democrats in Arizona, Nevada, New Mexico and Florida in 2006. There are some who believe they can win California and New York by winning over more of the Hispanic vote. Should that happen the Democrats will face being out of power indefinitely.

CHAPTER 7

Social and economic inequality in the USA

In this chapter we will consider the inequalities faced by the ethnic minority groups in the USA today including:

Economic Inequalities
◆ Income levels including welfare
◆ Unemployment rates
◆ Promotion

Social Inequalities
◆ Housing
◆ Family structures
◆ Education
◆ Health
◆ Crime
◆ Chemical abuse

The USA is the richest country in the world. Many Americans have lived the American Dream and have become very prosperous. However, the reality of life in the USA is that there are millions of people living in poverty in a society which is intolerant of poverty. The prevailing view in the US makes a virtue out of independence and self-help. Increasingly, the poor are being criticised for their poverty. It is a society where the majority endorses their government for cutting welfare and replacing it with workfare. The USA is a very unequal society.

SOCIAL AND ECONOMIC INEQUALITIES IN THE BLACK COMMUNITY_____

POVERTY IN THE BLACK COMMUNITY

There were three social and economic themes which affected the black minority in the second half of the twentieth century. There was a significant reduction in poverty in the black community. (See Figure 7.1.). However, despite improvement, Blacks at all levels continue to suffer greater disadvantage compared to Whites (See Table 7.1) and, any improvements have not been shared evenly throughout the black community.

There are two black communities. Middle-class Blacks have lived the American Dream and have experienced significant improvements in living standards. They are well-educated, and are in employment where they have well-paid jobs. They live in the traditional nuclear family.

Blacks who remain in the ghetto have become detached and rooted in their poverty and now form an underclass. They suffer from

Figure 7.1 Source: US Census Bureau

poor education and are often unemployed or working in low paid employment. As a result they live in poverty or may turn to crime or drugs. Over 80% of black families in the ghetto are lone parent families.

Improvement

There has been a marked reduction in the number of Blacks living in poverty over the past forty years. There were fewer than half the number of Blacks living in poverty in 2001 than there were in 1959. (See Figure 7.1.) Nevertheless, they have not achieved equality in US society. Blacks are the poorest of the main ethnic groups. Table 7.1 shows that 7.8% of Whites were

Poverty levels in the USA by race and ethnicity (%)				
	GENERAL POPULATION		**CHILDREN**	
	1990	**2001**	**1990**	**2001**
Non-Hispanic White	9.4	7.8	12.3	9.5
Black	31.9	22.7	44.8	30.2
Hispanic	28.1	21.4	38.4	28.0
API	12.2	10.2	17.6	11.5

Table 7.1 Source: US Census Bureau

classed as poor compared to 22.7% of Blacks. Therefore, three times as many Blacks lived below the Federal Poverty Level as Whites.

Why do Blacks face relatively high levels of poverty?

Black families are the victims of the poverty cycle. Being born poor generally leads to poor education, a low paid job, unemployment, single parent families and poverty which in turn leads to the children of these people being born poor. This repeats itself down the generations.

Black families in the ghetto suffer from low incomes due to unemployment and welfare dependency. Blacks face higher unemployment caused by lower educational attainment and discrimination in employment opportunities and in promotion. Another barrier to employment is that over 80% of families in the ghetto are lone parent families which means that most depend on welfare for their income. However, in recent years welfare payments have been reduced or removed as the result of welfare cutbacks and the introduction of workfare which has caused further reductions in black incomes. 80% of claimants receiving welfare payments are Black.

As Table 7.3 shows, Blacks are far more likely to be poor than any other group in the US. However, official figures for poverty underestimate the scale of the problem.

Income in the Black community

Poverty is linked to income and three times as many Blacks (14.6%) earned less than $10,000 compared with Whites (4.4%). Even middle-class Blacks earn less than middle-class Whites. Table 7.2 shows, that around twice as many Whites as Blacks earned over $75,000. In 2004, the median income for Blacks showed that they earned two-thirds of the white income. (Median income is the middle income; half of all incomes are higher and half are lower.) Black incomes then, remain significantly lower than incomes for Whites.

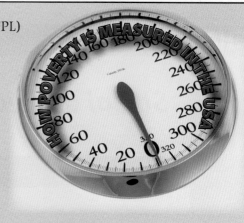

The Federal Poverty Level (FPL) was introduced in 1963–64. Officials calculated that an average family spent one-third of its income on food, so officials work out the average cost of a family's food budget then multiply it by three. However, today food spending accounts for less than one-fifth of the average US family's income. If the FPL was calculated to take account of current costs then the figure for average food spending should be multiplied by five not three.

In 2005, the FPL was calculated on the food costs of a family of four being $6,500. As a result of this the FPL was set at $19,500. However, a more accurate FPL would be $32,500 to reflect the current proportion of income spent on food. At $32,500 there would be far more people counted as poor and poverty rates would be far higher.

Another problem with the FPL is that all areas of the USA (except Alaska and Hawaii) are assumed to be the same even though the cost of living varies significantly throughout the USA. In Tennessee, for example, estimates suggest that a lone parent family with two children is poor if their income is less than $23,001, whereas in Indianapolis it is $29,388 and in Washington DC it is $52,061.

These estimates were calculated using the Self-Sufficiency Standard (SSS) which is an alternative and more accurate measure of poverty. The SSS is the income level necessary to meet a family's basic needs without public support and covers food, housing, clothing, child care, health care, transport and taxes. No eating out or takeaway meals or other luxuries for a lone parent with two children!

COMPARING INCOMES

Families earning over $75,000

White	29.3%
Black	15.6%

Table 7.2 Source: US Census Bureau

Families with incomes under $20,000

White	14.3%
Black	26.4%
Hispanic	18.9%
API	12.3%

(Federal Poverty Levels for a family of four in 2001 was $18,000)

Table 7.3 Source: US Census Bureau

Median Income

White	$48977
Black	$30,134

Table: 7.4 Source: US Census Bureau

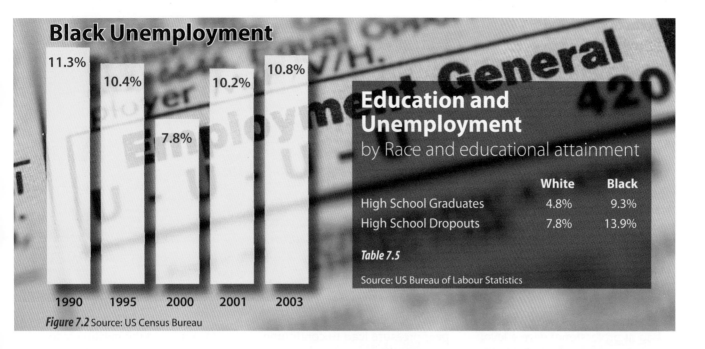

Black Unemployment

Year	Unemployment
1990	11.3%
1995	10.4%
2000	7.8%
2001	10.2%
2003	10.8%

Figure 7.2 Source: US Census Bureau

Education and Unemployment
by Race and educational attainment

	White	Black
High School Graduates	4.8%	9.3%
High School Dropouts	7.8%	13.9%

Table 7.5

Source: US Bureau of Labour Statistics

Unemployment in the Black community

Economic recession harms both Blacks and Whites but affects Blacks more than Whites. Blacks tend to be in lower skilled and marginal jobs and therefore are more likely to be the first to be paid off. Also, they may have least length of service and so suffer from last in, first out. From 1993, the US economy experienced an upturn and more work became available. The gap between Whites and Blacks began to narrow. However, in the late 1990s there was another downturn in the economy and black unemployment began to rise faster than white unemployment

Young people are affected more than other age groups. In 2003, the overall unemployment rate for Blacks was 10.8%, whereas the rate for those aged 20–24 was 19.1% and for those aged 16–19 was 29.8%. High levels of unemployment adversely affect the attitudes of the young. High unemployment helps promote negative attitudes to education and makes crime, gang membership and drug taking more likely.

Education and employment

Education is one of the most important factors in determining employment and income levels. Table 7.5 shows that high school dropouts, i.e. those who do not graduate from high school, are more likely to be unemployed than their contemporaries who do graduate. This is true for both Blacks and Whites.

Blacks are more likely to be unemployed across all levels of educational attainment compared to Whites. Even at Batchelor's Degree level, Blacks (4.5%) face nearly twice the rate of unemployment as Whites (2.8%). Clearly, discrimination is another factor which affects Black rates of employment and unemployment.

Income and education

Income is also determined by educational attainment. The highest earners are those who have professional degrees—people such as doctors and lawyers. Blacks who live in the ghetto experience many problems with their education and this puts them at a disadvantage.

Schools with large numbers of ethnic minority students are more likely to be in buildings which have problems with their fabric. 48% of schools with less than 5% minority students have at least one problem

(roof, heating, ventilation etc.) compared to 59% of schools with more than 50% minority students

The same schools also often lack equipment. In 2000, 85% of schools with less than 5% minority students had Internet access compared to only 64% of schools with more than 50% minority students. They often face teacher shortages, particularly teachers from an ethnic minority background. Research indicates that students tend to learn better if taught by someone from their own ethnic background. The standard of teaching in ghetto schools is often poor because more able teachers are attracted to the best schools.

Added to this is the negative attitude towards education in the ghetto. A significant proportion of the students see little value in education and do not want to learn so set out to disrupt those who do. Consequently, black dropout rates are higher than for most other groups.

Education in the US, more so than in the UK, costs money. Poor Blacks, therefore, cannot compete for the expensive university and college courses. Blacks are underrepresented in subjects and courses which may lead to highly paid employment such as maths, science and engineering, and on legal and medical courses.

Discrimination and Employment

Discrimination is obviously a factor in employment. Blacks are more likely to be unemployed at each level of education. If there was equality of opportunity in the USA, then Blacks would not be twice as likely to be unemployed as Whites. Furthermore, if there was no discrimination then Blacks and Whites would have the same income if they had the same qualifications. However, it is clear from Table 7.6 that at every level of educational attainment, Blacks earn far less than their white counterparts.

The problem seems to be particularly bad at professional degree level where demand for the individual's skills should be most critical. However these involve personal services such as doctors and lawyers where a person's most intimate secrets are opened up. In general the white population appears to want the best white doctor, not the best doctor. These are also professions where tradition controls access to the top posts. So in long-established legal firms partnerships may not be on offer to Blacks whose abilities may be used on the less well-paid rungs of the ladder.

THE CYCLE OF POVERTY AND THE BLACK UNDERCLASS

To improve living standards people need access to a good education. They also need role models to demonstrate the value of success, people like themselves who have used education to succeed. However, Black middle-class flight has taken potential role models out of the ghetto, and what remains is negative peer group pressure towards education.

The poverty of the ghetto has created a negative cycle of pressure which undermines people's belief that they can work hard and improve their lives. The barriers of poor education, unemployment, substance abuse, crime, limited work opportunities and negative

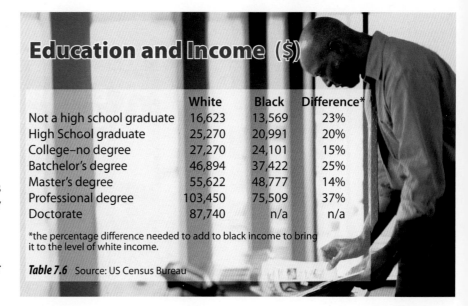

Education and Income ($)

	White	Black	Difference*
Not a high school graduate	16,623	13,569	23%
High School graduate	25,270	20,991	20%
College–no degree	27,270	24,101	15%
Batchelor's degree	46,894	37,422	25%
Master's degree	55,622	48,777	14%
Professional degree	103,450	75,509	37%
Doctorate	87,740	n/a	n/a

*the percentage difference needed to add to black income to bring it to the level of white income.

Table 7.6 Source: US Census Bureau

peer pressure lead to continuing poverty which goes on down the generations. This cycle of poverty has created a black underclass.

A large black underclass emerged in the USA in the second half of the twentieth century. When middle-class Blacks took advantage of the education system and Affirmative Action Programmes to leave the ghetto, many more were left behind. According to the Urban Institute, membership of the Black underclass is identified by several characteristics. It consists of single female-headed households who are marginally educated (high school dropouts or less) and therefore chronically unemployed. As a result they are either welfare dependent or criminal recidivists (always in and out of jail) or both.

Urban Institute statistics indicate that the Black underclass increased from 900,000 in 1980 to 2.7 million in 1995 which was approximately 8% of the black population of the US. Given that there have been cutbacks in welfare since 1995 and that poverty in the ghetto has increased, the Black underclass must be considerably larger today.

Welfare and poverty

The 1996 *Welfare Act (Personal Responsibility and Work Opportunity Reconciliation Act 1996—PRWO-*

RA) replaced the existing federal-funded programme with Temporary Assistance for Needy Families (TANF). TANF, commonly known as welfare, is the monthly cash assistance programme for poor families with children under the age of 18. The federal government provides a level of funding to each state which has to design and operate its own system.

Nevertheless, each state system must have certain features. There is a five year lifetime limit on welfare. A person can only claim welfare for up to five years throughout their entire life. If someone is unemployed for three years then gets a job then once more becomes unemployed, at that point the maximum time they can be on welfare is two years. After five years of claims they receive no more welfare. Also, each recipient must do some work in return for their welfare. The work is chosen by the state and cannot be turned down on the grounds that it is too far away or it does not match the claimant's skills or the claimant has family commitments. There is child support for lone mothers or fathers.

Finally, there must be welfare-to-work training. Welfare claimants are required to undertake training to acquire the skills necessary to obtain work. Hence the system is called workfare.

The effects of these changes

The number of families and individuals receiving TANF fell rapidly. Between 1996 and 2001 the number of families receiving cash assistance fell by over 50% from 4.4 million to 2.1 million.

There has been a significant increase in the number of single parents who have left welfare and now work. Studies of families who have left welfare show that about 60% of former welfare recipients are employed, while 40% are not. Those employed generally earn low wages and often remain poor. Most earned between $6 and $8.50 per hour and in addition many lost access to Medicaid and food stamps.

The Food Stamp Programme enables needy families to purchase essential food items in local shops with food stamps which they are given instead of cash. It is means tested and usually it can be claimed if the family is receiving other types of welfare. Between 1996 and 1999, there was an increase in the number of elderly and disabled households claiming food stamps. At the same time there was a drop of 8 million individuals claiming food stamps. Therefore it can be inferred that more than 8 million families with children stopped getting food stamps. Black family incomes have been the worst hit by these welfare reductions. 80% of families receiving TANF are black compared to 17% for Whites and only 1.3% for Hispanics.

Some observers argue that these changes have benefited families. Many single mothers were forced to find jobs because they ran out of welfare. According to the Manhattan Institute Report, the poverty rate for single mothers fell from 40% in 1996 to 32% in 2001. In Illinois, mothers returning to work increased household incomes by $1,000 per month.

However, other indicators show the changes harmed the poor. In 2001, the US Conference of Mayors reported that hunger and homelessness had risen sharply in US cities

Families receiving TANF (millions)

	Families	Individuals
1996	4.4	12.3
2000	2.3	5.9
2001	2.1	n/a

Table 7.7

Recipients of Food Stamps (millions)

	Households	Individuals
1996	10.6	25.9
1999	7.7	18.1

Table 7.8

Source: US Census Bureau

despite economic growth: "Hunger remains a very real problem in America and that problem has gotten worse over the past four years". In 2001 a survey of twenty seven US cities found that requests for emergency food assistance had risen 23% and requests for emergency shelter were 13% up.

The proportion of children classed as extremely poor—50% below the poverty line—increased between 1996 and 2001 at a time when the US economy was improving. A medical journal reported that between 1999 and 2001 there were "dramatic increases in food insecurity, the risk of being underweight and a 30% increase in the risk of hospitalisation for infants and toddlers in six urban hospitals." These problems were in families which had "lost welfare for failing to comply with welfare rules."

In 2003 the *Welfare Act* was amended. It increased the level of compulsion in the system and reduced the finance available for support. It increased the pressure on the poorest and most vulnerable groups, especially in the Black underclass. Welfare recipients were required to work forty hours per week rather than thirty hours and by 2007, 70% of welfare recipients

have to hold jobs, an increase from 50% previously. Welfare spending was to be held at $16.5 billion which was the same as 1996. Legal immigrants were banned from welfare but remained eligible for food stamps. Mothers on welfare were therefore required to do more work but the support programmes, child care, transport costs and job training had their funding frozen and therefore eroded by inflation.

HOUSING

Far more Whites own their own homes than Blacks. Fewer than half the Blacks in the USA are homeowners. Blacks find it harder than Whites to get a mortgage. A study undertaken in Boston found that Blacks were refused mortgages twice as often as Whites. This is evidence of discrimination in the housing market. Due to where they live and where they wish to buy property Blacks and other minorities fall victims to redlining. Financial institutions such as banks and mortgage brokers 'draw' a red line around certain areas of a town where they believe they will have difficulty getting loans repaid. As these are often the areas where Blacks, Hispanics and poorer Asians live, they will have difficulty securing mortgages in these areas. However, the main

Home ownership by race

	White	Black
Owner	64%	47%
Renter	29%	50%
Other	7%	3%

Table 7.9 Source: US Census Bureau

reason for Blacks failing to secure mortgages is that they have lower incomes than most other groups.

Consequently, the majority of Blacks are forced to rent and in the cities of the North and West most will rent in the inner city. Most accommodation in the inner city is for rent because property prices are too high. Federal housing programmes in the 1970s knocked down old housing to build 'the projects'. The projects were large-scale housing programmes which built high density housing in enormous blocks with very few facilities. They helped to create more social problems than they solved. The projects helped to reduce the housing stock available to buy and sell which helped push up the value of the housing that remained.

Segregation in Housing

According to the US Bureau of Census, the least segregated metropolitan areas for Blacks were in the South, South-west and California—Orange County, San José, Phoenix, Norfolk (Virginia), Tampa and San Diego. Among the most segregated metropolitan areas in the USA were Detroit, Milwaukee, New York, Newark, Chicago, Cleveland, St Louis and Philadelphia. These are large cities in the North and Midwest. The only Southern city to appear on the list was New Orleans.

Housing in the metropolitan areas of the North and Midwest be-

came heavily segregated as a consequence of 'White Flight' which took place from the 1950s to the 1970s. With the freedom created by the motor car and the building of motorways out to the new suburbs, Whites left the inner cities in their millions to escape the cost of living and the pollution of inner city life. They also left to avoid living next to the growing population of Blacks.

These suburbs became segregated. Many Whites used a variety of tactics to keep black families out. Some communities used intimidation or controlled the buying and selling of local homes through the residents' committee. The majority of Blacks could not afford to move out to these suburbs but for those who could afford it and who also overcame white opposition to settling in these areas, studies have shown that once black occupancy reached 8% of a suburban area white flight began again.

So, a typical northern city would have a central business district where there might be a few extremely wealthy people living in penthouse or executive apartments. This would be surrounded by a series of inner city segregated ghettos. Beyond the city limits there would be a ring of independent suburban commuter communities which would also be segregated.

FAMILY LIFE IN THE BLACK COMMUNITY

Blacks experience two distinct types of family life. The 30% who form the Black middle class have the traditional family with two parents looking after the children. However, in the ghetto, over 80% of black families are single parent families. Only 36% of black children live with both parents and over two-thirds of children born in the black community are born to unmarried mothers. Only 11% of families in the ghetto are married black couples with children.

Most families in the ghetto are single parent families and are headed by a woman. For the Black underclass, marriage as an institution for parenting children is rapidly disappearing. In the suburbs black family life follows the traditional American pattern and most families have parents who are married or cohabiting.

In the ghetto the lifestyle has created a dependency culture. There is restricted access to employment. There are few permanent males of working age in households. It is

Births to unmarried mothers

White	26.8%
Black	68.9%

Table 7.11

Single Parent Families

	White	Black
● mother	16%	48%
● father	4%	5%

Table 8.10 Source: US Census Bureau

The United State of America

common for women to have several children while they are still in their teens, often by a succession of males, and to end up in households of three or more generations. Few work and until recently most were dependent on welfare throughout their lives.

Respect for women in the ghetto has all but disappeared. Men father children and move on. Their children, particularly the male children, have no respect for the female head of the family. Increasingly, girls have lost respect for their mothers. Many join girl gangs for protection and companionship, but also to get the respect as females that they see is missing in their mothers' circumstances. In 1990 girls formed 10% of gangs in the USA but by 1995 this had grown to 15%. Girl gangs are involved in drug dealing and violence and challenge boy gangs to protect their territory.

In 1997, the Million Women March was a mass demonstration in Philadelphia in reaction to the social and economic problems that black women faced. They were showing that they were fed up with crime, unemployment, teenage pregnancy and the other social problems of the ghetto. 700,000 black women joined the demonstration from all over the USA which had the message 'we will no longer tolerate disrespect.' It was an indication of the scale of the problem, but following the demonstration little changed and black women continue to face overwhelming problems in the ghetto.

CRIME IN THE BLACK COMMUNITY

Most crime occurs in the inner cities. More Blacks are involved in crime, either as perpetrators or as victims, than any other group. Blacks are eight times more likely than Whites and three times more likely than Hispanics to be held in prison or jail. 47% of all jail inmates are black despite being just over 12% of the population.

Children under 18 by presence of parent

	Both parents	Mother only					Father	No parent
		Divorced	Separated	Never married	Widowed	Total		
White	74%	8%	4%	5%	1%	18%	5%	3%
Black	36%	9%	9%	32%	1%	51%	4%	9%
Hispanic	64%	6%	8%	12%	1%	27%	4%	5%

Table 7.12 Source: US Census Bureau

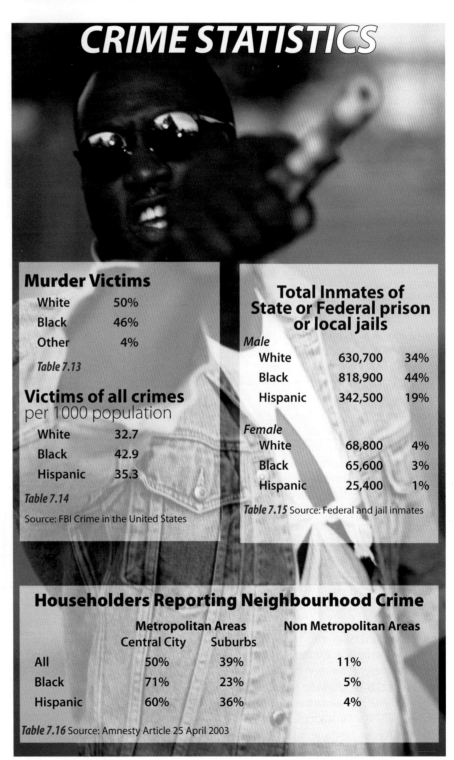

CRIME STATISTICS

Murder Victims

White	50%
Black	46%
Other	4%

Table 7.13

Victims of all crimes
per 1000 population

White	32.7
Black	42.9
Hispanic	35.3

Table 7.14

Source: FBI Crime in the United States

Total Inmates of State or Federal prison or local jails

Male

White	630,700	34%
Black	818,900	44%
Hispanic	342,500	19%

Female

White	68,800	4%
Black	65,600	3%
Hispanic	25,400	1%

Table 7.15 Source: Federal and jail inmates

Householders Reporting Neighbourhood Crime

	Metropolitan Areas		Non Metropolitan Areas
	Central City	Suburbs	
All	50%	39%	11%
Black	71%	23%	5%
Hispanic	60%	36%	4%

Table 7.16 Source: Amnesty Article 25 April 2003

The reason for the greater incidence of crime in the inner city is related to unemployment, drugs and street gangs. During the 1990s, crack cocaine spread through the ghetto. People took crack cocaine as an escape from poverty whilst others supplied it to make money. At a time when an unskilled worker could earn $200–$300 a week in a fast food job, major dealers could earn $5,000 to $10,000 a day tax free.

Gangs controlled territory and provided protection for drug dealers who paid them with guns and drugs. Gangs fought to control territory in order to protect their income and feed their habit and this led to a rapid escalation in violence. In the economic upturn of the mid to late 1990s, several metropolitan areas did see a reduction in gang violence. However, the reductions were marginal and violence is still a part of everyday life in many black neighbourhoods.

Race and Justice in the USA

The figures show that Blacks are more likely to be arrested for serious crime than non-serious crime because of the level of crime in the inner city. It is also clear that Blacks are more likely than Whites to be sentenced to death. A report by Amnesty International, *Death by discrimination: the continuing role of race in capital cases*, highlighted the fact that black defendants convicted of killing Whites have been sentenced to death fifteen times more often than white defendants convicted of killing Blacks.

The report stated that "80% of the more than 840 people put to death in the USA between 1976 and 2003 were convicted of crimes involving white victims, compared to the 13% who were convicted of killing Blacks". It went on to say that some 200 African Americans were executed for the murder of white victims, "fifteen times as many as the number of Whites put to death

for killing Blacks, and at least twice as many as the number of Blacks executed for the murder of other Blacks."

Kate Allen, Amnesty International's UK director, said, "At least one in five of African Americans executed since 1977, and a quarter of the Blacks put to death for killing Whites, were tried in front of all-white juries". The Amnesty International survey, based largely on recent investigations carried out by individual states, suggests that race remains a powerful factor when American juries decide whether to send convicts to death row, but that the race of the victim is often more important than the race of the murderer.

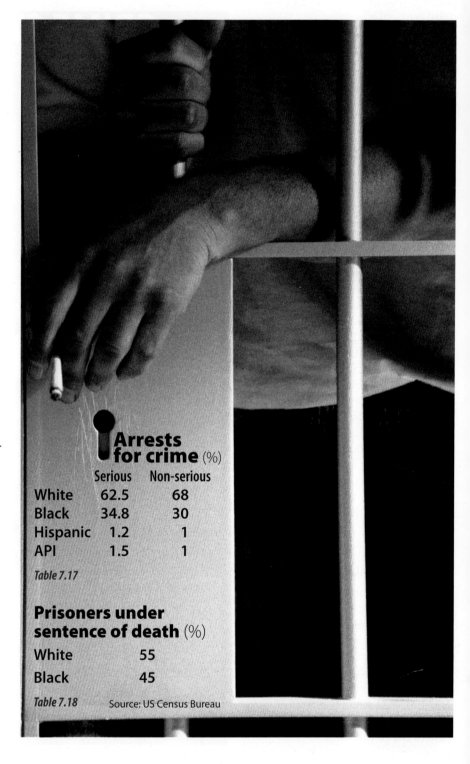

Arrests for crime (%)

	Serious	Non-serious
White	62.5	68
Black	34.8	30
Hispanic	1.2	1
API	1.5	1

Table 7.17

Prisoners under sentence of death (%)

White	55
Black	45

Table 7.18　　Source: US Census Bureau

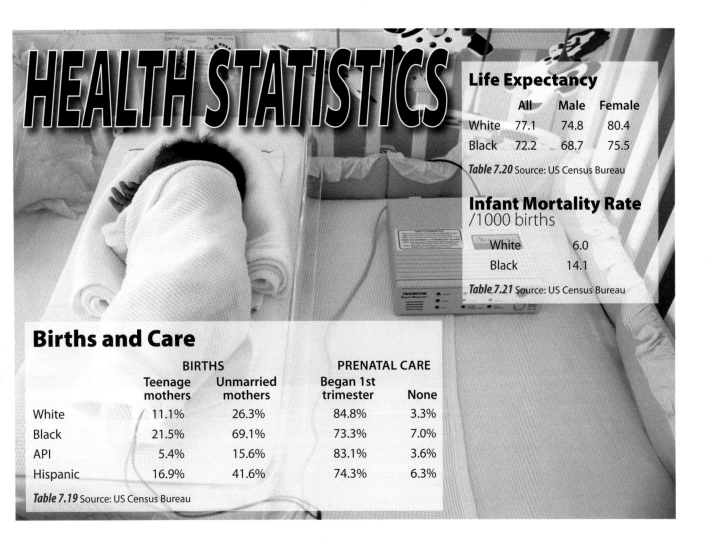

HEALTH STATISTICS

Life Expectancy

	All	Male	Female
White	77.1	74.8	80.4
Black	72.2	68.7	75.5

Table 7.20 Source: US Census Bureau

Infant Mortality Rate
/1000 births

White	6.0
Black	14.1

Table 7.21 Source: US Census Bureau

Births and Care

	BIRTHS		PRENATAL CARE	
	Teenage mothers	Unmarried mothers	Began 1st trimester	None
White	11.1%	26.3%	84.8%	3.3%
Black	21.5%	69.1%	73.3%	7.0%
API	5.4%	15.6%	83.1%	3.6%
Hispanic	16.9%	41.6%	74.3%	6.3%

Table 7.19 Source: US Census Bureau

HEALTH IN THE BLACK COMMUNITY

Between 1990 and 2000, life expectancy for Blacks improved from 69.1 years to 72.2 years. Nevertheless, it still lags behind life expectancy for Whites by about five years. The black infant mortality rate is more than double that for Whites. Blacks then, suffer from more ill-health than Whites.

On average Blacks have less access to health insurance and so get inadequate health care. In 2001, a quarter of Blacks in the USA had no medical insurance whereas fewer than one in ten Whites had none. In other words, more than twice as many Blacks as Whites had no health insurance and therefore limited access to medical care.

The lack of health care is made worse by unhealthy lifestyles in the ghetto. There are twice as many black teenage mothers as white and nearly 70% of all black births are to unmarried mothers. These children have low birth weight because their mothers do not have a healthy diet and smoke, drink or take drugs during pregnancy. Twice as many black babies are born without any prenatal medical care.

Poverty is another reason for continuing ill health. Poor quality housing that is damp and overrun by vermin adds to the problems of poor diet and substance abuse. Obesity is a major threat to health in the US and is a particular problem in the Black community.

Crime and gangs have increased the rates for murder and gunshot wounds in the ghetto. The most common cause of death for black males in their teens and twenties is being shot.

Finally, AIDS is a particular health problem in the Black community because of lifestyle. There are more cases of black people with AIDS reported in the USA than there are white. Currently Blacks account for 40.2%of aids cases in the USA and between 1981 and 2000, Blacks accounted for 47% of all reported cases of AIDS in the USA. Overall, Blacks have the worst levels of ill health and enjoy least access to treatment of all the ethnic minority groups.

People without Health Insurance

	All	Children
Non-Hispanic White	9.7%	7.3%
Black	24.5%	13.6%

Table 7.22 Source: US Census Bureau

AIDS Cases

White	114,846	39.2%
Black	117,890	40.2%
Hispanic	57,722	19.7%
API	2,324	0.79%

Table 7.23 Source: US Census Bureau

HISPANICS AND ECONOMIC AND SOCIAL INEQUALITIES

HISPANICS AND EQUALITY

The causes of Hispanic poverty and black poverty are different. Immigration has a big impact on Hispanic poverty, whereas black poverty has more to do with discrimination and racism. Immigrants usually start at the bottom of society in the lowest paid jobs and the worst social conditions. Due to the education system their children get better paid jobs and become upwardly mobile, or else they join with others in their family to start their own businesses. Many Hispanics are upwardly mobile and integrate into life in the USA, for example many Hispanics marry white people. The poverty in the Hispanic community is thus largely fuelled by the next group of immigrants.

Black poverty, on the other hand, is more permanent and is due to racism and discrimination. It has become institutionalised by society. While Hispanics also face discrimination it is not to the same extent as Blacks because the Hispanics do not depend as much on white society. Hispanics tend to be more self-reliant. Many become entrepreneurs and start their own businesses and may employ family and friends which means they do not depend on Whites for jobs and promotion.

Poverty in the Hispanic Community

Nevertheless, there are still many Hispanics who are disadvantaged, live in poverty and face unemployment, limited education and poor health. The barrio is the Hispanic equivalent of the ghetto.

The number of Hispanics living below the Federal Poverty Line fell between 1990 and 2001, but the poverty levels for all other groups fell too. Hispanics are over three times more likely to be poor when compared to Whites, but only marginally less likely to be poor compared to Blacks.

Farmworker Francisco Palacios cuts celery in California in November 2005. The farm has only about half of the seventy farmworkers needed to work the fields. As farmers nationwide complain about labour shortages, and pressure the Bush administration for a massive guest worker programme to bring in Hispanic workers, civilian groups and the Border Patrol increase efforts at the border to stem what they claim is an unchecked flow of illegal immigrants.

Poverty Levels in the USA (%)

	General Population		Children	
	1990	2001	1990	2001
Non-Hispanic White	9.4	7.8	12.3	9.5
Black	31.9	22.7	44.8	30.2
Hispanic	28.1	21.4	38.4	28.0
API	12.2	10.2	17.6	11.5

Table 7.24 Source: US Census Bureau

Poverty is not evenly distributed throughout the Hispanic subgroups. Puerto Ricans and Mexican Americans are more likely to suffer from poverty than Cubans. Mexican Americans and Puerto Ricans have a large influx of poor economic migrants who increase the poverty statistics whereas the Cubans have a relatively stable population. Very few Cubans are poor immigrants and they have developed a significant middle class. Many are second or third generation Americans who have grown up in the USA and who have lived the American Dream in business as entrepreneurs.

Hispanics are more upwardly mobile than Blacks. Furthermore, Hispanics are more readily accepted in white communities. Studies have shown that white flight takes place when black occupation reaches 8%, while for Hispanics it is closer to 20%. Hispanics become middle class by starting their own businesses or by working in blue-collar jobs and pooling their income with the extended family. With their pooled resources they can extend their business ventures or invest in housing.

Median Income

		Percentage of white income
Non-Hispanic White	$46,305	
Hispanic	$33,565	72%
Black	$29,470	64%

Table 7.25 Source: US Census Bureau

In 2001 the median income for Hispanics was only 72% of that for Whites but it was still higher than Black median income.

Why are Cubans better off than other Hispanic groups?

Miami has become the centre of trade, shopping and culture for the wealthy and powerful from Central and South America. It is the centre for finance and banking because many banks in Central and South America are not as stable as US-regulated banks. In Miami the 'savings' of politicians, businessmen and drug cartels are safer. Florida's Cuban entrepreneurs provide marketing services, consultancy work, legal assistance and transport for Latin America.

Approximately 30% of US trade with Latin America goes through Florida (around $31 billion in 2000). It is the business capital and major banking centre for Latin America. There are many foreign trade offices and fifty two foreign consulates in Miami. The city has a geographical advantage because of its proximity to Central and South America to which it is closer than Los Angeles. It has another advantage because the middle-class migrants from Cuba were skilled and saw the opportunities.

Finally, Latin American businessmen are attracted to Miami because of its sophisticated infrastructure and the fact that it has the same language and culture as they do. It is also 'neutral turf' for groups that are at war with each other in their native countries and it is both politically and economically stable. Many powerful Latin Americans have bought second homes in Miami.

Many Cubans established businesses in Florida. Among Hispanics they are the most prosperous group although a large proportion of them still live in poverty.

Education in the Hispanic Community

Hispanics are more likely to drop out of high school than Whites or Blacks. (See Table 7.26) However, they tend to be less dependent on education generally or on Affirmative Action to get jobs in the public sector or in middle management. They are far more likely than Blacks to set up their own businesses where they employ family and friends. Many leave school early and go into a family business. A lot of these enterprises start with the extended family pooling its resources. This explains why, despite Hispanics dropping out of education earlier than Blacks, fewer are unemployed.

Again the Cuban population is better off than other Hispanic groups. Cuban educational attainment is closer to that of Whites whereas Mexican Americans have the highest high school dropout rates and only 7% graduate from college.

People living below poverty level

25.8%
24.1%
22.8%
17.3%
7.7%

| Puerto Rican | Mexican American | Hispanic | Cuban | Non-Hispanic White |

Figure 8.3

Dropout and Graduation Rates (%)

	High School		College	
	Dropout	Graduate	Dropout	Degree
White	15.1	33.4	17.4	34.1
Black	21.5	35.2	20.0	23.3
Hispanic	43.0	27.9	13.5	15.6

Table 7.26 Source: US Census Bureau

Educational Attainment (%)

	High School Graduate	College Graduate
White	84.9	26.1
Mexican American	51.0	6.9
Puerto Rican	64.3	13.0
Cuban	73.0	23.0

Table 7.27 Source: US Census Bureau

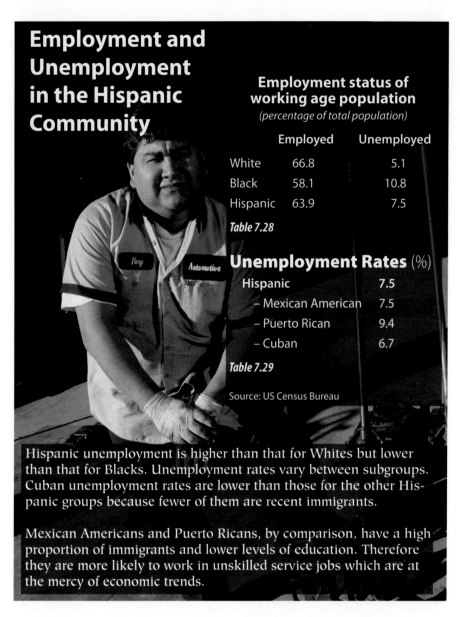

Employment and Unemployment in the Hispanic Community

Employment status of working age population
(percentage of total population)

	Employed	Unemployed
White	66.8	5.1
Black	58.1	10.8
Hispanic	63.9	7.5

Table 7.28

Unemployment Rates (%)

Hispanic	**7.5**
– Mexican American	7.5
– Puerto Rican	9.4
– Cuban	6.7

Table 7.29

Source: US Census Bureau

Hispanic unemployment is higher than that for Whites but lower than that for Blacks. Unemployment rates vary between subgroups. Cuban unemployment rates are lower than those for the other Hispanic groups because fewer of them are recent immigrants.

Mexican Americans and Puerto Ricans, by comparison, have a high proportion of immigrants and lower levels of education. Therefore they are more likely to work in unskilled service jobs which are at the mercy of economic trends.

Hispanics and Health

Hispanics, compared to other groups, are less likely to have health insuranceas many are economic migrants working in low income jobs and so cannot afford it. They also have no residency rights which would allow them access to Medicaid. Hispanics are more likely to than Whites to die from stroke, chronic liver disease and cirrhosis, diabetes, HIV, homicide, cancers of the cervix and stomach and obesity. These problems are linked to income, lifestyle and employment. Hispanics have some of the poorest statistics for diet, alcohol intake, smoking and lack of health screening. The problems of language and a different cultural attitude to the use of traditional medicine rather than conventional medicine also contribute.

Hispanics and Housing

Between 1991 and 2001, the number of Hispanic households increased by 57% in the US. During that time the Hispanic home ownership rate increased until it peaked at 47% in 2001 since when it has dipped slightly. The main problem facing Hispanics is being able to afford a home as housing costs have increased faster than incomes. The average Hispanic household spends more than one-third of its income on housing. More than twice as many Hispanics as Whites report problems with the quality of the buildings they live in.

A report by the US Department of Housing and Urban Development (HUD) found that between 1989 and 2000 both Blacks and Hispanics experienced a decrease in the level of discrimination they encountered when trying to a buy a home. There was also a modest decrease in discrimination toward Blacks trying to rent, but there was no evidence of a reduction in discrimination towards Hispanic renters.

The main form of discrimination experienced by Hispanics and Blacks is being told that houses are unavailable when they are available to non-Hispanic Whites. They are also shown fewer available houses than Whites. Housing agents give Hispanics less help with getting finance and between 1989 and 2000 there was an increase in the incidence of quoting Hispanics higher rents for properties than the rents quoted to other groups.

Family Lifestyles in the Hispanic Community

Children under 18
by presence of parent (1998)

	Both	Mother only	Father only	Neither
White	74	18	5	3
Black	36	51	4	9
Hispanic	64	27	4	5

Table 7.30 Source: US Census Bureau

The family is more central to life in the Hispanic community than in the black underclass. There are fewer births to unmarried mothers in the Cuban community than in the white community. However, among Puerto Ricans and Mexican Americans there is less stability because these communities are younger and more transient and family ties are less strong. Nevertheless, family life in these groups is still stronger than in the black underclass.

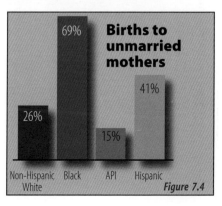

Births to unmarried mothers

Non-Hispanic White 26% — Black 69% — API 15% — Hispanic 41%

Figure 7.4

Victims of Crime
(Rate per 1000)

42.9
35.3
32.7

White   Black   Hispanic

Figure 7.5

Jail Population by race (%)

43.8%
39.8%
14.7%
1.6%

White   Black   Hispanic   Other

Figure 7.6

Inmates in State or Federal Prison
(per 100,000)

4810
1740
649

White   Black   Hispanic

Figure 7.7

Sources:
FBI Crime in the United States and Federal and Jail Numbers

Crime in the Hispanic Community

Hispanics are more likely to be the victims of crime than Whites but less likely than Blacks. The proportion of the Hispanic population in jail is three times higher than the proportion of whites who are in jail.. Many Hispanics in the barrio become involved in criminal activity for the same reasons that Blacks become involved in criminal activity in the ghetto.

A large number of poor Hispanics, with help of their extended family, work hard and avoid crime. Many more Hispanics are upwardly mobile and so provide role models for others in the community. Socially, Hispanics find it much easier to integrate although many are still discriminated against. One-third of US-born Hispanics marry non-Hispanic partners.

ASIANS

Asians have become very successful in the business world and in education and are noted for their drive and ambition. Many recent immigrants have opened businesses and have been responsible for regenerating rundown areas. For example, many Koreans have opened shops in the ghetto and have brought services to areas which would otherwise lack them.

Asians also do well in the sunrise industries such as computer design, software and other electronic industries. There are many Asians who have become successful in other scientific areas such as genetics and in education as lecturers and professors in colleges and universities.

On average, Chinese, Japanese and Koreans have done better in the United States than Cambodians, Vietnamese and Laotians. In recent years, Filipino women have been the largest single group of Asian immigrants and most arrive as brides or nurses. Others have arrived to work in sweatshops in the cities and once established they have brought in other members of their family.

Income levels

Asians have higher median income levels than Whites which is a reflection of their economic success. The average income for Asians is much higher than that of other ethnic groups. Asian per capita income is lower than for Whites because the number of poor immigrants lowers the average, but second generation Asians rapidly improve their income levels.

Median Income	
Non-Hispanic White	$46,305
Asian	$53,635

Table7.31

Per Capita Income	
Non-Hispanic White	$26,134
Black	$14,953
Asian	$24,277
Hispanic	$13,003

Table 7.32

Money Incomes 2001 (households)		
Less than	$15,000	$75,000+
Asian	12.3%	34.4%
White	14.3%	26.2%

Table 7.33

Source: US Census Bureau

Education

Graduates

	High School Graduate	College Graduate
White	84.9%	26.1%
Asian	85.7%	43.9%

Table 8.34 Source: US Census Bureau

Asians have done far better in education than any other group. Culturally they appear to value education more highly. The ending of Affirmative Action for university entrance in California led to far more Asian undergraduates taking places than their proportion in the population would suggest.

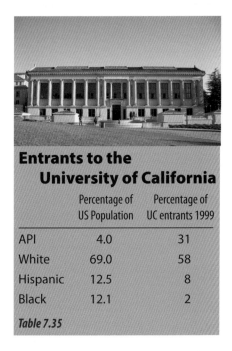

Entrants to the University of California

	Percentage of US Population	Percentage of UC entrants 1999
API	4.0	31
White	69.0	58
Hispanic	12.5	8
Black	12.1	2

Table 7.35

When Texas introduced a law requiring its universities to accept the top 10% of students from each of its high schools irrespective of the quality of the high school graduates, white parents moved their children out of the 'best' schools because they feared the competition from Asian children. Traditional white flight saw parents remove children from inner city schools because they feared deteriorating education due to integration with large numbers of poor immigrants. The new white flight is different. Parents are not fleeing the 'worst' schools, but the 'best.' Parents are afraid their children will not make the top 10% at their local high school.

One mother chose not to send her daughter to Bellaire High School in Houston, one of the area's highest performers, because she said "I don't think she can compete with the Asians." 17% of the students at Bellaire are Asian. Some Asian families have homes in other areas of Houston but rent apartments in the Bellaire school zone because they see it as the best school.

Education is highly prized in the Asian community, particularly among the Chinese and Japanese. Proportionately far more Asians are currently entering and graduating from colleges and universities than Whites which in the future will lead to Asians earning higher incomes and becoming the wealthiest group in the USA. Asians are doing well under the 10% rule. They make up an estimated 18% ot the new undergraduates at the University of Texas.

Asians and Health

Asians in America live longer and have a lower death rate than any other group. The main health problems for Asians are stomach cancer (from eating foods like pickled vegetables, dried fish and Kimchi), carbon monoxide poisoning, tuberculosis and leprosy. Asians have the lowest rates of death by 'modern causes' such as AIDS and cancer. This is most likely due to the high level of self-discipline found in Asian culture where few births are due to teenage pregnancies or are to unmarried women. Few drink or take drugs when pregnant. Equally, few engage in activities which might lead to AIDS. Finally, many have a general aversion to risky occupations and sports which contributes to a low rate of accidents.

Asians and Housing

A US Department of Housing and Urban Development report found that Asian and Pacific Islanders looking for properties to rent experienced adverse treatment compared to Whites in over 21% of cases. Asian and Pacific Islander prospective homebuyers experienced consistent adverse treatment relative to Whites 20% of the time. Systematic discrimination occurred in housing availability, with financial assistance, and in agent encouragement.

CHAPTER 8

Affirmative Action

WHAT IS AFFIRMATIVE ACTION?

Affirmative action was a series of programmes and measures designed to overcome discrimination in employment and education. Affirmative Action Programmes gave minorities and women special consideration in employment, education and contracting decisions.

In employment, organisations implementing Affirmative Action Programmes generally set goals and timetables to achieve diversity and used recruitment and preference as ways of achieving those goals. In education, affirmative action enabled colleges and universities to provide some form of extra preference for minority candidates to counterbalance the poor quality education they had experienced up to that point.

Affirmative action decisions were generally not supposed to be based on quotas, nor were they supposed to give any preference to unqualified candidates. Finally, they were not meant to harm anyone through 'reverse discrimination.'

In employment, companies which wanted contracts from the Federal government or state governments had to have Affirmative Action Programmes to eliminate discrimination in hiring or promotion. Large firms such as Coca Cola or Ford had to have written programmes designed to change the profile of their workforce to match the population profile in the particular area in which they were operating. The population profile in New York would be different from that in Texas.

In education there were two types of affirmative action attempted. In schools there was busing and for universities and colleges, the programmes centred on admission procedures. Busing describes a series of programmes to transport children around towns in order to create a greater race balance in schools. It created resentment and hostility in parents and children rather than integration and understanding and led to middle-class flight among both black and white parents. It was very expensive and diverted funds away from improving education in other ways. In 1995 busing was effectively ended following a Supreme Court decision. Busing is an example of a failed AAP.

One of the main features of affirmative action was the involvement of the Supreme Court. The history of affirmative action is littered with legal challenges, many of which were appealed all the way to the Supreme Court. In 1978, Allan Bakke, a white mature student, was denied a place on a medical course in California despite having higher qualifications than the minority students who were accepted. He successfully argued that a university admissions policy which relied on reserved places for minority groups (a quota) was reverse discrimination. The Supreme Court ruled that universities could not use quotas to set aside places for minority students but it could consider race as one factor in choosing between qualified applicants for admission.

The Effect of ending Affirmative Action on UCLA entry (%)				
	Black	Hispanic	Asian	White
1996	7	15	15	62
1999	2	8	31	58

Table 8.1

Whites did not always benefit from the ending of AAPs. When the University of California ended Affirmative Action for student admissions, Black and Hispanic student admissions suffered but the main beneficiaries were Asians. Asians doubled their numbers of admissions to over 30% of new undergraduates in 1999.

In 1996, Proposition 209 abolished all public service AAPs in "employment, education and contracting" in California. The Supreme Court refused to hear a challenge to Proposition 209 so it was put into effect. One of the consequences was that the University of California stopped using race as a factor in admissions.

From 1998 onwards many other states, such as Texas, Washington, Georgia and Florida, abolished AAPs. Although Affirmative Action as an on-going programme to help the minorities has largely been undermined there are places where some forms of programme still exist.

In 2003, there was a legal challenge to the programme for admissions used by the University of Michigan. Michigan gave minorities twenty points for being minorities on a 150-point scale for admission. The policy was challenged and the challenge was supported by the Bush administration which demonstrated its hostility to AAPs. The Attorney General (the top US government law officer) appeared in court on behalf of the students making the challenge. President Bush described Affirmative Action as "quota systems that ... exclude people from higher education ... (and) are divisive, unfair and impossible to square with the Constitution."

The Supreme Court ruled that Michigan University could take race into account when allocating student places but said that the system of awarding extra points to ethnic minorities was unconstitutional. This ruling shows how confused the situation with AAPs is in the USA.

SHOULD AFFIRMATIVE ACTION PROGRAMMES CONTINUE?

Arguments for Ending Affirmative Action

✗ 'Angry white men' blame affirmative action for robbing them of jobs and promotions.

✗ Many white middle-class liberals feel that the past thirty years has done enough. Minorities should stand on their own feet. White children suffer in a time of economic downturn.

✗ It is reverse discrimination.

✗ In 1996 in the vote on California's Proposition 209, 54% of Californians voted to end sexual and racial preferences in public employment, contracts and education.

✗ The Republican Party opposes Affirmative Action Programmes and won the 2000 and 2004 elections with that policy.

✗ Minorities have seen rapid improvements in their social and economic situation over the past thirty years.

✗ Affirmative action has not been successful in creating a 'colour blind society'—social and economic disadvantage persists.

✗ Minorities would have made greater advances without AAPs. Some argue that AAPs created a dependency culture in the Black community. Had they been left to develop without government interference then just like the Hispanics they would have developed a culture of enterprise which would have helped many more of them.

Arguments for Continuing with Affirmative Action

✔ Minorities have made great advances due to AAPs.

✔ Despite advances, minorities still lag significantly behind Whites. Minorities have lower paid jobs and still face active discrimination.

✔ President Clinton argued that the job of ending discrimination remains unfinished, and strongly defended affirmative action. "Mend it, but don't end it."

✔ The Black Caucus is still powerful in Washington and supports the continuation of AAPs.

✔ When the University of California was banned from using affirmative action for admissions, the Berkeley campus had a 61% drop in admissions of Black, Hispanic and Native American students, and UCLA had a 36% decline.

✔ AAPs have helped to make the US a more tolerant society.

HAVE AFFIRMATIVE ACTION PROGRAMMES BEEN SUCCESSFUL?

Yes
- Minorities have made great advances in their social and economic circumstances.
- The US is a more tolerant society.
- Ending affirmative action led to fewer Blacks and Hispanics entering the University of California.

No
- Minorities would have made greater advances without AAPs.
- Blacks and Hispanics are still not equal to Whites.
- Reverse discrimination occurs when AAPs are in force.
- Busing was a disaster for both white and minority communities.
- The USA is still not a tolerant society.
- Employers claim they are forced to employ less capable workers just because of their colour and ethnic background.

The Republic of South Africa

CHAPTER 9

The rainbow country

Any study of South Africa must include the impact of the apartheid years (1948–1994) during which the white minority denied the black majority their political, social and economic rights. A legacy of vast inequalities between the races in terms of income, living standards, health care, education and employment opportunities remained.

THE LAND AND THE PEOPLE

South Africa is five times the size of the United Kingdom with a population three-quarters that of the UK. Due to its size, it has different climates and landscapes in different parts of the country. Much of the west of the country is desert, while the south, around Cape Town, has a Mediterranean climate. South Africa is divided into nine provinces. (See page 81.)

Its population of 45 million is made up of numerous ethnic groups and this is reflected in the recognition of eleven official languages. Black South Africans make up 79% of the population. (See Table 9.3.)

Boers, British and Africans

In 1652 a settlement was established by the Dutch East India Company to supply fresh provisions for their trading ships. Before the appearance of the Dutch, the land had been inhabited by two main tribes, the San and the Khoikhoi—often referred to as Bushmen and Hottentots respectively.

By 1806 the British government had decided to control Cape Colony and consequently took it over. The resultant increase in immigration from Britain established two distinct white communities—the Afrikaners (Boers) and English-speaking Whites (Anglos). Their attitudes to the Cape were quite different. The Anglos saw it as a colony of the British Empire, but the Afrikaners saw it as their home and country.

Between 1836 and 1846, therefore, thousands of Boers left Cape Colony and Natal in the Great Trek to establish the independent republics of Transvaal and the Orange Free State. Britain left these Afrikaner republics alone as they had no strategic or economic value. This changed, however, with the discovery of diamonds in 1867 and gold in 1886 in the Transvaal and the Orange Free State. In 1867 Britain proceeded to annexe the Afrikaner republics. This eventually led to the Boer War 1899–1902 in which Boer hostility towards the Anglos was fuelled by the British use of concentration camps and a scorched earth policy. The Afrikaners' humiliation was complete when many of them were forced into waged labour as their farms failed.

British dominance ended in 1948 when the Afrikaner National Party won the election and began its policy of apartheid and total white control of all aspects of life.

SOUTH AFRICA'S ECONOMY

South Africa is a middle income emerging economy with an abundant stock of natural resources. It is served by a modern infrastructure,

South Africa's Mineral Wealth

	World Production		World Reserves	
	Rank	%	Rank	%
Gold	1	23	1	45
Vanadium	1	51	1	45
Chrome Ore	1	36	1	69
Alumino Silicates	1	34	1	37
Manganese Ore	3	12	1	81
Platinum	1	48	1	56
Vermiculite	1	43	2	40
Antimony	4	12	2	5
Diamonds	5	11	2	21
Fluorspar	4	6	3	12
Titanium	2	20	2	17

Table 9.1 Source: Official Yearbook of South Africa 2000

South African Development Community

Selected Countries	2003 GDP US$b	2002 GDP US$ per capita	Population 2004 (m)
Democratic Republic of Congo	7.0	90	53.6
Tanzania	8.9	280	36.2
Angola	10.0	650	13.9
Malawi	1.5	160	10.5
Mozambique	2.4	210	19.4
Zambia	3.1	330	9.8
Zimbabwe	9.4	570	11.4
South Africa	**156.9**	**2,520**	**45.7**

Table 9.2 Source: World Bank, 2004

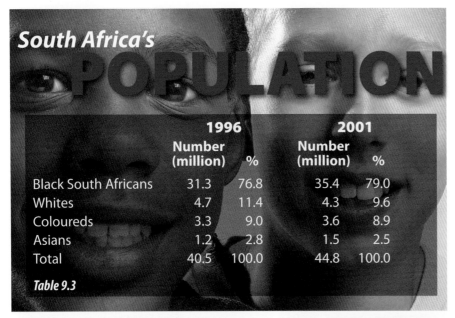

South Africa's POPULATION

	1996		2001	
	Number (million)	%	Number (million)	%
Black South Africans	31.3	76.8	35.4	79.0
Whites	4.7	11.4	4.3	9.6
Coloureds	3.3	9.0	3.6	8.9
Asians	1.2	2.8	1.5	2.5
Total	40.5	100.0	44.8	100.0

Table 9.3

Population by province

	1996	2001	Growth (%)
Eastern Cape	6,302,525	6,436,763	2.1
Free State	2,633,504	2,706,775	2.8
Gauteng	7,348,423	8,837,178	20.3
KwaZulu-Natal	8,417,021	9,426,017	12.0
Limpopo	4,929,368	5,273,642	7.0
Mpumalanga	2,800,711	3,122,990	11.5
Northern Cape	840,321	822,727	-2.1
North West	3,354,825	3,669,349	9.4
Western Cape	3,956,875	4,524,335	14.3
South Africa	40,583,573	44,819,778	10.4

Table 9.4

The population of South Africa is growing, especially among the black South African community. In contrast, the number of Whites is decreasing. It is estimated that almost one million white people left South Africa in the period 1995 to 2002. The new census results, published in July 2003, show that the South African population increased from 40.5 million people in 1996 to 44.8 million in 2001, a growth of 10%. South Africa is made up of numerous ethnic groups, with the main racial groups being Blacks, Whites, Coloureds and Asians.

Distribution of the population

by language most often spoken at home

(number of speakers in millions)

isiZulu	10.6
isiXhosa	7.9
Afrikaans	5.9
Sepedi	4.2
English	3.6
Setswana	3.6
Sesotho	3.5
Xitsonga	1.9
SiSwati	1.1
Tshivenda	1.0
isiNdebele	0.7
Other	0.2

Table 9.5 Source: 2001 Census

South Africa has eleven official languages, IsiZulu being the most popular language. The number of people who speak Afrikaans or English as their home language has declined.

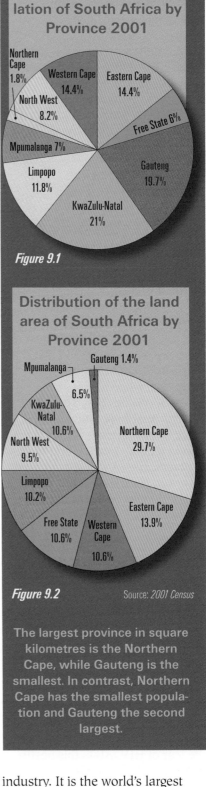

Distribution of the population of South Africa by Province 2001

Northern Cape 1.8%
Western Cape 14.4%
Eastern Cape 14.4%
North West 8.2%
Free State 6%
Mpumalanga 7%
Gauteng 19.7%
Limpopo 11.8%
KwaZulu-Natal 21%

Figure 9.1

Distribution of the land area of South Africa by Province 2001

Gauteng 1.4%
Mpumalanga 6.5%
KwaZulu-Natal 10.6%
North West 9.5%
Northern Cape 29.7%
Limpopo 10.2%
Eastern Cape 13.9%
Free State 10.6%
Western Cape 10.6%

Figure 9.2 Source: *2001 Census*

The largest province in square kilometres is the Northern Cape, while Gauteng is the smallest. In contrast, Northern Cape has the smallest population and Gauteng the second largest.

---

ensuring an efficient distribution of goods to major urban areas. The country has well-developed financial and legal sectors with a stock exchange that ranks among the ten largest in the world. Unemployment is still a major problem with 50% of the population living below the poverty line. Massive economic inequalities still exist between

Whites and black South Africans. South Africa is one of the most unequal countries in the world, alongside the USA, China and Brazil, in terms of wealth distribution among its citizens.

South Africa is the wealthiest country in Africa in terms of natural resources and its manufacturing

industry. It is the world's largest producer of gold. (See Table 10.1.) Large-scale commercial farming ensures an abundant supply of food. This is an excellent achievement as only 12% of the land is suitable for cultivation. In the less fertile areas pastoral farming dominates, with sheep rearing and cattle ranching particularly strong.

South Africa is the region's economic superpower. (See Table 9.2.) It accounts for 85% of southern Africa's energy consumption and 90% of its Gross Domestic Product (GDP). South Africa's GDP is $156.9 billion. In contrast, the combined GDP of the other thirteen countries is $16.9 billion.

ILLEGAL IMMIGRANTS

The official census of South Africa's population did not include the millions of Africans who have flocked to South Africa to escape poverty and persecution. It is estimated that there are over five million illegal immigrants living in South Africa. It is ironic that while highly skilled and educated Whites leave for countries such as Australia, and educated black South Africans flock to London to take up nursing and teaching posts, they are being replaced by a workforce that South Africa, with an unemployment rate of 40%, does not need.

Most refugees originate from the Democratic Republic of Congo, Rwanda, Angola, and, increasingly, Zimbabwe. South Africa deports between 600 and 1,000 Zimbabweans every week, but it is a losing battle as they simply return. It is estimated that there are as many as two million Zimbabweans in South Africa escaping from the tyranny of their leader, Robert Mugabe. Illegal immigrants face great hostility from South Africans and when one adds the fear of HIV /AIDS this hostility turns to 'xenophobia', fear of foreigners. The view in 2004 of the then Home Affairs Minister, Chief Buthelezi, still reflects public opinion: "The presence of illegal aliens impacts on housing, health services, education, crime, drugs, and transmissible diseases. Illegal immigrants who are HIV positive cannot receive free treatment from a clinic and must pay privately for anti-HIV

While there are significant inequalities in South Africa based on race, there are also significant inequalities between urban and rural areas in South Africa. The 2001 Census, published in July 2003, highlights the fact that regional inequalities are still a feature of South Africa, as outlined in the selected statistics below.

Percentage of households in each province with access to piped water	
Eastern Cape	62.4
KwaZulu-Natal	73.2
Limpopo	78.0
North West	86.2
Mpumalanga	86.7
Free State	95.7
Northern Cape	96.6
Gauteng	97.5
Western Cape	98.3
South Africa	84.0

Table 9.6

Households in each province with no toilet facility (%)	
Eastern Cape	30.8
Limpopo	23.3
KwaZulu-Natal	16.2
Northern Cape	11.2
Mpumalanga	10.3
North West	9.7
Free State	9.6
Western Cape	7.7
Gauteng	3.6
South Africa	13.6

Table 9.7 Source: Census 2001

In the Eastern Cape, 62% of households had access to piped water, either in the dwelling, on-site, or from a communal tap, compared with 98% in the Western Cape.

In the Eastern Cape three in every ten households did not have access to a toilet facility

Population aged 20 and above in each province with		
	no education	tertiary qualifications
North West	19.9	5.9
Mpumalanga	27.5	5.9
Northern Cape	18.2	6.1
Eastern Cape	22.8	6.3
Free State	16.0	6.3
Limpopo	33.4	6.8
KwaZulu-Natal	21.9	6.9
Western Cape	5.7	11.2
Gauteng	8.4	12.6
South Africa	17.9	8.4

Table 9.8

Unemployment rate among those aged 15–65 in each province	
Limpopo	48.8
KwaZulu-Natal	48.7
Eastern Cape	54.6
North West	43.8
Mpumalanga	41.1
Free State	43.0
Gauteng	36.4
Northern Cape	33.4
Western Cape	26.1
South Africa	41.6

Table 9.9

In Limpopo just over a third of those aged 20 years and above had not received any education. In South Africa as a whole fewer than one in ten people had tertiary qualifications.

drugs at a cost of R300 a month, a price few can afford. A 2003 government-sponsored research study of refugees and asylum seekers discovered that only 10% had been issued with identification cards, which provided access to the health system. The remaining 90% had been waiting for more than three years for asylum status.

PROFILES OF THE PROVINCES OF SOUTH AFRICA

PROVINCE/Capital   GAUTENG/Johannesburg

Principal Language	Afrikaans (25%), English (16%), isiZulu (18%)
Population	8.8 million (19% of total)
Area Km²	18,810 (1.6% of total)
% of GDP	38
Agriculture & Industry	Gauteng is South Africa's engine room, where about 40% of the country's GDP is generated. Gauteng means 'place of gold' and this is a highly urbanised and industrialised area. It is a magnet area for a large inflow of migrant labourers who settle in the townships and shanty towns.
Comment	Pretoria, the administrative capital of South Africa, is situated in the province. The sprawling townships, such as Soweto, are struggling to overcome the social and economic legacy of apartheid.

PROVINCE/Capital   NORTHERN CAPE/Kimberley

Principal Language	Afrikaans (66%), isiXhosa (6%), Setswana (19%)
Population	0.8 million (1.8% of total)
Area Km²	361,800 (29.7% of total)
% of GDP	2
Agriculture & Industry	Extremely rich in mineral wealth with Kimberley being the diamond capital of the world. Other major minerals are copper, manganese and marble.
Comment	It covers the largest area of South Africa and has the smallest population. It is a semi-arid region with low summer rainfall and is the home of the San (bushmen) people who live in the Kalahari area of the Northern Cape.

PROVINCE/Capital   WESTERN CAPE/ Cape Town

Principal Language	Afrikaans (62%), English (20%), isiXhosa (15%)
Population	4.5 million (10.6% of total)
Area Km²	129,379 (14.4% of total)
% of GDP	14.8
Agriculture & Industry	Food basket of South Africa with a harvest of top grade fruits, vegetables and meats. Head offices of many South African businesses are in Cape Town. 95% of its population is urbanised.
Comment	Cape Town is the legislative capital of the country. Western Cape has the highest literacy rate in the country.

PROVINCE/Capital   FREE STATE/Bloemfontein

Principal Language	Afrikaans (15%), isiXhosa (9%), Sesotho (57%)
Population	2.7 million (6.7% of total)
Area Km²	129,480 (10.6% of total)
% of GDP	6.8
Agriculture & Industry	'The granary of the country' with 31% of the potentially arable land of South Africa. Its main economic base is mining.
Comment	It lies in the heart of South Africa and is the third largest province. Its agricultural sector has been affected by the drought experienced in the late 1990s.

PROVINCE/Capital   NORTH WEST/Minabatho

Principal Language	Afrikaans (9%), isiXhosa (6%), Setswana (59%)
Population, millions	3.3 (8.1% of total)
Area Km²	116,190 (9.5% of total)
% of GDP	5.5
Agriculture & Industry	Main economic base is mining with its major agricultural products being maize and sunflowers. High unemployment levels in the province contribute to the poverty experienced by many of its citizens.
Comment	At present it has no major airport. It is developing its tourist industry through national parks.

PROVINCE/Capital   EASTERN CAPE/Bisho

Principal Language	Afrikaans (10%), English (4%), isiXhosa (82%)
Population	6.4 million (14.4% of total)
Area Km²	169,600 (13.9% of total)
% of GDP	7.6
Agriculture & Industry	Not rich in minerals but includes rich agricultural and forestry land. The urban areas of Port Elizabeth and East London are based primarily on manufacturing.
Comment	Includes the former Homelands of Transkei and Ciskei.

PROVINCE/Capital   LIMPOPO/Pietersburg

Principal Language	Sepedi (57%), Tshivenda (12%), Xitsonga (23%)
Population	5.3 million (12% of total)
Area Km²	123,280 (10% of total)
% of GDP	3.7
Agriculture & Industry	Extremely rich in minerals including coal, copper, asbestos, iron ore and platinum. Produces sub-tropical fruit and its Bushveld is cattle country. Unemployment is high. The per capita income is by far the lowest in the country. Contains the three former Homelands of Venda, Gazankulu and Lebowa.
Comment	The province is the country's gateway to the rest of Africa as it shares borders with Botswana, Zimbabwe and Mozambique. This province has the Savannah Biome, an area of mixed grassland and trees (Bushveld).

PROVINCE/Capital   MPUMALANGA/Nelspruit

Principal Language	isiNdebele (11%), SiSwati (30%), isiZulu (24%)
Population	3 million (7% of total)
Area Km²	78,370 (6.4% of total)
% of GDP	8.1
Agriculture & Industry	Produces sub-tropical fruits and its tree plantations supply half of the country's total timber needs. It is rich in coal reserves and the country's three biggest power stations are based in the area.
Comment	Mpumalanga (formerly Eastern Transvaal) means 'place where the sun rises'. The province attracts migrant labour from neighbouring states, especially refugees from Mozambique. Suffers from extreme levels of poverty and low levels of literacy.

PROVINCE/Capital   KWAZULU-NATAL/Pietermaritzburg/Ulundi

Principal Language	Afrikaans (2%), English (16%), isiZulu (79%)
Population	9.4 million (21% of total)
Area Km²	92,180 (7.6% of total)
% of GDP	14.9
Agriculture & Industry	Rapid industrialisation in recent times. Durban is one of the fastest growing urban areas in the world. Huge gap between the urban and rural per capita income.
Comment	The only province with a monarchy specifically provided for in the 1993 Constitution. Ulundi is the traditional capital of the Zulu monarchy.

Limpopo

Mpumalanga

North West   Gauteng

Northern Cape

Free State   LESOTHO   KwaZulu-Natal

Eastern Cape

Western Cape

SOUTH AFRICA

2010 FOOTBALL WORLD CUP

South Africa will host the 2010 FIFA World Cup with Johannesburg probably hosting both the opening and final games. While rugby is the sport traditionally associated with the Whites, football is the most popular sport among black South Africans. Recently crowds of 100,000 people, almost all black, squeezed into Johannesburg's Soweto football stadium to watch the local derby between the Kaiser Chiefs and the Orlando Pirates. This explains South Africa's enthusiasm for holding the finals and the pride of the people at being chosen.

Below is an extract from FIFA's website about the 2010 Finals with some interesting comments about Johannesburg.

Johannesburg (affectionately known as Jo'burg) has a population estimated at 7

" million people and is the largest city in sub-Saharan Africa. Johannesburg is a large, sprawling city. It is the powerhouse for the country's economy, and owes its existence to the discovery of gold in 1886. Mine dumps, many disused or reclaimed, can be seen ringing the city. Johannesburg is interesting and unique in many ways. At almost all traffic lights, informal traders sell a wide range of goods to motorists—including clothes, CDs, cellphone accessories and more. Hawkers (informal traders) also ply their trade along the side of the road in many places, where one can stop and purchase a variety of original crafts, furniture and other goods. This is also one of the greenest cities in the world and has been called the world's largest man-made urban forest. Trees line suburban streets, including the distinctive Jacaranda tree which flowers in spring.

Jo'burg is a constantly changing city. Since the first democratic government was voted into power in South Africa in 1994, a black middle class has begun to emerge which is both wealthy and sophisticated. Jo'burgers are confident people and many are entrepreneurs. The city is also a cultural 'melting pot' and is an exhilarating and vibrant place.

The city and its surrounds present a fascinating contrast between First and Third World. In the middle and upper-class suburbs, the 'haves' live in homes with gardens, often with swimming pools, and a high level of security including electric fencing and burglar alarms. In contrast, the 'have nots' live in cheap housing, or shacks, in informal settlements known as townships.

This disparity of incomes has contributed to increasing crime levels. However, Johannesburg is not a dangerous place to visit if the tourist follows certain guidelines. Some parts of Jo'burg are not appropriate to visit at all, especially not after dark, and due caution over the security of one's person and belongings should be exercised at all times. "

Two views of Johannesburg

CHAPTER 10

The apartheid years 1948 – 1990

In 1948 the white voters placed their trust and future in the apartheid policies of the National Party. The vision of a 'White only' South Africa, which maintained the power and wealth of the white minority while condemning the non-Whites to low paid employment and limited political rights, appealed to the white electorate.

DIVIDING THE POPULATION

The first step in the National Party's development of apartheid was to define the races, or national groups, to which people belonged. This was done through the *Population Registration Act* (1950) which decreed that all people were to be racially classified into three main groups with subdivisions. These are shown in Table 10.1.

The majority black South African population was divided into eight tribal groups. The Coloureds were made up of two main groups. There were descendants from relationships between Whites and the original African inhabitants of the Cape, the San and Khoikhoi. These constituted Cape Coloureds. There were also the Asians, or Indians, descended from Indian workers who were brought from India to work, especially in Natal, in the nineteenth century. Whites were divided into English-speaking and Afrikaans-speaking, with the latter controlling the country

The Coloureds were not given a Homeland to live in. They were forced to live in Coloured townships on the outskirts of towns and cities. By 1980, over 116,000 Col-oured and Indian families had been forced to leave their homes and move to these designated areas.

DIVIDING THE LAND

Having divided the population, the National Party began to divide the land to define where the different groups could live and exercise their individual and political rights. The 1950s saw the creation of the Homelands policy which defined the territory which Whites saw as the traditional land of the black South Africans. It was in these Homelands or Bantustans that the black South Africans would be entitled to exercise citizenship rights.

The aim was to develop the Homelands into independent countries with governments elected by the black South Africans recorded as being citizens of that Homeland. This meant that when Transkei became 'independent' on 26 October 1976, every black South African with 'Xhosa' stamped in his or her passbook lost his or her South African citizenship. The same thing happened to those labelled 'Tswana' when Bophuthatswana became 'independent' on 6 December 1977. By 1985 two other Homelands, Venda and Ciskei, had also become independent. (The four Homelands were collectively known as the TBVC countries.)

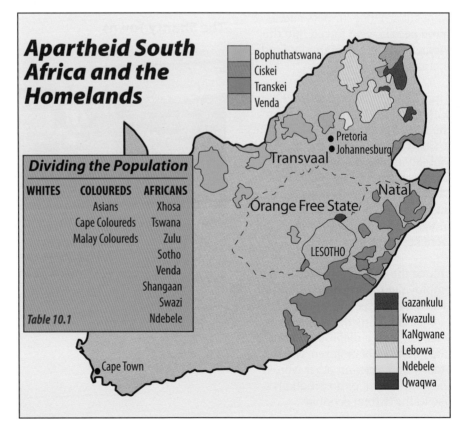

Apartheid South Africa and the Homelands

Bophuthatswana
Ciskei
Transkei
Venda

Pretoria
Johannesburg
Transvaal

Natal

Orange Free State

LESOTHO

Gazankulu
Kwazulu
KaNgwane
Lebowa
Ndebele
Qwaqwa

Cape Town

Dividing the Population

WHITES	COLOUREDS	AFRICANS
	Asians	Xhosa
	Cape Coloureds	Tswana
	Malay Coloureds	Zulu
		Sotho
		Venda
		Shangaan
		Swazi
Table 10.1		Ndebele

The Homelands

Comprising no more than 13% of the total land in South Africa, the Homelands were expected to support almost 73% of the population, or twenty one of the twenty eight million people living in the country. On the most fertile soil and with the most modern farming techniques this would be an awesome task— and these conditions did not exist in the Homelands.

However, the quality of the land allocated to the Homelands varied. The largest, Bophuthatswana, had a very large amount of desert and semi-desert, with only 6–7% of the land considered suitable for arable farming; the rest was suitable only for livestock grazing. The quality of even the best land in the Homelands was diminished by the demands placed upon it as more and more black South Africans were forcibly resettled there. Most black South Africans in the Homelands were subsistence farmers and as more people were forced into the Homelands, the demand for land increased.

The Homelands were fragmented, with pockets of land cut off from the rest of the Homeland by 'white' areas. This weakened the economic viability of the Homeland. The borders were arbitrarily drawn to satisfy white requirements. This ensured that most major towns, industrial and mining developments were kept out.

Due to the shortage of land and employment many black South Africans had to seek work outside the Homeland. Thus the Homelands were left with a disproportionately large number of children, women, elderly and sick—in other words, those who were of no productive use to the 'white' economy.

The Townships

Most black South Africans who qualified to stay in 'white South Africa' under Section 10 regulations were housed in one of the many townships. These were housing areas for the black South African labour force which was required by local industry and they were usually situated on the outskirts of an urban area. Soweto, situated twelve miles south-west of Johannesburg and housing well over one million black South Africans, was an example of one such township.

Most homes used candles, paraffin or gas lamps for lighting and coal stoves for cooking. Water was supplied to most houses by an outside tap from which residents carried supplies. Only 3% had running hot water and 7% had a bath or shower. Electricity was not common in houses.

The Shanty Towns

Many black South Africans lived illegally in squatter camps, or shanty towns, in the urban areas. Probably the best example of this was Crossroads, a vast squatter camp of about 4,000 'illegal' families, a few miles outside Cape Town. In such camps black South Africans were willing to flout apartheid's regulations in order to maintain family life. The camp flourished, with each household contributing to the cost of water, refuse disposal and education services. Crossroads reflected a demand from black South Africans to be allowed to live a normal life and a rejection of the single-sex hostels which were built to house migrant workers while their families were banished to the Homelands to face starvation.

EDUCATION

Education was used by the government to shape people to fit the apartheid mould. The Afrikaner view on the role of education was made quite clear by a future Prime Minister, Hendrik Verwoerd, in 1954 when he said, "The native must be taught from childhood that equality with Europeans is not for him. There is no place for him in the European community above the level of certain forms of labour." To the black South Africans it was simply a case of "the Boers wanting to indoctrinate African children into being perpetual slaves of the white man."

In 1959, segregation was extended to university education, with separate universities being established for Whites, Coloureds, Indians and Blacks. Access to universities was unequal, as demonstrated by the 1980 student roll which had 160,000 Whites, 16,000 Indians, 12,000 Coloureds and 10,500 black South Africans.

THE STRUGGLE AGAINST APARTHEID

1912   African National Congress (ANC) is formed to create national unity among blacks South Africans in their struggle for civil rights.

1950s   ANC becomes a mass movement and its leader from 1952–1960, Chief Albert Luthuli, supports peaceful non-violent change.

1955   ANC draws up a Freedom Charter.

1959   ANC suffers a blow when a splinter group from the ANC forms the Pan Africanist Congress (PAC).

1960   Sharpeville Massacre takes place—sixty nine demonstrators in a peaceful protest against the pass laws are shot dead by police. State of emergency declared with over 20,000 people being arrested. ANC goes underground and begins the armed struggle.

1964   Nelson Mandela, leader of the ANC, is captured and sentenced to life imprisonment.

1964–76   For more than a decade, black opposition lies crushed and dispirited.

1976   Soweto riots take place. Young people march in protest against the compulsory use of Afrikaans in schools. Over 700 black South Africans die and thousands leave the country to continue the struggle from abroad.

1977   Steve Biko, leader of the Black Consciousness Movement (BCM) dies in police custody.

1979–84   Rapid expansion in black trade unions. Cyril Ramaphosa leads this opposition to apartheid.

1984–88   Failure of Botha's reforms. ANC makes the townships ungovernable.

1989   President Botha resigns through ill health and is replaced by FW de Klerk.

1990   The ban outlawing the ANC and other political groupings is lifted. In February, Nelson Mandela is freed after being in jail for twenty seven years.

INTERNAL OPPOSITION TO APARTHEID

The apartheid system was not only opposed by Blacks and Coloureds but also by many Whites. Nevertheless, the main opposition came from the African National Congress (ANC) which was formed in 1912 with the goal of achieving civil rights for all non-Whites. Despite the brutality of the regime, the ANC continued to preach and argue for non-violent change until it was forced to go underground in 1960 and begin an armed struggle.

With Nelson Mandela and other leaders in jail, the ANC organised resistance from Zambia. The ANC carried out acts of sabotage against military and industrial targets and some isolated action against white civilians. The ANC also ensured that the townships would become ungovernable. Other organisations such as trade unions, church activists like Archbishop Desmond Tutu, and community rights organisations such as the United Democratic Front (UDF) spoke out against the apartheid system. The Zulu movement Inkatha, led by Chief Buthelezi, opposed apartheid through non-violent means and was accused by the ANC of being a puppet of the apartheid regime.

Steve Biko was leader of the South African Students Organisation and spread the gospel of Black Consciousness to instil self-confidence, pride and dignity in the young.

MODERNISING APARTHEID
1978–1990

The Soweto riots of 1976–77 were crushed by the security forces with an estimated 700 deaths. Many young black South Africans fled the country to prepare for armed resistance and were determined to return with bullets, not stones.

In 1978 PW Botha became the new President of South Africa and promised to introduce reforms. "We must adapt or die" was his message to the white electorate.

PW Botha hoped to create a larger non-black minority by including the Coloureds and Asians in decision making. He hoped that his economic reforms would create a black middle class which would benefit from the apartheid system. Botha also hoped that his reforms would promote a new international image of South Africa and that the United Nations and individual countries would end their economic sanctions against his country.

Reaction to Botha's Reforms

Botha's reforms were condemned by the black majority and even by the Coloured and Asian communities. Moreover, his reforms split his own party, with Dr Treurnicht, a member of Botha's cabinet, resigning along with fourteen other National Party MPs to form the Conservative Party.

The townships once again exploded and Botha was forced to declare a state of emergency before order was restored in 1989. Yet it was clear that the country was heading towards a savage war between the apartheid regime and its black opponents led by the ANC.

BOTHA'S REFORMS

Social

● Restaurants, transport and certain public facilities were opened to all races (end of petty apartheid).
● The hated Pass Laws were abolished.
● The laws prohibiting mixed marriages and inter-racial sexual relations were abolished.
● Sports and sporting facilities (excluding schools) were completely integrated.

Economic

● Black South Africans were now able to purchase their own homes under a ninety nine year lease and set up their own businesses in areas which previously had been exclusively white.
● Black trade unions were recognised and jobs were opened to all races.
● Electricity and other amenities were installed in the townships.

Political

● The vote was given to the Coloured and Asian communities. The Whites-only parliament was replaced by a tricameral parliament consisting of three separate chambers, one each for Whites, Coloureds and Asians.
● At the local level black South Africans were given greater control over the running of the townships with the setting up of local councils.
● South African citizenship was restored to all citizens including citizens of the Homelands.

ISOLATION OF SOUTH AFRICA

1974 United Nations suspends South Africa from its membership
1977 United Nations imposes an arms embargo against South Africa

1986 European Union and British Commonwealth impose a ban on the import of coal, iron, steel and gold coins from South Africa
1986 United States bans the import of South African iron, steel, coal, uranium, textiles and agricultural products

CHAPTER 11

Creating the rainbow nation

In August 1989, the ailing President Botha was replaced by FW de Klerk who, within a year, had brought apartheid to an end. He released Nelson Mandela, legalised the ANC and other political parties in February 1990, and scrapped the remaining apartheid laws. Negotiations began for a peaceful transition from white minority to black majority rule.

TRANSITIONAL ARRANGEMENTS

Negotiations were slow and painful, with the National Party reluctantly being forced to accept that it could not impose a settlement which would retain a built-in veto to protect white minority rights. Violence, especially in KwaZulu-Natal between ANC and Inkatha supporters, raised political tension and accelerated negotiations.

In 1993, the major political parties agreed to elections being held in 1994, and to an interim constitution. Under the agreement nine regional provincial governments were to be set up with each being responsible for areas such as education, law and order, and health. Central government would be responsible for foreign affairs and economic management.

Neither Inkatha, the Zulu movement led by Chief Buthelezi, nor the extreme right-wing white groups of the Afrikaner Volksfront were involved in the creation of the interim constitution. Inkatha wanted greater power to be given to the Provinces and was afraid of ANC dominance. The Afrikaner Volksfront, which included the Conservative Party and the AWB, was demanding a Volkstaat (homeland) for the Afrikaners and was against black majority rule.

Election Day

Finally, in April 1994, the silent political voice of the African people roared into life as millions of non-

FW de Klerk – the last white South African President

The Path to Peace and Freedom 1990–1994

1990	
2 February	The ANC and other political parties are legalised
11 February	Nelson Mandela walks out of Victor Verster Prison to freedom
6 August	The ANC suspends its armed struggle
31 August	The National Party offers membership to all races
1991	Hated apartheid legislation, such as the Group Area Acts and the Population Registration Act, is repealed
1992	
March	In the Whites-only referendum, 69% vote for the end of white supremacy
1993	
July	The Inkatha Freedom Party (IFP) and the white Conservative Party promise to boycott the April 1994 elections
1994	
19 April	Fighting continues in KwaZulu-Natal between Inkatha and ANC supporters, forcing de Klerk to declare a state of emergency. Inkatha agrees to take part in the elections and civil war is avoided
27 April	The elections take place without disruption

Whites turned up to vote for the first time. Nelson Mandela, leader of the ANC, stated without exaggeration that "Today is a day like no other before it" as twenty million fellow voters waited patiently in long excited queues to cast their votes.

The political violence promised by extreme Whites failed to take place. The only major violence took place before the voting began. White extremists planted bombs which killed twenty one people. The authorities reacted quickly and arrested thirty four members of the extreme right-wing group, the Afrikaner Resistance Movement (AWB).

1994 Election Analysis

✘ It was a triumph for democracy with the election remaining free from intimidation, fraud and violence.

✘ As expected, the ANC dominated the election, winning over twelve million votes and just failing to receive two-thirds of the votes (which would have enabled it to create a new constitution without consulting the other political parties). At the provincial level the ANC won seven of the nine provinces with narrow defeats in the Western Cape and Kwa-Zulu-Natal.

✘ The New National Party, by winning the support of Whites, Coloureds and Asians, gained an impressive 20.4% of the vote and thus a post of Deputy President. Its best performance was in the Western Cape where it won the provincial election.

✘ The Inkatha Freedom Party (IFP) gained a narrow victory over the ANC in KwaZulu-Natal and won control of the province. The results reinforced

The 1994 Election Results

Party	Number of votes cast	Percentage of the vote	Seats won
African National Congress (ANC)	12,237,655	62.6	252
New National Party (NNP)	3,983,690	20.4	82
Inkatha Freedom Party (IFP)	2,058,294	10.5	43
Freedom Front (FF)	424,555	2.2	9
Democratic Party (DP)	338,426	1.7	7
Pan Africanist Congress (PAC)	243,437	1.2	7
African Christian Democratic Party (ACDP)	88,104	0.5	2
Others	159,295	0.9	0
Votes counted	19,533,456		

Percentage poll 87%

Table 11.1

THE POLITICAL PARTIES

African National Congress (ANC)

The ANC, with its history of struggle against apartheid and the leadership of Nelson Mandela, had the overwhelming support of the black South Africans. It was a broad organisation which had strong ties with CO-SATU (Trade Unions) and the SACP (South African Communist Party). It had some support from the white and coloured communities. The ANC fought the election on the slogan 'A Better Life for All'. Inevitably, promises were made such as 'Build one million low cost homes by 1999', which raised the expectations and hopes of the black South Africans.

New National Party (NNP)

The National Party, led by FW de Klerk, changed its name to the New National Party and declared that it was now a party for all the people of South Africa. Its main support came from Whites and Coloureds.

Inkatha Freedom Party (IFP)

The IFP, under the leadership of Chief Buthelezi, only agreed to participate a week before the elections. Its main aim was to establish an independent Zulu state and it was unhappy with the Constitution which limited the powers of the provincial governments. Considerable tension existed between the ANC and Inkatha, which led to atrocities being committed by both sides during the 'peace' negotiations of 1991–94.

Democratic Party (DP)

Formed by Whites who had always opposed apartheid, it offered an alternative to voting for the NNP or the ANC. It was regarded as the party of the middle-class, English-speaking Whites.

Freedom Front (FF)

The FF represented the extreme right-wing Afrikaner movements and its goal was the creation of an independent Afrikaner state (Volkstaat). The most notorious right-wing group, the AWB led by Eugene Terre Blanche, boycotted the elections and threatened that black majority rule would lead to a 'race war'.

Pan Africanist Congress (PAC)

This was an extreme black South African political party which supported the seizure of white farms without compensation.

the status of the IFP (and the New National Party) as regional rather than national players. While the IFP gained 1.8 million votes in KwaZulu-Natal, its combined vote in the eight other provinces was only 214,000.

✗ The extreme parties fared badly. The Pan Africanist Congress (PAC) gained only 243,000 votes and five seats in the National Assembly. The Freedom Front, representing the Afrikaner community, gained 424,000 votes and nine seats.

THE RAINBOW GOVERNMENT

1994–1996 marked the high point of cooperation between the New National Party and the ANC within the Government of National Unity (GNU), a position which ensured political and social stability. The GNU's commitment to a mixed economy, combined with its policy of reconstruction, reassured both the domestic and the international business communities.

One of the first major tasks for the Constitutional Assembly, under the leadership of Cyril Ramaphosa, was to prepare a new constitution. Although de Klerk held the office of Deputy President and his Party had nine posts in the Cabinet, his influence on decision making was limited. The role of 'junior party' angered and frustrated the New National Party. It became clear that it could not protect what it called the 'cultural identity' of the Whites (although the ANC thought that these were 'privileges').

Symbols of the new order were the demotion of Afrikaans to minority language status on the broadcasting services and the opening of rural white schools to all races. Prior to February 1996, the national state-owned television had offered to share time equally between English and Afrikaans and this decision was seen as an attack on the Afrikaans language. It had also become clear that Nelson Mandela, while agreeing to set up a Volkstaat Committee within Parliament, had no intention of supporting an inde-

NELSON MANDELA

Nelson Mandela was born on 18 July 1918, the son of a tribal chief of the Xhosa nation. He graduated from the University College of Fort Hare and later set up a legal practice with Oliver Tambo in Johannesburg. Both men were leaders of the ANC Youth League which supported boycotts, strikes and acts of civil disobedience.

The introduction of apartheid in 1948 and the brutal use of force by the white regime made him question the ANC's policy of non-violence. In 1961, Mandela went underground to organise the military wing of the ANC. On 2 August 1962 he was sentenced to life imprisonment for attempting to overthrow the government by violent revolution. It was not until 11 February 1990 that he gained his freedom when he was released from prison by President de Klerk. He was reunited with his wife, Winnie, but their marriage ended and they were divorced in 1996.

Nelson Mandela was elected President of the new democratic South Africa in 1994 and he retained this post until 1999 when he retired from politics. Mandela preached reconciliation between the races and worked hard to create a new 'rainbow nation'.

"We enter into a covenant that we shall build a society in which all South Africans, both black and white, will be able to walk and talk, without any fear in their hearts, assured of their inalienable right to human dignity—a rainbow nation at peace with itself and the world."

Nelson Mandela during his inauguration speech, May 1994

pendent Afrikaner Homeland (Volk-staat). Furthermore, he maintained that cultural identity could only exist within the concept of the Rainbow Nation and not as an excuse to maintain white privileges.

Relationships with Inkatha and Chief Buthelezi were especially difficult. Although Inkatha was a member of the Government of National Unity, it spent much of its time boycotting Cabinet meetings and the drafting of the new constitution.

APPROVAL OF THE NEW CONSTITUTION 1996

May 1996 was marked by the passing of the country's post-apartheid constitution and the end of the New National Party's involvement in the Government of National Unity. The party had failed to win any concessions and only voted for the new constitution after the ANC threatened to call a national referendum if de Klerk vetoed the proposals.

While de Klerk condemned the new Constitution as sounding the death knell for multi-party participation in decision making, and as "majority domination", the ANC was jubilant.

Predictably, Inkatha's forty eight Members of Parliament boycotted the occasion and ten members of the Freedom Front abstained from voting. Inkatha did not follow the actions of the New National Party, however, and remained in the Government of National Unity until 2004.

The Decline of the New National Party

In August 1997 de Klerk resigned as leader in a futile attempt to enable the New National Party to reinvent itself. The remorseless disclosures from the Truth and Reconciliation Commission (TRC) (see page 110) of government-sanctioned atrocities by de Klerk and his colleagues (despite their denials) had turned de Klerk into a liability.

De Klerk was praised by Mandela, attacked by white extremists and remembered by the world as South Africa's Gorbachev who began a reform process which swept him from power.

SOUTH AFRICAN CONSTITUTION 1996

The Constitution includes a Bill of Rights which guarantees an extensive range of human rights. This includes equality before the law, the right to life including the abolition of the death penalty, and freedom of speech and religion.

Cyril Ramaphosa, architect of the new constitution

The Constitution provides for an independent judiciary. The Constitutional Court is the highest court in the land. It deals with the intepretation, protection and enforcement of the Constitution.It deals exclusively with constitutional matters. The Constitutional Court plays a crucial role in upholding the rights of the citizens of South Africa. (See page103.)

The Constitution makes clear reference to the need to address the inequalities created by Apartheid. Article 9.2 states: "To promote achievement of equality, legislative and other measures designed to protect or advance categories of persons disadvantaged by unfair discrimination may be taken."

This has enabled the government to pass legislation which discriminates against Whites. (See pages 94–5.)

Parliament

South Africa has a bicameral parliament consisting of a National Assembly (400 members) and the National Council of Provinces (NCOP). The council has two roles—namely that of an upper house and also as a body with special responsibilities to protect provincial interests. The NCOP consists of ninety delegates (ten from each province) and ten innovating delegates representing local government. Elections are held every five years based on a system of proportional representation.

The President and The Cabinet

The President is elected by the National Assembly from among its members. He or she is the executive Head of State, and leads the Cabinet. The President may not serve more than two five-year terms in office.

The Cabinet consists of the President, the Deputy President and twenty five Ministers. The President appoints the Deputy President and Ministers and may dismiss them.

CENTRAL GOVERNMENT

EXECUTIVE

President   Deputy President   Cabinet Ministers

PARLIAMENT (Legislature)

National Council of Provinces   National Assembly

Complimentary Institutions
Council of Traditional Leaders
Volkstaat Council (abolished 2001)

THE SOUTH AFRICAN CONSTITUTION
(adopted 1996)

PROVINCIAL GOVERNMENT
Nine Provinces each have a state government

EXECUTIVE AUTHORITY   LEGISLATIVE AUTHORITY

9 Premiers   9 Provincial Assemblies

9 Executive Councils

House of Traditional Leaders (in 5 of the 9 Provinces)

LOCAL GOVERNMENT

The South African Constitution:

- *Maintains unitary government.* "The Constitution of South Africa shall provide for the establishment of one sovereign state, a common South African citizenship and a democratic system of government committed to achieving equality between men and women and people of all races."

- *Supports cultural identity.* "The diversity of language and culture shall be acknowledged and protected, and conditions for their promotion shall be encouraged."

- *Offers limited powers to the Provinces.* The powers granted to the Provinces are to be used to improve the well-being of their inhabitants in accordance with the policies and priorities of the National Government.

Law Making

Legislation may be introduced in the National Assembly only by Cabinet members, Deputy Ministers or a member of a National Assembly committee. Bills amending the Constitution require a two-thirds majority in the National Assembly as well as a supporting vote of six of the nine provinces represented in the NCOP. Any Bill amending Section 1 of the Constitution, which sets out the state's founding values, requires a 75% majority in the National Assembly.

Houses of Traditional Leaders

Provincial governments have the right to set up a House of Traditional Leaders (Tribal Chiefs) and these have been set up in the Eastern Cape, KwaZulu-Natal, Free State, Mpumalanga and the North West. In April 1997 a National Council of Traditional Leaders was set up. Each Provincial House of Traditional Leaders nominates three members to represent it on the Council.

Volkstaat Council

The Volkstaat Council consisted of twenty members elected by the MPs who supported the establishment of an Afrikaner Homeland (Volkstaat). In 1996 it made its submission on self-determination for

South Africa's Parliament in Pretoria

the Afrikaner people. It proposed an Afrikaner Homeland or majority area incorporating parts of Gauteng, North West, Mpumalanga and the Free State—1% of the total South African land surface. President Mbeki abolished this Council in 2001.

Provincial Government

All provincial constitutions and laws must correspond with the National Constitution as confirmed by the Constitutional Court. Provinces have legislative powers over agriculture, cultural affairs, education except Higher Education, environment, health services, housing, local government, police, traditional authorities welfare services, urban and rural development.

CHAPTER 12

Social and economic issues in South Africa

LEGACY OF APARTHEID

The provision of the vote to all citizens of South Africa ensured that the black South African people would run their own country. The political legacy of apartheid was removed by this action. Much more difficult for the new government would be the removal of the social and economic inequalities between the races. This was the task which faced the new government, made all the more challenging by the overambitious programme of reform set out by the ANC in its election manifesto. "A job, a decent home and a chicken in every pot" were the expectations of those who voted for the first time. The legacy of apartheid which had created vast inequalities between the races, is outlined in the statistical survey which follows.

Education

The population growth within the black South African community is a challenge facing the government. Eleven million of the 28 million black African population are under the age of 16. The paradox which South Africa faces is that while it has an unemployment rate of 40%, it is desperately short of skilled and educated black South Africans.

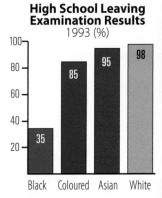

High School Leaving Examination Results
1993 (%)

Black 35 · Coloured 85 · Asian 95 · White 98

Figure 12.1

The culture of violence, with "no education before liberation" being the slogan for a generation of young black South Africans, contributed to the decline of educational standards. This was reflected in the low matriculation results achieved by black South African students. (See Figure 12.1.) Overcrowded classrooms and few resources are also factors which help to explain poor educational performances.

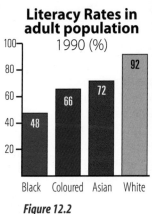

Literacy Rates in adult population
1990 (%)

Black 48 · Coloured 66 · Asian 72 · White 92

Figure 12.2

> " Apartheid has left a ghastly legacy. There is a horrendous housing shortage and high unemployment; health care is inaccessible and not easily affordable by the majority; Bantu education has left us with a massive educational crisis; there is a gross maldistrubution of wealth and an inequitable sharing of the resources with which South Africa is so richly endowed. Some 20% of the population owns 87% of the land. Then there is the hurt and anguish of those who have been victims of this vicious system, those who were forcibly removed from their homes, nearly 4 million people. Those whose loved ones were detained without trial or banned, or who died mysteriously in detention, such as Steve Biko, or at the hands of death squads.
> There is need of healing, of rehabilitation, of confession, of forgiveness, of restitution and reconciliation. Our beautiful land yearns for healing. "
>
> *(Archbishop Desmond Tutu, 1994)*

Health

While the Whites enjoyed an excellent Health Service, the non-Whites were condemned to a second-rate one which struggled to cope. The situation was worse in the rural areas of the Homelands. Poverty, hunger and disease, combined with a lack of doctors and nurses, explain the high level of malnutrition and under-nourishment among rural children.

The existence of a strong private health care sector also created inequalities between the races. In 1994, 90% of the white community relied on private medical care, while the vast majority of Blacks could not afford private care.

Health Inequalities (1990)

	Infant Mortality Rate (per 1000 births)	Life Expectancy (at birth)
Black	65	60
Coloured	35	62
Asian	14	67
White	8	72

Table 12.1

Population below Minimum Living Level (1990, %)

	RURAL	URBAN
Black	65	30
Coloured	45	20
Asian	45	8
White	3	1

Table 12.2

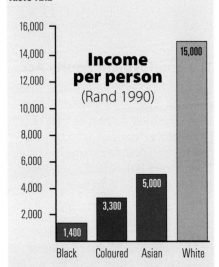

Income per person (Rand 1990)

- Black: 1,400
- Coloured: 3,300
- Asian: 5,000
- White: 15,000

Figure 12.3

Land

As Archbishop Desmond Tutu highlights, almost four million non-Whites were forcibly removed from their homes by the apartheid regime. The Homeland and Township systems (see pages 83–84) created squatter camps, shanty towns and sprawling townships such as Soweto where the majority of dwellings lacked basic amenities such as electricity and proper sanitation. In the rural areas many Blacks were forcibly settled in arid lands which could not sustain them. The outcome was malnutrition, disease and abject poverty.

Cyril Ramaphosa, then ANC General Secretary, stated in 1993 that "unless we settle the land question we tear South Africa to pieces." As part of the 1994 peace agreement between de Klerk and Mandela, the white farmers were guaranteed that their land would not be taken from them through nationalisation or expropriation policies.

"Things will not improve tomorrow or the next day, but I know my life is going to get better after this, because I voted to make it better."

Murial Ranganana, a widowed mother of six from the squatter camp of Crossroads

Legacy of Violence

The apartheid years created a culture of violence in South Africa both at the political level, with the ongoing antagonism between the ANC and Inkatha in KwaZulu-Natal, and at the domestic level with an explosion of violent crime. Leaving aside the issue of political violence, the crime wave which has engulfed South Africa can, ironically, be partly blamed on the dismantling of the rigid controls imposed by the security forces. The association of law enforcement and the rule of law with the apartheid regime has created a lack of respect within the black community for the police and the judiciary. E Webster, a South African sociologist, explains, "the capacity of key institutions like the police and judiciary to apply sanctions is weak because they have been discredited. That creates a no-man's-land where the old society is dead and the new not born and where people cease to distinguish between right and wrong and where normal rules of behaviour fall."

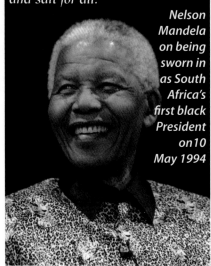

"We shall build a society in which all South Africans, both black and white, will be able to walk tall, without any fear in their hearts—a rainbow nation at peace with itself and the world. We must act together as a united people, for national reconciliation, for nation building. Let there be justice for all. Let there be peace for all. Let there be work, bread, water and salt for all."

Nelson Mandela on being sworn in as South Africa's first black President on 10 May 1994

RDP AND GEAR

The ANC election manifesto, which created the RDP targets, was far too ambitious. The Reconstruction and Development Programme (RDP) was to be delivered through a separate agency with its own Minister, Jay Naidoo, and its own funds. In 1996, the government closed down the RDP agency, transferring financial control back to the Treasury.

The new government had underestimated the timescale required to set up a new national ministry alongside the nine new provinces and local government structures. At the national level the first priority in education and health was to create national ministries. Fourteen separate education systems had to be dismantled and replaced with a National Department of Education. Local government elections did not take place until 1996. This delayed the reforms, especially in housing where, by the end of 1995, only 12,000 RDP houses had been built, compared to the promised 200,000.

A new policy, Growth, Employment and Redistribution (GEAR), was introduced, committing the government to an economic strategy similar to that of Prime Minister Blair in Britain. The government was prepared to upset the trade unions and the South African Communist Party by selling state-owned enterprises, such as electricity and gas, to the private sector. This policy of privatisation would provide income for the government to improve services. The downside was that private firms would raise prices and consumers would have to pay higher charges for essential services. This would place a heavy financial burden on the poorer sections of society.

In addition, GEAR encouraged growth and employment by providing economic stability, which encouraged foreign investment. GEAR also promoted a black enterprise culture. 'Wealthy, black and proud of it' is the slogan of the government. The creation of a privileged black elite has not been welcomed by all ANC members.

Has GEAR succeeded?

- The government highlights that GEAR has brought inflation down and has reduced the budget deficit from 8% in 1997 to 1.5% in 2004.
- The target is to raise growth to 4%, partly through the expansion of government expenditure into the creation of new roads, ports, energy and other infrastructure developments.
- Better credit rating and a more stable currency has drawn more private money into South Africa.
- The Trade Unions (COSATU) have protected the wage levels of their members but workers who are not in unions suffer from low wages.
- Strikes are a common occurrence in South Africa and tension remains between the 'Triple Alliance' of the ANC, SACP (South African Communist Party) and COSATU (Congress of South African Trade Unions). They accuse President Mbeki of "talking left and acting right". They are opposed to Mbeki's free-market GEAR policies and feel marginalised.

Mbeki is aware of the need to transform South African society. The shift of power which took place in the political field must now cover all aspects of economic and social life. To try to narrow the huge gap between Black and White, the government has embarked on a programme of Affirmative Action.

AFFIRMATIVE ACTION

Under Mandela's rule, firms and institutions, including the civil service, were encouraged "to hire and promote black employees". By 1998, 60,000 public servants—including many senior and middle level white officials—had accepted retirement packages from the Public Services. By 2002 this figure had increased to 120,000.

Mandela did not wish to antagonise the Whites and did not pass the legislation to compel employers or institutions to discriminate in favour of non-Whites. His successor, Thabo Mbeki, used Affirmative

POLITICS OF TRANSFORMATION

Thabo Mbeki, President of South Africa

"If you were speaking of national reconciliation based on maintaining the present situation, because you did not want to move at a pace that frightens the Whites, it means you wouldn't carry out the task for transformation. To avoid the anger that would be boiling among the black people, you've got to transform the society. Affirmative action ... is an instrument to get to a more equal society, broadly representative of South African population groups."

Action legislation to speed up the "transformation of South Africa's economic life".

There are two major pieces of Affirmative Action legislation—The *Employment Equity Act*, and the *Black Economic Empowerment Act*.

The Employment Equity Act

This *Employment Equity Act*, 1998, set up a directorate called 'Equal Opportunities' to ensure that organisations "demographically represent" the people of South Africa. The correct balance of a workforce is 75% black, 52% female, 5% disabled.

If someone complains that they have been discriminated against, the employer must prove his or her innocence. Under reverse discrimination black South Africans are entitled to preferential treatment in hiring, promotion, university admission and the awarding of government contracts.

Any company which has more than fifty employees is covered by this Act and can be fined up to £100,000 if it does not meet its terms. In an effort to strengthen monitoring and enforcement of the legislation, a National Roving Inspectorate Unit was set up in November 2005.

Black Economic Empowerment (BEE) Act 2004

Black Economic Empowerment (BEE) has the ambitious aim of placing more of the economy in black hands, in part by forcing the country's largest industries to set targets for promoting more black managers, training more black workers, using more black-owned suppliers and selling ownership stakes to black capitalists. The key objectives of BEE are:

● At least 40% of the companies listed on the Johannesburg Stock Exchange (JSE) should be black.

● At least 30% of private sector companies should be black-owned.

● Black people should hold at least 25% of the shares held on the JSE.

In a country with 40% unemployment and where half the population lives below internationally recognised subsistence levels, it is understandable that the government wishes to speed up the transfer of wealth to the black majority. In the public sector (education, health, housing etc.) great progress has been made in transferring executive and clerical posts to non-Whites. The government argues that BEE is

necessary to enable Blacks to enter key posts in the private sector. Under BEE any bank or company which wishes to receive government contracts must have the BEE charter in place.

Banks and companies are in the process of selling assets and equity to BEE companies headed by people such as Cyril Ramaphosa and Tokyo Sexwale. Critics of BEE argue that too few people benefit when large white firms hand over minority stakes to favoured black partners. Kgalema Motlanthe, the ANC General Secretary, created a political storm in October 2004 when he stated, "We see the same names mentioned over and over again in one deal after another." This comment by Motlanthe reflects the growing unease that BEE is not benefiting the Black majority. Significantly, in October 2004 Standard Bank chose Saki Macozoma and Cyril Ramaphosa as partners in a deal to boost black employment that netted each man around 200 million Rand (£17 million.) Zwelinzuma Vavi, a leading member of COSATU, argues that BEE helps only "a narrow group of individuals already rich through transactions of this type". He argues that banks should use their cash to build houses for poor Blacks, fund small black businesses and subsidise black farms.

The authorities are aware that black empowerment risks alienating the white population through what some Whites call 'reverse apartheid' at a time when many Blacks do not have the education or the vocational skills required to take over the running of the economy. (See page 97.) The hope is that eventually, once transformation has been achieved, affirmative action legislation can be abolished and appointments made on merit not colour.

Saki Macazoma — Patrice Motsepe
Cyril Ramaphosa — Tokyo Sexwale

THE CONTROVERSIAL FABULOUS FOUR

It is significant that former ANC leaders who fought against apartheid have crossed over from politics to the boardroom to become millionaires. The four who symbolise the new black elite are Cyril Ramaphosa, once touted as Mandela's successor, Tokyo Sexwale, former ANC provincial premier, Saki Macozoma, former political prisoner, and Patrice Motsepe who is married to an ANC minister. They are aware of the growing criticism coming from fellow Blacks, but they argue that their goal is to create a million black capitalists. They argue that while Whites comprise only 10% of the nation's 45 million people, they control 69% of the companies listed on the Johannesburg Stock Exchange. Of these, 27% are in foreign hands, and just 4% are controlled by Blacks. Macozoma argues that his work with the ANC helped to transform the colour of South Africa's government and now he's doing the same for its boardrooms. Macozoma states, "you need the same kind of person who was the bedrock of the ANC to be the bedrock of society that is based on a middle class. There is no way I would support a free enterprise system that tolerates poverty. But with five or six of us spread out through the economy, that can make a difference in a very fundamental way."

BEE: ACHIEVEMENTS AND CRITICISM

Achievements

✔ Almost 300,000 Blacks became middle income earners (between £8,000 and £15,000 annually) between 2002 and 2005.

✔ In 2005 Banking & Insurance Group First Rand finalised a £700 million empowerment deal that puts 10% of the company's shares in trusts established for black staff members and for poor rural woman and mine workers.

✔ In 2005 Anglo American, the mining group, appointed Lazarus Zim as its first black Chief Executive in charge of all its South African operations.

✔ To achieve government contracts, firms must now file a BEE scorecard to prove that they are promoting "previously disadvantaged individuals" including Blacks, Coloureds and Asians. The government spends R12 billion a year, much of which benefits black businesses and the black workforce.

Criticisms

✘ Many Black-owned firms win government contracts despite submitting higher bids (the government rule is that bids from previously disadvantaged individuals, PDIs, can be up to 10% higher than others). Having won the contracts they subcontract the work to their losing competitors. In effect the PDI/10 % rule constitutes a special tax on all taxpayers with the proceeds going to the black businessmen who win the contract.

✘ Several high profile black empowerment businesses such as NAIL, African Bank and Community Bank have collapsed.

✘ Many BEE activities simply enrich a small number of individuals and do not offer any economic benefits to the black majority. White businessmen give them directorships and shares to conform to BEE regulations. (See The Fabulous Four.). Eric Molobi, the chairman of Kagiso Trust, and former ANC activist, has been appointed deputy chairman of the Imperial Group, which has revenues of $3 billion a year.

EDUCATION

Under Mandela and Mbeki much has been done to improve the horrendous legacy of Bantu education. The government is aware that education and training are crucial for the creation of economic prosperity. There is a shortage of skilled and highly educated black South African workers, yet an abundance of poorly educated, unskilled black South Africans who face a lifetime of formal unemployment.

This explains why a company such as Sasol cannot find about 2,000 qualified mechanics, welders and riggers among South Africa's 4.6 million unemployed workers. It is estimated that South Africa needs to produce at least 13,000 engineers each year in order to cope with the skilled worker shortage, yet in 2004 the Engineering Council of South Africa registered just over 3,000 new engineers. Again it is estimated that only 40% of learners who enter Grade 1 at age 7 matriculate at age 18. Education is only compulsory until Grade 7, age 15, although many pupils drop out of school at the end of primary.

In 2004 the government invested 21% of the entire budget in education. At over 6% of the country's GDP, this is one of the highest rates of investment in the world. Yet while much has been achieved, there are still major shortfalls. (See page 97.) Fighting the culture of non-attendance and resistance to learning, the pressures caused by population growth, and the legacy of apartheid in terms of provision of resources between the races is a long uphill struggle, but one which is essential to enable South Africa to end poverty, unemployment and illiteracy among its people.

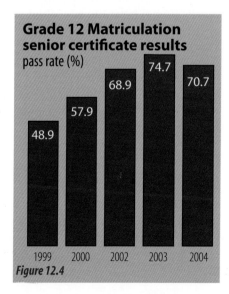

Grade 12 Matriculation senior certificate results
pass rate (%)

1999	2000	2002	2003	2004
48.9	57.9	68.9	74.7	70.7

Figure 12.4

MATRICULATION RESULTS

The pattern of matriculation results, while highlighting significant progress, still reflect large inequalities in performance in spite of a more equitable allocation of resources across schools and provinces. (See Table 12.3 & Figure 12.4.)

There has been a clear improvement even if the 2004 exam results were less impressive than those of 2003. Between 1999 and 2005 the

Grade 12 matriculation senior certificate results
(provincial results %)

Province	2003	2004
Western Cape	87.1	85.0
Northern Cape	90.7	83.4
Free State	80.0	78.7
Gauteng	81.5	76.8
KwaZulu-Natal	77.2	74.0
Limpopo	70.0	70.6
North West	70.5	64.9
Eastern Cape	60.0	53.5
Mpumalanga	56.0	NA *

Table 12.3

*Mpumalanga results were declared invalid because of cheating by teachers and students.

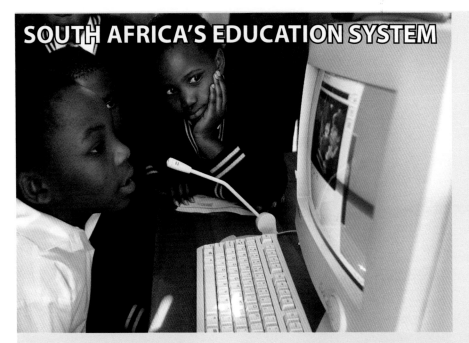

SOUTH AFRICA'S EDUCATION SYSTEM

South Africa has a single national Education Department and system. Provincial legislatures and governments have substantial powers to run educational affairs (excluding universities and technikons—further education colleges) subject to a national policy framework.

The *South African Schools Act,* 1996, ensures that no state schools are racially segregated. While former white schools now take in pupils of all races, many former black South African and disadvantaged schools have no white pupils and have the highest number of matriculation failures. (See Matriculation Results.) The Act also provided compulsory education for learners between the ages of 7 (Grade 1) and 15 (Grade 9). From Grade 10 to Grade 12, students either attend school or engage in Further Education and Training (FET). At present school students sit a matriculation exam in Grade 12 in six gateway subjects at either Standard or Higher level, results in these matriculated subjects being the benchmark for entry to Higher Education. In 2004 the government announced that it would merge Standard Grades and Highers to create one leaving exam.

Central to educational reforms is Curriculum 2005 which is an outcomes-based education package. It focuses on what pupils can do and on their levels of understanding with less emphasis on exams (25% of the final marks in the matriculation exams are now based on continuous assessment.) In July 2005 new reforms were announced for Grades 10–12. At Grade 10 new updated subjects will be established. The new curriculum will be introduced progressively over the period 2006–2009. There will be twenty nine subjects in all and schools will be expected to offer between fourteen and sixteen subjects.

South Africa's education system accommodates more than 14 million learners and there is a sizable and growing private sector. National norms and standards for school funding have been set to address the inequalities between the races. Schools are divided into five categories based on needs: the poorest 20% receive 35% of resources and the richest 20% receive 5% of resources. Education is not free in South Africa and school fees are paid by parents. This explains why many pupils from the poorest communities (and those who are disadvantaged most in their quality of life) do not attend schools. The Department of Education is considering exempting the poorest 30% of schools (all black South African) from fees. South Africa has a teacher shortage, made worse by the number of qualified teachers who actually teach and the number who have died from HIV/AIDS. It is estimated that 50,000 teachers have died from AIDS over the last five years.

exam pass rate went up from 48% to 70% and by 2003 all provinces had achieved a 55% plus pass rate.

However, the following statistics highlight the continuing problems facing South African education and the difficulties involved in creating a skilled and educated workforce.

- While black South Africans now make up 71% of all matrics who passed, only 5% of the whole African cohort achieved results which would gain them university entry. White students achieved 97% of the 'A+' (90% and higher) scores with 13% of the total number of candidates for the examination; Blacks received 88% of the 'F' grades and comprised 95% of candidates who failed.

- While 49,800 students sat Higher History, only 23,400 students sat Higher Mathematics.

- In the Western Cape, of the 4,260 Maths Higher Grade candidates, only 1,470 were Blacks. Even worse, only 305 black learners passed the exam.

UNIVERSITY AND TECHNIKON STUDENTS

Despite the shortcomings in attainment, a significant change has taken place in Higher Education. There is clear evidence of progress. Black South Africans now make up more than 60% of university and technikon students. The following statistics illustrate the progress made.

- The number of black students enrolling at universities and technikons increased by almost 101% between 1993 and 2002. By 2002 they were 60% of the total—compared with 40% in 1993.

- The number of coloured student enrolments increased in the same period by 34%; Indian students increased by 45%.

- In contrast the number of white students enrolled went down by 20% between 1993 and 2002 with their share of the total declining sharply from 46% to 26.5%

- At the other end of the educational spectrum one million learners achieved basic literacy between 1999 and 2002 through the government's Adult Basic Education and Training (ABET) programme. According to the government, literacy in South Africa has risen from 86% to 93%. However, significant provincial inequalities remain. (See Table 9.8.)

THE MODERNISATION OF SCHOOLS

In 2002 the Education Minister Kader Asmal openly stated that "the backlog (in upgrading schools) is still huge and the differentiation between rich and poor schools within the public system is still unacceptable". His priority in 2002, which was reiterated in 2005, was to improve the infrastructure of schools, to increase the number of pupils passing Grade 12 (matric) in maths and science, to ensure economic development and to increase the number of black students enrolling in further education and university. While progress has been made in improving basic infratructure within schools e.g. electricity, water, sanitation, much still needs to be done. (See Table 12.4.)

In the Western Cape, where educational provision and attainment is one of the highest in the country, only six primary schools are still without electricity and the guideline for class size is 35 to 38. (Teachers in Pretoria went on strike in 2005 to protest against class sizes of 60.)

National School Profile 2002

45% of schools were without adequate sanitation

12% of schools did not have any sanitation

34% of schools were without a telephone *(59% in 1994)*

34% of schools did not have water *(40% in 1994)*

40% of schools had no electricity *(60% in 1994)*

Regional Inequalities

No Running Water		*No Electricity*	
Western Cape	2%	Western Cape	4.5%
Northern Cape	2.5%	Eastern Cape	60.5%
Eastern Cape	40%	KwaZulu-Natal	57%
Limpopo	32%		

Table 12.4

Cameron Dugmore visiting a local school in the Western Cape

The following comment made in 2005 by Cameron Dugmore, Provincial Minister of Education, Western Cape, highlights the inequalities that exist within the school system.

" When I came into office, I found a situation where, for instance, some of our children still have to get up in the early morning hours to take a bus, and drive past an existing school in the town to an adjacent town of some 10 kilometres or further away. When one asks 'why?', the answer is that 'the school is full'. And yet the school to which the learners were being transported is doubly overcrowded. I found a situation where there were two schools in a town, one historically white with empty classrooms, low learner numbers and lots of resources. The other school in the historically disadvantaged community is normally overcrowded and has very few resources, with parents battling to keep up with the payment of school fees because of poverty levels. When one asks 'why not amalgamate?' the standard answer is, 'it will lead to the lowering of standards, safety concerns and overcrowding . … "

HEALTH

Under Mandela and Mbeki significant progress has been made in improving primary health care (PHC) in both urban and rural areas. For those not covered by medical aid schemes, free health care is provided at public PHC facilities such as clinics and community health care centres. Some 40% of all South Africans live in poverty and 75% of these stay in rural areas where health services are least developed. (See Table 12.5. Regional inequalities reflect the urban-rural divide. Gauteng and Western Cape are highly urbanised.) Malnutrition is a major problem in rural areas alongside outbreaks of cholera which occurred in KwaZulu-Natal in 2002. Three state-of-the-art hospitals have recently been built in the Eastern Cape, Gauteng and KwaZulu-Natal to tackle the poor hospital facilities available in urban areas.

A key weapon against ill health and disease has been the availability of a clean water supply. Over the last ten years, eight million South Africans have been provided with a clean water supply, leaving five million still to be connected. As with other things regional inequalities still exist in the percentage of households with no toilet facility. (See Table 9.7.) Child mortality rates double when there is no access to clean water.

In some areas clean water is provided through a metered system. This means that people have to pay for the water as in the photo on the left. Those who cannot afford to pay have to use a muddy puddle which has a high probability of being infected with diseases such as cholera as in the photo on the right. The government believes that private investment will be attracted to providing water if people have to pay for it.

There is a very strong private health service which inevitably reflects a racial imbalance in favour of Whites and ensures that they have access to better health provision. While 38 million people had access to the R33.2 billion public health sector, seven million people had access to the R43 billion private health sector.

PRIMARY HEALTH CARE

The primary health care programme offers a comprehensive range of services delivered by health professionals and associated organisations such as school and nutritional services. Water and sanitation services, both of which have an obvious connection to health, are also included.

The strategy embraces health education, nutrition, family planning, immunisation, screening for common diseases, HIV/AIDS education and counselling, maternal and child health, oral health and the provision of essential drugs.

Projects such as the National Primary School Nutrition for needy primary schoolchildren have improved educational achievement as well as health standards. Every day more than five million children in over 12,000 schools munch on a 'Mandela sandwich'. This has increased attendance at school and improved concentration and alertness levels.

Immunisation against tuberculosis, whooping cough, diphtheria, polio and measles is available free of charge to all children under the age of six.

In 2004 a massive Measles and Polio Immunisation Campaign took place which ensured that all children under the age of five received either their first or second measles or polio vaccine. This was part of the World Health Organisation (WHO) strategy to eradicate polio and measles by 2005.

Alongside the free health care programme for children under six and pregnant women, an impressive clinic building and upgrading programme has been implemented. 3,500 Primary Health Care Clinics have been built and more than 700 mobile clinics set up, providing basic health care in the most remote and isolated areas.

Distribution of Health Personnel
per 100,000 of the Population

Province	Doctors
Western Cape	36.8
Gauteng	34.5
Eastern Cape	12.2
Mpumalanga	17.2
KwaZulu-Natal	23.5
Limpopo	9.5
North West	12.1
Free State	24.5
Northern Cape	28.3

Table 12.5 Source: SA Health Statistics 2003

Essential Health Care for all South Africans: 2004

This government report confirmed that public health care had been chronically underfunded for the previous five years and that gross provincial disparities in spending persist. This underfunding has led to an excessive workload for staff, causing demoralisation and migration to the private sector or abroad. While health spending will increase in the period 2004 – 09, much of this increase will be spent on anti-retroviral treatment for HIV/AIDS.

The report estimates that the public health expenditure in 2002/03 was R928 per uninsured person, less than the R989 spent in 1997/98. Population growth and the spread of HIV/AIDS have contributed to this decline. Table 12.5 highlights the inequalities in medical staff and therefore funding between the provinces. Two of the wealthiest provinces, Western Cape and Gauteng, have more than three times the number of doctors as compared to Limpopo and the North West, two of the poorest provinces.

In reference to the draft charter covering the Public and Private Health Sector, the Minister of Health, Manto Tshabalala-Msumang, declared that its aim was to "remedy the wrongs of the past by improving access, equity and quality in healthcare, as well as levels of black economic empowerment." The target set by BEE (see page 95) was that by 2010 the healthcare workforce would be 60% black rising to 80% by 2014. Critics questioned this emphasis on racial quotas arguing that it would weaken, not strengthen, health provision.

HIV/ AIDS

The one regret Nelson Mandela has of his period in office is his failure to tackle the outbreak of HIV/AIDS in South Africa. Unfortunately his successor, Thabo Mbeki, has been very slow to react to the crisis. HIV/AIDS is the biggest health and social issue facing South Africa today and Mbeki has been criticised, even by Nelson Mandela, for his failure to accept that AIDS is caused by HIV. For this reason Mbeki refused to give free anti-AIDS drugs to all HIV-positive pregnant women and their children. Mbeki's former spokesperson, Parks Mankahlana, stated that saving these babies' lives would create a burden for the state as their mothers would die anyway.

In November 2001, a small group of AIDS activists, the Treatment Action Campaign (TAC), took the government to the highest court of the land, the Constitutional Court, to force it to provide the anti-AIDS drug, nevirapine, free to mother and child at birth. The Court ruled in favour of TAC and, in October 2002, the government announced that it would investigate ways of providing the anti-retroviral drugs that keep people alive—a dramatic reversal of policy. The nationwide civil disobedience campaign, led by TAC leader Zackie Achmat, had been successful. Achmat, who accuses Mbeki of stalling the implementation of the Court's ruling, has HIV. He had re-

Former South African President Nelson Mandela, right, and AIDS activist Zackie Achmat, wear 'HIV-positive' t-shirts on a visit to a Community Health Centre in Cape Town. Mandela, who remains South Africa's most revered public figure, has emerged as a champion of the fight against the country's rampant AIDS epidemic.

fused to take the drugs until they were available in all public hospitals. However, he was persuaded to take them by Nelson Mandela.

TAC has maintained its campaign and in the period 2003–05 staged sit-ins, marches on parliament and even launched culpable homicide charges against government Ministers for not doing enough to introduce the drugs. The government had set a target of treating 200,000 people by the end of March 2005. The number actually treated was only 42,000. Botswana (population 1.6 million) offers a model which South Africa can follow. Botswana has a horrendous AIDS epidemic, (see Table 12.6) with 36% of its population suffering from AIDS. However it provides free anti-retroviral drugs to its citizens. Many private firms in South Africa provide free anti-AIDS drugs to their workforce and are calling on the government to do more.

TAC is especially critical of the Minister of Health, Manto Tshabalala-Msumang who continually downplays the AIDS epidemic and the use of anti-AIDS drugs. In June 2005 she argued that AIDS sufferers should use traditional remedies such as garlic and olives. ANC sources have accused TAC of serving the interest of the pharmaceutical companies.

HIV Prevalence among 15–49 year olds (2000)		
	Prevalence of HIV (%)	Health Expenditure (US$ per head)
Botswana	36	381
South Africa	20	652
Malawi	15	39
Nigeria	7	31

Table 12.6 Source: Economist

AIDS Pandemic: The Present and the Future?

- Life expectancy has dropped from 62 to 48 and is expected to fall to 41 by 2009

- 35% of deaths among pregnant women are caused by AIDS

- Nearly five million children will be orphaned by 2016

- Between 4.5 million (government figures) and 6.2 million (independent figures) South Africans are infected with HIV/AIDS

- Almost 40% of women between 25 and 29 are infected by HIV/AIDS

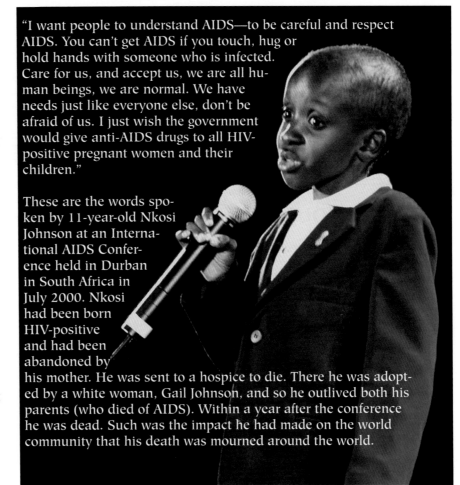

"I want people to understand AIDS—to be careful and respect AIDS. You can't get AIDS if you touch, hug or hold hands with someone who is infected. Care for us, and accept us, we are all human beings, we are normal. We have needs just like everyone else, don't be afraid of us. I just wish the government would give anti-AIDS drugs to all HIV-positive pregnant women and their children."

These are the words spoken by 11-year-old Nkosi Johnson at an International AIDS Conference held in Durban in South Africa in July 2000. Nkosi had been born HIV-positive and had been abandoned by his mother. He was sent to a hospice to die. There he was adopted by a white woman, Gail Johnson, and so he outlived both his parents (who died of AIDS). Within a year after the conference he was dead. Such was the impact he had made on the world community that his death was mourned around the world.

FIGURES OF DEATH

Health professionals and the South African government have been locked in a bitter struggle over the real scale of the HIV/AIDS epidemic. There is still a stigma attached to AIDS and many AIDS related deaths have been diagnosed as being other illnesses such as tuberculosis and influenza. This attitude is slowly changing, helped by the actions of political leaders such as Chief Buthelezi and Nelson Mandela. Both leaders publicly stated that their children had died of AIDS. In August 2004 Buthelezi buried both a son and a daughter and in January 2005 Mandela's son died of the disease.

This contrasts sharply with the actions and words of President Mbeki. In July 2003 at the UN General Assembly he told the Washington Post "I do not know anybody who has died of AIDS"

According to government figures, 4.5 million South African's suffer from HIV/AIDS. The South African Medical Research Council estimates that that the real figure is a staggering 6.2 million. Its work which was published in the journal *AIDS 2005* also suggests that the true death toll is nearly three times the official government statistics and this figure is in line with the UNAID's estimate of around 380,000 deaths a year.

Whatever the correct figures, both government and health professionals agree that there is a pandemic (widespread over the whole country) and that it is women especially in their mid to late twenties who are the hardest hit. Nearly 40% of women between 25 and 29 years were HIV-positive. In 1997, 149 men were dying for every 100 deaths among women. In 2003, that figure had dramatically changed to 77 male deaths for every 100 female deaths.

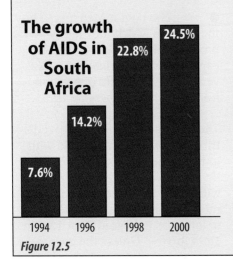

The growth of AIDS in South Africa

7.6% (1994)
14.2% (1996)
22.8% (1998)
24.5% (2000)

Figure 12.5

Life Expectancy in South Africa (years)

60.6 (1985-1990)
61.8 (1990-1995)
58.2 (1995-2000)
47.7 (2000-2005)
41.5 (2005-2010 (est.))

Figure 12.6

Providing decent housing was one of the biggest challenges facing the government.

LAND AND HOUSING

Mandela was aware of the enormous task his government faced in order to provide adequate housing. There was a distinct racial and urban-rural divide. These differences were still obvious in 2001. (See Tables 9.6 and 9.7 on page 80 and Figure 12.8 on page 105.) The situation was not helped by an influx of people into the cities from the rural areas.

It became clear that the 1994 election promise to deliver one million new homes over a five-year period was unrealistic. This figure was retained but was extended over a ten-year period with many of the houses being 'starter homes' rather than fully completed units. The target was achieved by December 2000 but still left a housing backlog of three million homes.

Progress has been made in providing basic amenities such as electricity and running water. The Community Water Supply Programme has brought clean water to over seven million mainly rural homes. Unfortunately, a culture of non-payment

of rents and amenities charges still persists. The situation has not been helped by the privatisation of services which has led to an increase in charges.

The government provides 6,000 litres of water per household per month free of charge to more than two-thirds of South Africa's population. While this is welcomed, the Anti-Privatisation Forum (APF) argues that an average family of six needs about 20,000 litres of water each month. Pre-paid water meters are being installed in the townships and this has created unrest among many residents. In Soweto and Johannesburg police had to protect workers installing pipes. Trevor Ngwane of the APF argues that water meters will reduce consumption of water below minimum hygienic levels. A parliamentary committee has recommended that water metres should not be installed in the homes of those considered "previously disadvantaged". However, it also recommended that the free basic water policy (of 6,000 litres) should exclude those who can afford to pay for their water supply.

Land Reform

Land reform, especially in the countryside, is a major issue. A new Department of Land Affairs was created in 1994 with the responsibility of developing and implementing a policy of land reform. The policy has seven main points.
- Compensation for those who lost their land because of apartheid laws.
- Redistribution of productive land to those who were disadvantaged.
- New land-holding rights to be established.
- Compensation to be paid to those whose lands are redistributed through the Settlement/Land Acquisition Grant.
- Creation of an independent Commission on Restitution of Land Rights as well as a Land Claims Court. Any claimant will have to prove that he or she was dispossessed after 1913 without financial compensation or alternative land being provided.
- The setting up of the Land Reform Pilot Programme to "establish mechanisms for state-assisted entry into the land market for the most disadvantaged sectors of rural society".
- The right for tenants to buy the land on which they farm and protection from eviction. This became an Act of Parliament in November 1995 despite opposition from the white farmers.

The original RDP promise of redistribution of agricultural land within five years was totally unrealistic. The revised target date of 2014 will not be achieved at the present rate of progress. Black ownership of land has increased from 13% in 1994 to 16%. Unless the govern-

Clean water for all households – but at what price?

ment was to resort to mass confiscation as Mugabe has done in Zimbabwe, it has virtually no hope of doubling black ownership of the land. (See 'Fears of white farmers'.) The government would argue that its record on dealing with the 80,000 redistribution claims is excellent. By July 2005, 62,000 land cases costing R4.4 billion had been settled, mostly in the cities. Most people in urban areas prefer cash compensation to land redistribution. This therefore partly explains the limited increase in black land ownership. A 2005 survey indicated that only 9% of Blacks who were not currently farming wished to do so. Rural claims are more difficult to settle; some need extensive mapping and a lengthy verification of claimants. The government has also increased the amount allocated to land claim settlements from 0.5% of government spending to 0.9%.

The 'willing buyer-willing seller' principle has been at the core of South Africa's land settlement, guaranteeing that land will be acquired by the state at fair prices and given to the landless Blacks. Tozi Gwana south Africa's chief land claims commissioner is considering setting a ceiling on land prices depending on the region and the land. Many white farmers have inflated the value of their land and have received extravagant prices for their farms. Delegates at the August 2005 Land Summit rejected the willing buyer-willing seller policy. The government immediately announced that it would review the present system and use its powers to force white farmers to sell their land if negotiations broke down. In September 2005, the Commission on Restitution of Land Rights stated that an expropriation notice would be served on Hannes Vissar, the owner of a cattle and crop farm in North West province. The land is to be returned to the descendents of the original owners of the land. Vissar turned down the government's offer, saying the land was worth double that amount. Mr Vissar stated he intended to fight the decision in court.

The ANC is also considering setting up a commission to examine the impact of foreigners buying up land in South Africa. Europeans have bought large stretches of coastal land as well as farms inland for hunting. The Cape Town coast is littered with luxury golfing estates and in the northern provinces of Limpopo and the North West huge game reserves have been created. Solid fences, necessary to keep game such as giraffes in, are effec-

A SUCCESS STORY

In a Cape Town valley, former ANC guerillas have part-ownership of the finest olive farm in South Africa. The estate's manager, John Scrimgeour, whose grandfather emigrated from Skye, highlights the success of this venture. " We are a community, part-`owned by workers who have security of tenure on their farm homes for life. Since they acquired shares, productivity has increased and profits have increased. We must transform this country completely. But do we have enough time left? We must do this on a really large scale across South Africa. Unless we do, we will be in a Zimbabwe situation for sure."

tively keeping people out. Many local black people are crammed into nearby squatter settlements with meagre land on which to grow crops or farm cattle.

FEARS OF WHITE FARMERS

The Afrikaner farming community is concerned that recent events in Zimbabwe where the government orchestrated nationwide land invasion of white farms will encourage further attacks on their property. Since 1994 more than 1,500 farmers and their families have been murdered. Farmers claim that this is an organised attack on white farms with unemployed Blacks being paid £200 a time to ambush and kill. A recent government enquiry denied that this is the case and claimed that the high murder rate of farmers reflects South Africa's high murder rate— over 25,000 South African's are murdered every year.

At the grassroots level there has been a significant increase in militancy with the formation of the Landless People's Movement and a series of threatened land invasions. The Pan Africanist Congress (PAC) regards Mugabe as an African hero and encourages land invasions. Supho Makhombathi, representing landless impoverished farm labourers, urges action: "We are still living in slavery. We have given the government an ultimatum to give us land or we will simply follow the examples of our brothers in Zimbabwe and invade."

The government has reassured white farmers that there will be no seizure of their farms. In May 2005 the Constitutional Court, , in a landmark judgement, upheld farmers' property rights. In 2000, 400 squatters invaded the land of Braam Duvenhage. By October 2004 the numbers had swelled to 40,000— a third of them alleged to be illegal immigrants. The squatters renamed the farm as the Gabon informal settlements. They lived in makeshift homes with primitive sanitation from pit toilets and access only to a single tap. The Chief Justice, Pius Langa, also ruled that the state had a duty to ensure progressive access to housing or land for these squatters. He stated: "Land invasions of this scale are a matter that threatens more than the property rights of a single property owner. Because of their capacity to be socially inflammatory, they have the potential to have serious implications for stability and public peace."

CRIME

The fear and impact of crime is one issue that unites all races. While many Whites seek safety in their walled estates, ordinary black and coloured South Africans protect their families as best they can. The availability of guns is a major problem. You can buy an AK47 rifle in any taxi queue for £30. On average, fifty five murders take place every day—twenty seven are caused by guns.

Why has there been a crime explosion in South Africa?

- The dismantling of the rigid controls imposed by the security forces in the apartheid years has brought crime into the former white suburbs.
- The apartheid years created a culture of violence at the political level between the ANC and Inkatha in KwaZulu-Natal.
- The association of law enforcement and the rule of law with the apartheid regime has created a lack of respect for the police within the black community.
- The vast inequalities in terms of wealth in South Africa have created a 'war' between the 'haves' and the 'have nots'.
- A massive influx of poor people from the countryside to the towns and the arrival of illegal immigrants (estimated at four million) from other African countries has created a group in society who ignore its laws.

What action has the government taken?

- The police force has been reformed, corrupt officers have been weeded out and salaries have improved.
- The police budget has been significantly increased and the number of police officers has increased from 119,560 in 2002 to 156,760 in 2006. A new elite force, known as the Scorpion, has been set up to tackle organised crime.
- According to the government, its action has led to a decline in the number of murders. (This, in part, can be explained by the decline in the number of political murders between ANC and IFP supporters.)
- Communities have set up their own vigilante groups, especially in the black South African and Coloured townships. The leaders of PAG (People Against Gangsterism and Drugs), a Muslim vigilante group, were acquitted in March 2002 for the murder of drug lord Rashaad Staggie. In the wealthy suburbs, private security guards patrol the streets and Alsatian dogs are trained to attack Blacks only.

Murder rates in South Africa
Ratio per 100,000 of the population

	Year 1995	2003
Eastern Cape	73.1	47.0
Free State	54.3	33.2
Gauteng	81.7	59.1
KwaZulu-Natal	92.9	58.1
Mpumalanga	43.8	33.0
North West	44.8	31.0
Northern Cape	84.4	48.6
Limpopo	19.7	12.1
Western Cape	84.3	84.8
RSA TOTAL	69.6	47.4

Table 12.7

The ending of political violence between ANC and Inkatha supporters explains the murder rate decline in KwaZulu-Natal. Western Cape has the highest murder rate

Selected Crimes in South Africa (per 100,000)

	Murder	Attempted Murder	Rape
1995	68.1	72	126
1999	52.5	58	122
2001	48.0	55	121
2004	42.7	49	115

Table 12.8

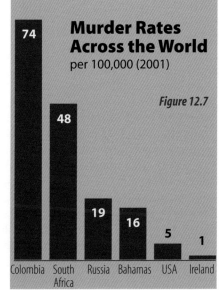

Murder Rates Across the World
per 100,000 (2001)

Figure 12.7

74 — Colombia
48 — South Africa
19 — Russia
16 — Bahamas
5 — USA
1 — Ireland

CRIME DOWN–PUBLIC FEAR UP

While the government highlights the reduction in crime figures, the public does not share the government's perception that the streets are safer.

Numerous surveys and studies indicate that the public believes that crime has increased in the past seven years despite government figures showing a drop in crime.

In a 1998 survey, 60% of South Africans said they felt very safe walking in the areas where they live during the day. This figure dropped to only 25% in 2003. These views differed largely by race with only 11% of Indians and 35% of Whites feeling very safe during the day, compared to a majority of coloureds (62%) and Blacks (64%) feeling very safe.

The murder of Marike de Klerk, (the former wife of the last white President FW De Klerk) in December 2001, shocked the white community. Like many Whites Marike De Klerk lived in her elegant home surrounded by a fence topped with razor wire with 24-hour security. Unfortunately for Marike, the security guard in the complex in which she lived was part of the gang that burgled her apartment.

Gun Control in South Africa

A new *Firearms Control Act* (2005) has created controversy in South Africa. The law makes it harder to legally own a weapon. All weapons must be registered every two years under a complex regulation system. The government argues that with 4.5 million guns in private hands, tighter gun control is necessary to reduce the horrendous murder rate. In 2004 a local rugby hero shot dead his teenage daughter, mistaking her for a car thief. Under the new regulations owners must now prove they can store and use guns responsibly and explain to the police why they need a weapon for self-defence.

Critics argue that this Act will force many to buy illegal arms. Already, illegal arms outnumber licensed weapons by ten to one in townships. The Afrikaner community is outraged. Piet Botha, the son of former white President PW Botha, declared that he will emigrate if he is denied a gun licence. He and his wife each carry a gun and a knife, and their children can handle guns. He says guns are essential to protect his family. He believes this because one of his best friends was shot dead in his garden, five attempted burglaries of his Pretoria home have taken place and he has twice been attacked by muggers.

Many gun shops are now closing down and gun control groups, both white and black, condemn the government's action. A spokesperson for the Black Gun Owner's Association pointed out that the death penalty was abolished in 1994 and people need to defend themselves against the criminals. He stated,

> "We Blacks only want arms for self-defence—after all crime is worst in the townships. The trouble is that the government is clearly targeting white gun owners and they really aren't the problem any more. The extremist white right is dead and buried. It's criminals, murderers and rapists who we have to defend our families against."

Distribution of those aged 20 and above in each population group by highest level of education completed

	Black	Coloured	Asian/ Indian	White	Average
Higher Education	5.2	4.9	14.9	29.8	8.4
Grade 12/Std10	16.8	18.5	34.9	40.9	20.4
Some secondary	30.4	40.1	33.0	25.9	30.8
Completed primary	6.9	9.8	4.2	0.8	6.4
Some primary	18.5	18.4	7.7	1.2	16.0
No schooling	22.3	8.3	5.3	1.4	17.9

Table 12.9 Source: 2001 Census

THE 2001 CENSUS

The findings of the 2001 census showed a gradual improvement in the social and economic position of Blacks over the previous five years. However, this improvement was not shared equally: class has become an issue. The new black and coloured middle classes have lifestyles and wealth equal to those of their white colleagues. The losers are the poor, uneducated and rural Blacks who have made limited progress.

Black women made huge inroads in the highest and lowest skills sectors, increasing their number at executive level by 60%. Black South Africans gained another 40,000 executive and management jobs between 1996 and the end of 2001.

There was a dramatic rise among middle-class black 'associate professionals' including police officers, teachers and junior government officials from 178,585 jobs in 1996 to 486,731 in 2001.

There is still a division between Whites and non-Whites as indicated in Tables 12.9–12.11 and Figure 12.8.

Access to piped water by population group of the household head

99.3%   99.2%   97.6%   80.3%   84.5%

White   Asian/ Indian   Coloured   Black   Total

Figure 12.8

A woman collects water from a communal tap servicing the Imizamo Yethu community near Cape Town in 2002. Over the past eight years the government has given seven million South Africans access to clean water, mostly in poor rural areas, and municipalities have hooked up another three million. The South African campaign is part of a global United Nations drive to supply clean, safe water.

Households with selected household goods by population group of the household head (%)					
	Black African	Coloured	Indian or Asian	White	Total
Radio	68.7	75.3	91.0	94.7	73.0
Television	44.2	73.6	91.0	92.6	53.8
Computer	1.8	9.4	27.9	46.0	8.6
Refrigerator	39.9	73.2	96.2	97.6	51.2
Telephone in Dwelling	12.0	43.2	74.8	78.6	24.4
Cellphone	24.6	31.0	58.9	74.6	32.3

Table 12.10 Source: 2001 Census

Unemployment rate among those aged 15-65 by sex and population group			
	Males	Females	Total
Black	43.3	57.8	50.2
Coloured	25.7	28.6	27.0
Indian/Asian	15.7	18.7	16.9
White	6.1	6.6	6.3
Average	35.8	48.1	41.6

Table 12.11 Source: 2001 Census

THE GAP IS CLOSING

In a controversial speech President Mbkei referred to South Africa as being a land of two nations—one white and rich, the other black and poor. While there are still significant inequalities between the races (see 2001 census on page 105), progress has been made through the BEE programme. (See page 95.)

It is true that rich, white South Africans have retained their wealth since apartheid ended, but many uneducated Whites have sunk into poverty and white beggars are a common sight in South African cities.

Poor Whites have also had to adjust to the influx of black families into what were once White-only neighbourhoods. John Mbeki illustrates the advancement of the black, skilled workers. He has moved with his wife and four children from a squatter house and has bought a house in what was once a white area. As a turner and fitter, his prospects are better than those of many of his new neighbours. John is shocked by the way many poor Whites live, but he has little sympathy. As he says, "I suffered to get where I am, but for them there's no excuse. They've had all the opportunities. It's not that I don't feel compassion. It's just that it's our time now. They've had theirs."

Evidence of the emergence of a black elite can be found in the number of Blacks now living in the wealthiest suburbs of South Africa's cities. Houghton, the grandest suburb in Johannesburg, has among its growing number of black residents Nelson Mandela and former Regional Premier Tokyo Sexwale.

This emerging black middle class has enrolled its children in the schools in the suburbs, rather than in the township schools. The loss of such talent, wealth and role models further impoverishes life in the townships. Mr Mugadi, the editor of the black magazine *The Tribute*, is aware of the impact of the flight of the black elite. One Sowetan wrote to *The Tribute* accusing "black yuppies" of "scurrying away into the comfort and safety of white suburbia" rather than using their talents "to liberate their people". However Mr Mugadi does not blame the black elite. "You can't glorify and have a sentimental attachment to the townships as if they were our creations: they were imposed on us by apartheid."

Soweto continues to have its 'Beverly Hills' and can boast that Winnie Mandela still lives there. Nevertheless, the majority of the new elite are leaving—black success means leaving the townships and comes at a cost to those left behind.

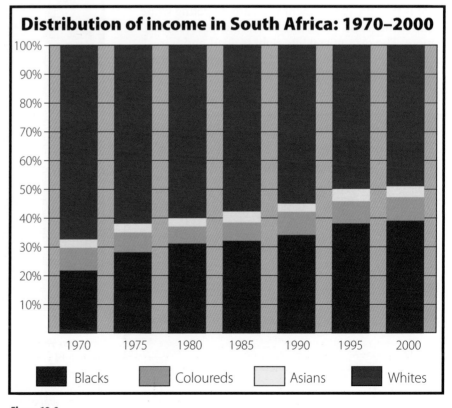

Figure 12.9

WHAT PROGRESS HAS BEEN MADE WITH TRANSFORMATION SINCE 1994?

Distribution of Income

The gap between the rich and poor in all race groups has grown since 1994.

The growth in inequality is linked to the emergent black middle class and growing unemployment among the lower deciles of the black population (unemployment increased from 36.2% in 1994 to 46.6% in 2002)

● Redistribution of income between the races has taken place.

● Between 1975 and 2000 the black share of income rose from 22.3% to 38.3%.

● White share of income declined from 67% to 49.9%.

● Coloured share of income increased from 7% to 8.1%.

● Indian income increased from 2.8% to 4%.

A growing black middle class

■ The emergent black middle class is the largest component in an increasingly multiracial national middle class.

■ The Public Service has made substantial progress in achieving employment equity goals.

■ Black representation in the public services increased from 76% in 1995 to 86% in 2001.

■ The proportion of senior black managers increased from 37% to 55% and the proportion of Blacks in middle management rose from 41% to 64%.

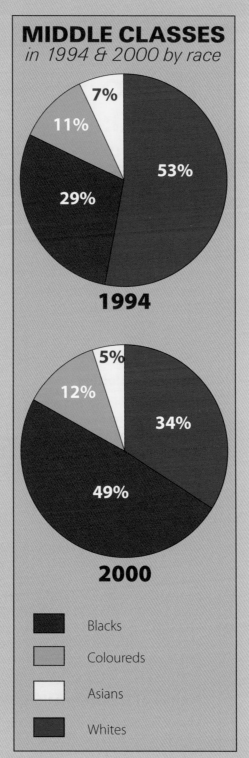

MIDDLE CLASSES
in 1994 & 2000 by race

7%
11%
29%
53%

1994

5%
12%
49%
34%

2000

■ Blacks
■ Coloureds
□ Asians
■ Whites

Figure 12.10

CHAPTER 13

Political issues in South Africa

The 1994 and 1999 elections were both outstanding success stories for the ANC, and South Africa can claim to be a politically stable country, a far cry from the fear of civil war which faced the country in 1994.

1999 GENERAL ELECTION

The election result was a personal triumph for Thabo Mbeki. The ANC increased its support, winning 66.3% of the vote and just failing to achieve a two-thirds majority which would have enabled the ANC to change the Constitution. In contrast, the election was a disaster for the New National Party and a disappointment for the new party, the United Democratic Movement. The Democratic Party emerged as the official opposition, benefiting from the collapse of the New National Party.

The ANC, once again, controlled seven of the nine provinces and shared power in KwaZulu-Natal with Inkatha. In the Western Cape, the former stronghold of the National Party, the ANC won the most votes (see Table 13.2), but a coalition between the New National Party and the Democratic Party prevented the ANC from taking office. The Afrikaans-speaking Freedom Front witnessed a significant decline in support, dropping from nine to three members of the National Assembly.

As stated, the election was a disaster for the New National Party with its support falling from 3.9 million in 1994 to 1.9 million in 1999. The party which ruled South Africa from

THABO MBEKI:

PRESIDENT OF SOUTH AFRICA

Thabo Mbeki was born on 18 June 1942 in the Eastern Cape. His father, Govan, was a close ANC comrade of Nelson Mandela and was in prison with him. Thabo followed in his father's footsteps and joined the ANC Youth League. In 1962 he went into exile and gained a university degree in England.

Political Activities

He travelled widely and after a spell in Moscow joined the South African Communist Party. On his return to Zambia, he became secretary to the national executive of the ANC. He won the power struggle against Cyril Ramaphosa to become Nelson Mandela's successor. In 1997 he became President of the ANC and in 1999 became President of the Republic of South Africa.

Personality and Policies

While he lacks the charisma of Mandela, he is an able administrator and he did increase the ANC's percentage of the vote in 1999. Despite his communist past, he supports the market economy and partnership with private enterprise. His privatisation policies (see page 115) have brought him into conflict with the Trade Unions (COSATU) and the SACP (South African Communist Party). He has also been criticised for his lack of action over AIDS and his failure to condemn Robert Mugabe in Zimbabwe.

Politics of Transformation

Mandela concentrated on allaying the fears of the non-black communities. He was aware that if the white community felt threatened, the extreme right-wing groups, such as the AWB, would wage a 'race war'. In contrast, Thabo Mbeki is aware of the need to transform South African society. The shift of power which took place in the political field must now cover all aspects of economic and social life.

1948 to 1994, and had been part of the Government of National Unity, was now reduced to the status of a minority party. It also lost overall control of the Western Cape and was forced to form a coalition with the Democratic Party.

THE RISE OF THE DEMOCRATIC PARTY

The Democratic Party, traditionally the home of white, English-speaking liberals, achieved a huge increase in its vote from the 2% gained in 1994. Its leader, Tony Leon, had displayed a high profile in the 'Mandela parliament', had criticised ANC action and had highlighted ANC corruption. The Democratic Party campaigned under the slogan of 'Fight back' and, untainted by the sins of apartheid, had won over white former National Party supporters and some middle-class Blacks. The Democratic Party criticised the ANC for not doing enough to combat South Africa's high crime and unemployment rates and promised to act as a watchdog over a powerful ANC.

Political Opposition to the ANC

The attempt by the other political parties to form a united front against the ANC was deemed to have been achieved in July 2000 when the two white-dominated political parties, the Democratic Party (DP) and the New National Party (NNP), along with the Federal Alliance, agreed to form the Democratic Alliance (DA) and to fight the December 2000 local government elections as a united front. Tony Leon, leader of the DP, was appointed leader, with Marthinus van Schalkwyk, leader of the NNP, becoming deputy leader.

The success of the DA in the December 2000 local government elections, failed to extinguish the growing tension between Tony Leon, van Schalkwyk and their respective parties. Van Schalkwyk resented the fact that posts in the new party were predominantly given to Democratic Party members, and was unhappy that he had not been

appointed leader. Tension came to a head in October 2001 when Peter Marais, the NNP Mayor of Cape Town, was expelled from the Democratic Alliance by Tony Leon for deception. Van Schalkwyk refused to support Tony Leon and withdrew from the Democratic Alliance.

Van Schalkwyk began talks with the ANC and, on 1 December 2001, the NNP announced that it was joining the Government of National Unity as a junior party. In return for the merger, van Schalkwyk became the new Premier in the Western Cape, enabling the ANC to join the provincial government, and two of his senior colleagues were given two deputy ministerial posts in the National Government. The ANC gained most from this merger. It further divided and weakened political opposition and it enabled the ANC to share power in the Western Cape and to gain control of Cape Town.

Tony Leon condemned the move and predicted that many NNP members would stay with the Democratic Alliance. He stated, "We're going forward and forward. It is obvious to everyone now that the NNP is about to disappear into oblivion."

Political Situation 1994–2004

■ The danger of civil war from extreme white groups or Zulu Nationalists, feared in 1994, did not happen. There was a resurgence

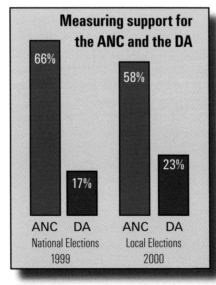

Measuring support for the ANC and the DA

ANC 66% DA 17%
National Elections 1999

ANC 58% DA 23%
Local Elections 2000

Figure 13.1

of terrorist acts by extreme Whites in 2002. The government arrested thirty Afrikaners who were charged with treason. Inkatha is still in the Government of National Unity with Buthelezi Minister of Home Affairs.

■ A peaceful transition of political power from Whites to Blacks has taken place and, more importantly, a peaceful transition of power from Mandela to Mbeki reflects the political stability which exists in South Africa.

■ The Truth and Reconciliation Commission has forced both Whites and non-Whites to come to terms with, and to go forward from, the evils of the apartheid years.

■ South Africa has established itself as a democratic country with a liberal, written Constitution. The rule of law exists and it has a free press, radio and television which can criticise the government and expose corruption.

■ The ANC is the only national party with strong electoral support in all of the nine provinces. (It holds power in seven of the provinces and shares power in one.) In contrast, all of the other political parties have regional power bases, for example Inkatha in KwaZulu-Natal and the Democratic Alliance in the Western Cape.

■ Voting in South Africa is based on racial background. The ANC is mainly a black political party, Inkatha is Zulu, and the Democratic Party and New National Party are white and coloured (including Asians).

THE 2004 ELECTION

The election result was a further personal triumph for Thabo Mbeki. The ANC won a landslide victory, gaining almost 70% of the vote in South Africa's third democratic elections, its biggest win in ten years of power. For the first time ever it was the largest party in all of the nine provinces and, most importantly, it gained control of KwaZulu-Natal, ending ten years of IFP rule in the province. The Democratic Alliance consolidated its position as the official opposition while the NNP suffered electoral annihi-

THE TRUTH AND RECONCILIATION COMMISSION 1996–2002

The Truth and Reconciliation Commission (TRC), chaired by retired Archbishop Desmond Tutu, was set up to establish as complete a picture as possible of the "causes, nature and extent of the gross violations of human rights committed between 1960 and 10 May 1994".

The Commission travelled round South Africa listening firstly to the heartbreaking stories of those who had lost their loved ones. The Commission had the power to grant an amnesty to anybody whose crime had a political objective as long as they admitted their wrongdoing.

In general the black South African population, with the exception of supporters of Chief Buthelezi, welcomed the Commission. The white community had their reservations, especially supporters of the NNP and extreme right-wing white organisations. Victims of apartheid had the opportunity to share their grief with the nation and to discover what had happened to their loved ones. Ordinary Whites could no longer pretend that apartheid was simply a bad system which had made mistakes. The hearings, aired on television, shocked and horrified the nation. The revelations damaged the National Party and led to the resignation of de Klerk.

In October 1998 the Commission presented its interim findings. While the Report accused the National Party, especially PW Botha, and the Inkatha Freedom Party of being responsible for the bulk of the apartheid-era atrocities, it also accused the ANC of human rights abuse. The only member of the ANC directly named was Winnie Madikizela-

Mandela.

In 2002 the TRC's final two reports were given to President Mandela with a request that the government carry out its legal obligation to provide reparation to the 22,000 victims who testified to the Commission. Finally, in April 2003 the government announced that it would give a £30,000 payment, which fell short of what the Commission had recommended. The government also stated that it would not take out any lawsuit against corporations or support any taken out by victims of apartheid.

- During the period of its existence, the TRC received some 21,000 statements.
- It received 7,100 applications for amnesty and granted 1,100 while refusing 6,000.
- Among those rejected were the five police officers responsible for the death of Steve Biko and the killers of Communist Party leader, Chris Hani.
- The government has been very slow in paying out compensation to the 21,000 victims.
- In a 2001 opinion poll, 76% of black respondents believed the TRC had done a good job but only 37% of Whites agreed.

lation, even losing out to the newly formed Independent Democrats.

The opposition parties fought the election on the ANC's so-called record of failure. (See ANC 'Failed Record'.) However, according to political commentator, Chris Landsberg, "People did not vote on whether the ANC had delivered on its previous election promises: they voted with their hearts". This explains the landslide victory of the ANC. For the first time the party won the majority of seats in all nine provinces—only in KwaZulu-Natal and the Western Cape did the ANC not achieve absolute majorities and in these provinces the ANC is ruling in coalition governments. The election now enables the ANC to change the Constitution if it so wishes (a two-thirds majority in the National Assembly is necessary).

As stated, the Democratic Alliance (DA) strengthened its position as South Africa's official opposition party, its 12.4% of the national vote up from the 9.6% it won in 1999, giving it fifty parliamentary seats. The DA had high hopes of forming a coalition government in KwaZulu-Natal, but the ANC's excellent result was a blow to both the DA and the Inkatha Freedom Party. The vote for the Inkatha Freedom Party continued to fall and, for the first time, the party lost control of KwaZulu-Natal. Nevertheless, the DA was the only political party apart from the ANC to win seats in all of the nine provinces.

Once again, the election was a disaster for the New National Party with its support falling from 3.9 million in 1994 to 251,000 in 2004. The party suffered the humiliation

ANC
'Failed Record'

- The destruction of more than one million jobs.
- Unemployment rising to over 40%.
- Redistribution of only 3% of the land.
- The delay of the roll-out of a comprehensive HIV/AIDS treatment programme in the face of the highest infection rate in the world.
- The disconnection of water, electricity and other services in poor communities unable to pay 'commercial rates' as a consequence of the privatisation programme.

of receiving fewer votes than the new Independent Democrats led by the charismatic Patricia de Lille, a former member of the Pan Africanist Congress (PAC).

GOVERNMENT OF NATIONAL UNITY (GNU)

The ANC once again dominated the Government of National Unity. The NNP's leader, Marthinus Van Schalkwyk, was given the lowly post of Minister of the Environment and Tourism and some of his colleagues received deputy ministers posts. The ANC deliberately attempted to humiliate the IFP leader, Chief Buthelezi. Mbeki offered posts of deputy ministers to two IFP members while ignoring Buthelezi who had been a Minister in the GNU since 1994. The IFP declined the posts which were then offered to members of the United Democratic Movement (UDM).

In KwaZulu-Natal, IFP agreed to join a power- sharing government with the ANC. Initially the IFP had threatened to contest the results in the courts but decided to drop its protest. The IFP was concerned with the high number of postal votes (over 360,700) which, it argued, favoured the ANC and were part of a deliberate strategy to register ANC voters who did not reside in KwaZulu-Natal. The IFP received three ministers' posts as well as the post of Deputy Speaker. The agreement ended the fear of political violence re-emerging in KwaZulu-Natal.

In the Western Cape, the NNP joined the ANC in the running of the province. For the first time an ANC member was appointed Premier, thus ending ten years of the NNP holding the highest post in the provincial government.

The Death of the New National Party

In August 2004 the NNP's federal council announced that members should join the ANC and fight all future elections under the banner of the ANC. Its leader, Marthinus Van Schalkwyk, encouraged NNP Members of Parliament to cross over to the ANC "within a few weeks". The Party ceased to exist in September 2005.

The Democratic Alliance MP, Helen Zille, accused van Schalkwyk of destroying his party and abandoning his voters in return for a Cabinet position. Pieter Mulder, leader of the extreme white party Freedom Front Plus, urged NNP Members of Parliament to cross over to his party rather than the ANC.

Electoral Turnout

The electoral turnout based on registered voters showed a significant decline from almost 90% in 1999 to 76.7% in 2004—a figure still far higher than turnout in the UK or the USA. However, when one looks at turnout as a percentage of voting age population, a different picture appears. In the ten years since black South Africans first received the vote, the number voting has declined from 86% to 57.8%. Almost 12 million South Africans did not vote in the elections; in contrast the number in 1999 was 6.5 million. It is clear that many South Africans, of all races, and especially the young, do not wish to engage in political activity.

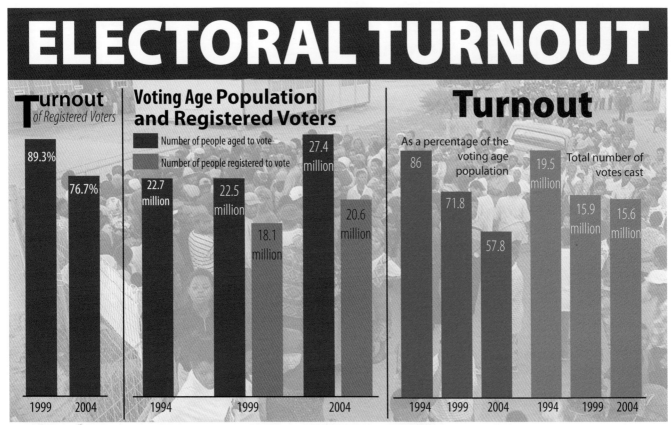

Figure 13.2

In 1994 there was no register of electors

**Phumzile Mlambo-Ngcuka
(Deputy President of South
Africa)**

Phumzile Mlambo-Ngcuka was born in November 1955 and after graduating in 1981 taught for two years in KwaZulu-Natal. In 1990 she became Director of a Rural Development programme. She entered politics in 1994, becoming part of the first ever group of black Members of Parliament. She became a member of the Reconstruction and Development Programme (RDP) Select Committee and in 1996 was appointed Deputy Trade and Industry Minister. In 1999 Mbeki appointed her Minister of Minerals and Energy. With this background she has strong links to South African business. The sacking of Jacob Zuma as Deputy President (see page 118) enabled her to become South Africa's first ever female Dep-

uty President, with the possibility of becoming President in 2009.

Significantly, her husband Bulenlani Ngcuka, was the National Director of Public Prosecutions who found there was a prima facie case of corruption against Jacob Zuma. Her appointment has therefore not been welcomed by those loyal to Jacob Zuma. Women are well represented in the ANC's ranks in par-

liament. In 1997 the ANC resolved that 33% of its candidates on election lists would be women and intends to increase this to over 40% in the 2007 local government elections. Mbeki has so far appointed twelve women as Cabinet Ministers and four as Premiers in the provincial governments. (As president of the ANC, it is Mbeki who appoints the Premiers rather than the rank and file ANC members.)

National Assembly Election Results:
1999 and 2004

Party	SEATS 1999	SEATS 2004	VOTES (%) 1999	VOTES (%) 2004
ANC	266	279	66.3	69.9
Democratic Party	38	50	9.6	12.6
Inkatha FP	34	28	8.6	6.9
New National Party	28	7	6.9	1.7
UDM	14	9	3.4	1.7
Independent Democrats	–	7	–	1.7

Table 13.1

Selected provincial results

Table 13.2

Western Cape

1999

Party	Votes	Seats
ACDP	44,323	1
ANC	668,106	18
DP	189,183	5
NNP	609,612	17
UDM	38,071	1

2004

Party	Votes	Seats
ACDP	53,934	2
ANC	709,052	19
DA	424,832	12
ID	122,867	3
NNP	170,469	5
UDM	27,489	1

KwaZulu-Natal

1999

Party	Votes	Seats
ACDP	53,745	1
ANC	1,167,094	32
DP	241,779	7
IFP	1,196,955	34
MF	86,770	2
NNP	97,077	3

2004

Party	Votes	Seats
ACDP	48,892	2
ANC	1,287,823	38
DA	228,857	7
IFP	1,009,267	30
MF	71,540	2
UDM	20,546	1

THE AFRIKANER COMMUNITY

The Afrikaner community feels threatened by the ANC. Their desire to establish their own volkstaat—a white homeland—has totally failed. The Freedom Front has no influence in parliament as it is not represented in the government. Mandela had set up a Volkstaat Council to discuss Afrikaner self-determination but this was abolished by Mbeki in 2001.

The collapse and dissolution of the New National Party in 2005 further weakened their political influence. The last white President of South Africa and former NNP leader FW De Klerk, condemned the decision to merge with the ANC.

There is deep anger and frustration among the Afrikaner community over the erosion of their culture, especially the Afrikaans language. A primary school in Northern Cape (where the majority of people speak Afrikaans) lost its legal right to teach only in Afrikaans, even though the judge accused the authorities of wanting to phase out all Afrikaans schools in the province. Stellenbosch and other Afrikaans universities have lost their status as Afrikaans-medium institutions.

Only 3% of all schools in South Africa are now single medium Afrikaans school. In 2005 the Western Cape, by then controlled by the ANC with the demise of the NNP, attempted to force Mikro Primary school to accept pupils who could not speak Afrikaans. The Cape High Court supported the school.

In the Western Cape, Afrikaans is the language of the large coloured population as well as the Afrikaans-speaking Whites. The Afrikaner community is concerned about the events in Zimbabwe and the government's measures to reduce their rights to hold arms. (See page 105.) The attacks on white, mostly Afrikaner farms continues. (700 farms were attacked and 140 farmers were killed in 2001.) The changing of place names from Afrikaans to African names has also infuriated the Whites. In 2005, the South African National Geographical Names Council approved the name change of Pretoria to Tshwane.

Dan Roodt, an Afrikaner journalist, stated, "What nation-building really means in South Africa is the complete destruction of Afrikaans culture and the Afrikaner identity." This frustration and anger led to the re-emergence of white, right-wing terrorist attacks in 2002. A group called Warriors of the Boer Nation set off nine bombs in Soweto, killing one black South African woman. The government's reaction was swift: over thirty Afrikaners were arrested with a number standing trial, accused of treason.

South African white supremacist supporters, holding a Nazi flag, listen to their leader Eugene Terreblanche, unseen, at a rally held in downtown Pretoria, South Africa, on 16 December 2005. A few hundred followers of the Afrikaner Resistance Movement (AWB) gathered as the rest of the country was celebrating the Day of Reconciliation.

ORANIA—AN AFRIKAANS OUTPOST

Apartheid lives on in Orania, an exclusive haven for Afrikaners who reject the new South Africa. The Whites-only town of Orania is situated in the vast open semiarid desert of the Northern Cape. It takes a seven hour drive from Johannesburg to reach the isolated community of 500 inhabitants. One of its citizens was Tammie Verwoerd, the widow of the architect of apartheid, Hendrik Verwoerd.

Orania is a private community where the Afrikaners have an opportunity to ignore the realities of the new South Africa. The community is a former ghost town bought by the right-wing Freedom Front. 'Strictly private' warns a sign nailed at the entrance to the fenced town. The town museum displays relics of Afrikaner glory and the Boer flag of the old Transvaal Republic flies on top of the hill.

Life is frugal and harsh—there are no opulent houses, tennis courts or private swimming pools. Orania is self-sufficient and resourceful; its citizens grow their own food, clean their own streets, educate their children and worship together in the community hall. Orania has no black servants, gardeners or council workers to carry out the manual tasks.

Its citizens deny that they are racists. Lida Strydom Kontreiwinkel, a mother of three small children, and her husband John gave up their farm in Northern Natal because of the constant threat from thieves. "We were thinking of emigrating to Canada and then we stopped over in Orania. It was very peaceful. People did not talk about crime. We don't belong to the Freedom Front. I have three children and when they are so small you have to protect them." Lida and John now live in a caravan on the plot of land they bought to farm pecan nuts.

Annamaria Boshoff, an elderly lady, is happy to end her days in Orania and dreams of a Boerstaat. "I don't feel at home in the new South Africa. It's not my country any more. It's not our government, the culture is different, the religion is different. We can't have the whole country, that is impossible; we're too small a nation. We just want a country of our own."

In April 2004 Orania launched its own currency to a cautious reception by the reserve bank. The currency is only acceptable in the town and is regarded as an example of the community's desire for autonomy and self-determination.

Orania has no black servants, gardeners or council workers to carry out the manual tasks.

Orania aims to ensure that Afrikaner culture is passed on to the next generation.

The following extract from a speech made in February 2005 by Dr Pieter Mulder, leader of the Freedom Front, highlights the frustration of the Afrikaners.

"Where are the equal rights for Afrikaners? Mr Mbeki says that South Africa belongs to all who live in it. But is this true for black and white? For ten years I have listened to speeches in this assembly in which Whites are accused of racism, while Blacks do no wrong.

Mr De Gouveia, a 70-year-old Afrikaans farmer was robbed, had a rope tied round his neck and was fastened to a vehicle which dragged him to his death.

Four young men were arrested, some were 15 years old. What motivates them to act like this? They weren't in the struggle. Yesterday the Indian shops in Phomolong in the Free State were destroyed, while the black-owned shops were not touched. Prejudice or racism?

The ANC is guilty of creating this climate. Read the ANC website. If you do not join the ANC, you are an enemy according to these documents.

'South Africa belongs to all who live in it, black and white,' says the President. We support it. But then I received a letter from a young South African who last week was affected by affirmative action. A qualified Clinical Army Psychologist, his contract was not renewed as 'the quota for black psychologists had to be filled and he, unfortunately, is white.'

The ANC claim to know what is best for the Afrikaners and other minorities. We pay more taxes than anybody else but cannot even determine how a single cent will be spent."

Dr Mulder meets members of the Freedom Front Youth branch in London in 2005.

INKATHA FREEDOM PARTY

The IFP's poor showing in the 2004 elections highlighted divisions within the party and led to criticism of Chief Buthelezi's tight control of the party. The end of the party's participation in the Government of National Unity (GNU) and the loss of control in KwaZulu-Natal are clear evidence of the erosion of party support, especially in urban areas. The IFP's emphasis on tribal authority and the importance of the Zulu monarchy ensures that it has strong support in rural areas. However, the growth of urbanisation, creating a less deferential population, has led some party activists to demand that the party modernises and considers a change in leadership (Buthelezi is over 70).

National Chairperson, Ziba Jiyana, was suspended from the party in August 2005 for daring to suggest that that the IFP lacked internal democracy and was being run in a dictatorial fashion. Rueben Mhlongo, a political analyst, stated, "There are two factions in the party, one loyal to the leadership of Mangosuthu Buthelezi and another pressing for democratisation."

The IFP is concerned that its ANC partners who dominate in the KwaZulu-Natal government, will undermine the cultural and national identity of the Zulu people. Buthelezi attacked the provincial government's KwaZulu-Natal Traditional Leadership and Governance Bill which he said did not recognise the role of the traditional leaders and "completely ignores the very notion of a Zulu nation, a Zulu monarchy and a Zulu kingdom."

"In a few years, it is likely that features of our Zuluness will be denied and they will try to foist upon us a uniform sense of Africanism."

Towards a One-Party State?

The fears of the country drifting towards becoming a one-party state, expressed by the opposition in 2003, became a swift march in 2004 and 2005. The emphatic victory in the 2004 election followed by the dissolution of the

"We need stronger opposition not a stronger government."
Tony Leon, 14 August 2003

"I am very worried … if we are not careful we are going to have a one-party state."
Chief Buthelezi, 2003

Mangosuthu Buthelezi (R) leader of the Inkatha Freedom Party (IFP) with Tony Leon (L) leader of the Democratic Alliance (DA), the main opposition party, during their joint rally in Soweto in 2003. The rally was held in response to the decision by the IFP and the DA to form a 'Coalition for Change' to offer a strong democratic alternative programme to the ruling ANC government to stop the "drift to a one-party state".

NNP in 2005, gave the ANC over 70% of the seats in the assembly. (286 seats to the DA's 50.) It now has the power to rewrite the Constitution and one such act might be to change the Constitution to allow the President to run for a third term. The two provinces—Western Cape and KwaZulu-Natal—which offered an alternative to the ANC and a protection of minority rights are now led by a dominant ANC. Politics in South Africa are based on race and, as the latest census figures display, the black South African population is increasing rapidly which was reflected in the 2004 election results. The government's commitment to Black Transformation and the all-embracing influence of the ANC in all sections of society are regarded as being detrimental to minority rights.

The Democratic Alliance has made attempts to attract more black voters. In August 2004 it put forward a black candidate for a 'safe' local government seat. The DA lost narrowly to the Freedom Front which increased its vote from 2% in 2000 to 47% in the above election. This further supported the view that race decides voting preferences. There

is also a great deal of hostility between Tony Leon, leader of the DA, and Thabo Mbeki, who regards any criticism as being racist inspired.

THE ANC UNDER MBEKI

The 'triple alliance' between the ANC, SACP (South African Communist Party) and COSATU (Congress of South African Trade Unions) is still intact despite criticisms of Mbeki's free-market economic policies. The government's attempt to control wage rises, to restructure public services and to introduce privatisation of essential services such as electricity, has heightened tension. Life in the black townships has deteriorated over the last eight years and the fruits of affirmative action programmes have not been distributed to the poorest sections of society in South Africa.

Mbeki has also been criticised by COSATU for his controversial views of AIDS and for the government's purchase of weapons worth $5.5 billion.

COSATU has also been critical of Mbeki's failure to condemn the actions of Robert Mugabe in Zimbabwe. Mbeki prevented a COSATU delegation from visiting Zimbabwe in 2004.

The electoral system and party structures strengthen Mbeki's powers and stifle debate within the party. Any ANC politician who criticises ANC policies will not be elected as an MP. The party list system used in the PR elections ensures that it is the party leaders and not the public who decide who will become an MP. Mbeki appoints not only his ministers but the nine Premiers of the provincial governments thus weakening the powers of the Provinces. Mbeki's intolerance of criticism (see page 117) further creates a climate of blind obedience to the leadership.

The ANC's relations with COSATU have been further strained by the escalation in strike action by low paid workers. A three-day strike by local government workers in August 2005 (prior to the local government elections) was followed by an autumn and winter of discontent. The Secretary General of COSATU, Mr Vavi, stated that "the apartheid wage gap is increasing" and that "workers have little reason to celebrate the gains of democracy as the rich have become richer and the poor poorer".

Judiciary and Media

Critics of those who argue that South Africa is moving towards a one-party state, highlight not only the democratic electoral system and the numerous political parties, but also the existence of an independent judiciary, a free press and active pressure groups such as TAC (see page 100) and COSATU. They rightly claim that South Africa is not Zimbabwe.

Administration of Justice

As highlighted on page 90 the Constitution grants judicial authority to its courts which are independent and subject only to the Constitution and the law. The Constitutional Court has already played an important part in monitoring the activities of the government. (See availability of the anti-AIDS drugs page 100 and the land rights of white farmers, page 103.)

An issue of concern to many commentators is the future independence of the judiciary. The dominance of white judges in the higher levels of the judiciary, especially the Constitutional Court, has led to demands from the ANC that the judiciary must reflect "the racial and gender composition of South Africa." This campaign of white judge bashing was witnessed in the trial of Schabir Shaik when the judge was called a 'white racist' by members of the Communist Party which is affiliated to the ANC. (See page 118.) Democratic Alliance (DA) Justice spokesperson Sheila Camerer stated that "the Constitutional Court is internationally recognised as one of the shining lights of South Africa's first decade of democracy and the ANC must leave it alone."

In April 2005 judges reacted angrily to proposed new legislation that would give the Department of Justice and Constitutional Development control of the administration

of courts, together with the power to reprimand judges.

The Media

South Africa has a thriving free and independent press with liberal newspapers such as *The Mail and Guardian* keeping a close and critical watch on the actions of the government. (The newspaper was a fierce critic of the apartheid government in the 1980s.) Ironically, an article which highlighted the R11 million of taxpayers' money being giving to the ANC for its 2004 election campaign by oil company Imvine failed to appear in print. A 'gagging order' by the courts prevented the newspaper from printing the article. The judge placed the rights of privacy above the constitutional rights of free press and freedom. The newspaper hit the streets with the word 'gagged' in large red letters across its front pages (See page 116.)

Television plays an important role in maintaining the culture and languages of South Africa. The impartiality and independence of the South Africa Broadcasting Company (SABC) is an issue of major debate in South Africa. Its former white executives have been replaced by black employees committed to the goals of black transformation. The SABC televised the ANC's launch of its 2004 election campaign. Tony Leon has accused the SABC of "becoming a virtual propaganda arm" of the ANC.

CORRUPTION

In December 2002, President Mbeki promised to "fight crime and to root out corruption". Unfortunately, events in 2003 were to embarrass Mbeki as prominent members of the ANC were accused and found guilty of corruption. (See Mismanagement or Corruption on page 118).

Tony Yengeni, Chief Whip of the ANC, and Winnie Madikizela-Mandela, were both charged with corruption. The Democratic Alliance Leader, Tony Leon, accused Jacob Zuma, the Deputy President, of ac-

MBEKI'S INTOLERANCE THREATENS CRITICAL DEBATE

Desmond Tutu, second only to Nelson Mandela as the face of the struggle for the emancipation of black South Africans from the apartheid regime, has become a thorn in the side of President Mbeki. He has also brought to the surface the climate of intolerance created by the President. Mbeki's weekly newspaper column has become a vehicle for personal attacks on individuals. It is claimed that this demeans the President of South Africa.

Archbishop Tutu's crime was to question Black Economic Empowerment (BEE) and to accuse the President of stifling debate among his party members over issues such as AIDS and Zimbabwe and of being prejudiced against the Whites. Mbeki, in his weekly online newsletter, called Tutu a "charlatan and a liar". Christine Quanta, a close associate of Mbeki, accused Tutu of being a "black ventriloquist amplifying the message of the white right." In contrast others supported Tutu. Thembani Sonjica wrote in *The Mail and Guardian* that "Archbishop Tutu's criticism of ANC sycophants is long overdue. Carrying an ANC membership card in one hand and a gold credit card in the other, they desire to be Ministers, high government officials and MPs. The gravy train is riding high and fast with all the fat cats singing Africa has returned to us. We need people like you, Milo Tutu, very few speak the truth in this country."

cepting payment from a French arms company.

In international terms, South Africa has an excellent record on tackling corruption and is ranked well above most other African countries by corruption monitors. A recent international survey in *The Economist* magazine, on public trust of politicians, made interesting reading: the South African public trusted their politicians more than the British public! The fact that South African politicians are not above the law displays the strength of South Africa's democratic system.

The Sacking of Jacob Zuma

Jacob Zuma speaking at a UN meeting as Deputy President of South Africa.

Accusations against Jacob Zuma, the Deputy President, first surfaced in 2003 when he was accused of receiving R500,000 from a French arms company and of offering to protect it from official probes. Despite being investigated by the Scorpion (the elite police unit), and the then National Director of Public Prosecutions, Bulenlani Ngcuka who stated that there was a 'prima facie' case to show that Mr Zuma had taken a bribe, no legal charges were brought against him.

A close friend and financial adviser of Jacob Zuma, Schabir Shaik, was charged in 2004 with corruption and fraud and was found guilty in June 2005.The trial focused closely on the financial link between

Zuma and Shaik; the latter gave Zuma more than R1 million in gifts or loans.The Judge, Hilary Squires, stated that Zuma must have been aware of bribes sought by Schabir Shaik on his behalf and that "their relationship was generally corrupt".

The Opposition Parties immediately called for Zuma to resign or be dismissed to protect the integrity of the government. In contrast, the Young Communist League of South Africa (YCL), urged Zuma not to resign as he had not been the one on trial. The YCL attacked Judge Squires claiming he was a white racist and called for his sacking. This attack on the independence of the Judiciary was not supported by Mbeki. (See Judiciary page 116.)

Despite strong opposition from the ANC Thabo Mbeki sacked Zuma and declared to Parliament that it was best for "our young democratic system that Mr Zuma should go". (Zuma remained as Deputy President of the ANC.) The Trade Union movement and the Communist Party were unhappy with this decision. President Mbeki appointed Phumzile Mlambo-Ngcuka as the new, and first female, Deputy President of South Africa.

The crisis facing Jacob Zuma intensified in December 2005 when he was charged by the Johannesburg Magistrates Court following allegations of rape made against him by a 31-year-old woman.

MBEKI ON CORRUPTION

It is clear that there are some people who believe that our liberation and the establishment of the democratic order have opened the doors for them to engage in corrupt practices, to enrich themselves at the expense of the people. We must state that these are parasites who are waging a war against the people. It is the task of all our members to declare war against these parasites.

MISMANAGEMENT OR CORRUPTION

March 2003
Tony Yengeni, former Chief Whip of the ANC, was sentenced to four years in prison for defrauding parliament.

April 2003
Winnie Madikizela-Mandela was found guilty of eighty five fraud charges and given a jail sentence.

2004–05
Forty current and former MPs were arrested and accused of falsifying their travel expenses.

January 2005
3,900 public employees in KwaZulu-Natal faced arrest for claiming social grants to which they were not entitled.

June 2005
Deputy President Jacob Zuma was dismissed from office after a Judge declared his relationship with his former adviser Schabir Shaik "was generally corrupt". Shaik had been found guilty of corruption.

The People's Republic of China

CHAPTER 14

Background

China is the third largest country in the world, by area, after Canada and the Russian Federation. It is bordered by twelve countries. The 1.3 billion citizens of China make up one-quarter of the world's population, making it the most populated country in the world.

China is important because of its economic potential. It has deposits of most minerals including oil and gas and it is the world's biggest coal producer. The Chinese workforce is the largest in the world. China has the potential to overshadow the economy of any other country, both

The People's Republic of China

500 km

0   500 Miles

Karl Marx

The philosophy (ideas) of Communism were developed by Karl Marx, a nineteenth century German philosopher. Marxist theory states that the flow of history is inevitable. All countries pass through certain stages of economic, social and political development.

Marx predicted that the first countries to experience Communism would be the most advanced industrial countries in the nineteenth century such as the UK and Germany, but in 1917 Russia was the first country to undergo a Communist Revolution. It was led by Lenin who was a follower of Marx. Lenin argued that, with strong leadership and control from the Communist Party, Russia could by-pass the capitalist stage and move directly to the classless Communist society. This was called Marxist-Leninist theory. The Chinese version of Communism is a variation of Marxist-Leninist Theory.

MAOISM

Mao Zedong adapted Marxist-Leninist theory to suit conditions in China. He believed that the revolution would start in the countryside as poor peasants rose in revolt against the oppression of their landlords. Mao built up support in rural areas and established his People's Red Army whose job it was to lead the peasants in dealing with the landlords. In areas under their control, the Red Army established rural soviets (peasants' groups) to run affairs. This was to form the basis of Chinese Communism. On 1 October 1949 the People's Republic of China (PRC) was proclaimed with Mao as its leader.

As the USSR (Russia) was the first Communist state, it was used as the model to build Communism in China. Initially, therefore, China concentrated on large-scale industrial projects to build up the country's strength. However, by the mid-1950s Mao had begun to develop his own model of Communism based on the peasants.

MAO'S MASS LINE

Mao's Mass Line was his political model for the development of China. This tried to take account of the ideas of the population in China. The masses were to be led by the Communist Party which would be a strong, well-disciplined organisation, responsive to the ideas and wishes of the masses and accountable to the masses for its actions in an on-going process. It would take the thoughts of the masses and concentrate them into usable ideas for running the country and the government. These would then be given back to the people as Communist Party policies.

This process was meant to produce continual change in the running of China. Government policies would be relevant to the peasants' needs and would always be able to adapt to changing circumstances in China.

as a consumer and as an industrial producer.

It is the largest remaining communist controlled country and its military might is awesome in terms of both nuclear weapons and a large conventional force. One of the permanent seats on the UN Security Council is occupied by China and it has influence well beyond its own borders.

China is a society undergoing great change. In the 1970s, factions within the leadership of the Communist Party of China (CPC) became acutely aware that economic and social pressures might undermine and destroy their control. For this reason they embarked on reforms which involved loosening economic and social controls in the country while retaining their strong political grip.

By the late 1970s, the CPC had largely organised the provision of basic housing, health, food supplies, clothing etc. to the population. However, the people were now ready to demand a standard of living beyond the basics. If this was not forthcoming then it was feared that discontent would develop and threaten the leadership role of the CPC. The Chinese economy therefore had to be modernised in such a way that political control was maintained.

THE COMMUNIST PARTY

The Communist Party gained popular support by curbing inflation, restoring the economy and rebuilding many war-damaged industrial factories. The authority of the Party reached into every part of Chinese life. The Party maintained its strong control by having strong military forces, a government that reacted to directions from the Party and many Communist Party members in organisations such as the workplace.

The Communist Party dominates every level of government and administration. Every key post is filled by Communist Party members, who decide who should get all other jobs. Although in theory the government and the Communist Party are different organisations, in practice they are one and the same. Over the years the Communists have gradually removed all opposition to their policies. Mao Zedong was responsible for various purges of people who showed any signs of disagreeing with his policies. In the 1950s and 1960s opponents and critics of the system simply vanished into prisons or forced labour camps. Often the people who disappeared included some who had been former officials of the Communist Party or high-ranking military officers.

Mao Zedong did not accept criticism of his government and its policies. Any criticism was viewed as 'counter-revolution'. Under his leadership the Communist Party played a dominant role in every aspect of people's lives. It controlled their friendships, their leisure activities and even the number of children they had!

By the time of his death in 1976 Mao had become a 'God' in the eyes of the Chinese people. In fact they were probably very frightened of what the future might hold because Mao had been such a dominant influence on their lives.

DENG'S CHINA

Deng Xiaoping ruled China from 1978 until his death in 1997. While Mao's slogan was 'Serve the People', Deng's was 'To get rich is glorious'. He encouraged people to run their own businesses and to enjoy the profits of their work. In the countryside he ended the commune system whereby everyone worked for each other in their village and replaced it with the household responsibility system. Under this sys-

tem peasants were allowed to have their own land and were encouraged to sell their products and animals. His vision was to transform China from a backward nation into an industrial giant. He launched the Four Modernisations which brought wealth and prosperity to China by encouraging the countries of the West to invest in China (see pages 123 – 126) and also ended China's isolation.

The Communist ideology of total state control of industry and agriculture was replaced with a more free enterprise, capitalist system. Deng created a system where market forces mixed with socialism to create 'socialism with Chinese characteristics'.

While overall living standards have improved, not all Chinese citizens have been part of this prosperity. There are now great differences between rich and poor in the new China. (See pages 127 and 131.)

In the political field, Deng will not be remembered for his reforms. He ensured that China would remain a one-party totalitarian state. In 1989 he ordered troops to open fire on unarmed protesters in Beijing's Tiananmen Square.

Tiananmen Square in more peaceful times. It was the centre of 'democracy' protests in 1989 which were quelled by the army intervening.

CHAPTER 15

China's economy

The economic policies carried out by Deng Xiaoping have been continued by his successors, Jiang Zemin and Hu Jintao. His economic reforms, such as the 'Four Modernisations' and the 'Great Leap Outwards', transformed China's industry and agriculture and opened up strong economic links with other countries.

The economy of China is the second largest in the world as measured by purchasing power parity (PPP), with a Gross Domestic Product (GDP) of US $8.092 trillion. (The PPP measures how much a currency can buy in terms of an international measure, usually dollars, since goods and services have different prices in different countries.) However, China's huge population of 1.3 billion results in a relatively low per capita income of $6,193 at PPP. As of 2005, China is regarded as the fastest-growing major economy in the world.

Since 1978 the People's Republic of China (PRC) government has been reforming its economy from a Soviet-style centrally planned economy to a more market-oriented economy. This is being done within a rigid political framework controlled by the Communist Party of China. It is called 'Socialism with Chinese characteristics' and is one type of mixed economy.

To this end the authorities have switched to a system of household responsibility in agriculture in place of the old collectivisation. They have increased the authority of local officials and factory managers in industry. They have also encouraged the growth of the private sector where they have permitted a wide variety of small-scale enterprises in services and light manufacturing. Furthermore, they have opened the economy to increased foreign trade and foreign investment. The government has emphasised raising personal income and consumption and introducing new management systems to help increase productivity. It has also focused on foreign trade as a major vehicle for economic growth. The result has been a massive rise in GDP since 1978. (See Figure 15.2.)

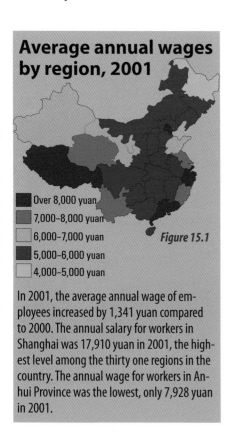

Average annual wages by region, 2001

- Over 8,000 yuan
- 7,000–8,000 yuan
- 6,000–7,000 yuan
- 5,000–6,000 yuan
- 4,000–5,000 yuan

Figure 15.1

In 2001, the average annual wage of employees increased by 1,341 yuan compared to 2000. The annual salary for workers in Shanghai was 17,910 yuan in 2001, the highest level among the thirty one regions in the country. The annual wage for workers in Anhui Province was the lowest, only 7,928 yuan in 2001.

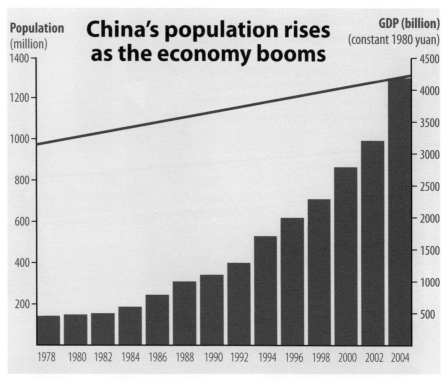

Figure 15.2

CHINA'S BOOMING ECONOMY

The number of mobile phone users in China continues to expand at over 3 million new subscribers per month, reaching 372.8 million at the end of August 2005. In July 2005, China reported 368 million users, meaning the figure increased by 4.8 million during August. There were 342.3 million fixed-line telephone users in China at the end of August 2005.

Retail sales

According to China's World Trade Organisation commitment, the retail market has been fully opened to foreign retailers since 11 December, 2004. All previous limitations on the location and number of outlets have been lifted. Official statistics show that 302 foreign retailers with 3,903 outlets have been approved to run businesses in China.

China's retail sales pick up pace–2004

China's retail sales grew at their fastest pace in five months during October 2004, driven by demand for clothes, cosmetics and computers.

Rising wages are helping consumer demand at a time when the government is trying to rebalance the economy and ensure that its boom is sustainable.

Foreign companies such as the US giant Wal-Mart and Carrefour, from France have opened stores in China and are planning on increasing their presence in one of the world's biggest and fastest growing markets.

According to the national statistical office, sales of food, clothes and household merchandise all rose more than 18% in October. Car sales increased by 2.1%, while sales of jewellery and precious metals jumped 25%.

With increasing concern that China's economy was heading for trouble following spectacular growth, the government has limited investment and lending, and last month raised interest rates for the first time in nine years.

RETAIL SALES ($billion)

481 — 2002
329 — 1997

1997   2002

Figure 15.3

GM to boost China car production

The world's biggest car maker, General Motors, says it plans to invest more than $3 billion and double its capacity in China over the next three years. This means that it will make 1.3 million vehicles a year, against Volkswagen's expansion target of 1.6 million.

China is the fastest growing vehicle market in the world. Virtually the whole of Shanghai's taxi fleet is made up of locally built Volkswagen saloons. Nevertheless, General Motors—the top manufacturer worldwide but behind VW in China—also holds a substantial place in the market. Its much bulkier locally made Buicks are favoured by officials and executives.

In April 2005, China's car production and sales figures slackened, partly because of government curbs on credit.

Car Production (000)

1,090 — 2002
400 — 1997

1997   2002

Figure 15.4

SUMMARY OF THE CHANGING CHINESE ECONOMY

1949: When the People's Republic of China (PRC) was established, peasants seized property and killed landlords. Nearly half of China's arable land was distributed to poor peasants.

1950–1957: Agriculture was collectivised and private property was abolished. The government set quotas for how much grain peasants could keep and fixed low prices for the state portion. In 1953 the First Five-Year Plan was adopted, with an emphasis on heavy industry, especially steel.

1958–1960: In an effort to create steel that would speed China's industrialisation, people melted woks, tools, and bed frames in backyard furnaces, but the steel they produced was useless. Some farmers over-reported farm output and the state took grain based on false figures, using it to pay off Soviet debt and to feed the population in the cities. China's economy did not advance, and 30 million people starved to death.

1961–1965: Mao left the government in the hands of pragmatists after his disastrous Great Leap Forward, and they initiated programmes of careful economic growth which worked. China became increasingly prosperous.

1966–1976: The Cultural Revolution was a time of intense internal confusion and isolation from the rest of the world. The economy was in a shambles as all economic pragmatists were purged from the government.

1977–1979: Deng Xiaoping wrested power from Hua Guofeng and by 1978 had outlined an ambitious programme for economic reform, including dismantling the communes and allowing peasants to produce food for private sale. This 'household responsibility system,' produced bumper crops. An open-door trade and investment policy was introduced.

1980–1984: Special Economic Zones (SEZs) allowed China to accept foreign capital and adopt foreign technologies in controlled phases. Massive construction projects and high wages lured people from all over China to the SEZs. In the countryside, the first markets in decades opened to sell surplus produce. Small factories made goods that were in short supply, fuelling the national economy.

1985–1987: State-owned factories were inefficient and were heavily subsidised by central government. Agricultural output was exploited to support the failing state-owned enterprises (SOEs), reducing profits for farmers. Rural unemployment increased as factories could not absorb the people who had been freed from collective farming. The economy entered a period of high speed growth, with high inflation and corruption.

1988–1989: Workers in SOEs, used to an 'iron rice bowl' of jobs, housing, and benefits for life, were encouraged to become entrepreneurs, but few dared. Workers watched inflation eat into their fixed wages and became angered by government profiteering and corruption.

1990–1991: The Shanghai Stock Exchange was allowed to open.

1992–1996: Deng pushed SEZs to accelerate their reforms. China's economy boomed, yet problems mounted. Urban SOEs were losing money and draining capital from the state budget. Foreign companies did not invest inland, creating a large disparity in income between coastal regions and the rest of China. Millions were unemployed, and village factories often could not pay their workers.

1997: On 1 July Hong Kong was handed back to China after 150 years of British colonial rule. Beijing inherited one of the world's most vibrant capitalist economies and an international financial centre. In September Jiang Zemin consolidated his power following Deng Xiaoping's death. The Party began to focus on reform of SOEs through mergers, acquisitions, bankruptcies, and share issues.

1998–2000: By 1999, with 1.25 billion people and a GDP of $3,800 per capita, China's was the fastest growing economy in the world, and also the second largest after the US. Nevertheless, the country remained poor, lacking the monetary and fiscal controls to manage its vast economy. The government turned to banks to provide failing SOEs with loans, but they were not repaid. The banking system was threatened.

2001–2003: After China joined the WTO (World Trade Organisation), foreign investment surged to a record high. Strong growth masked internal disparities between cities and rural areas, coastal and interior regions. Cuts in tariffs and changes in rules streamlined business, but the huge state-owned sector remained deeply troubled and extremely difficult to reform. In 2003 the spread of the deadly SARS virus had a severe impact on China's economy.

TENTH FIVE-YEAR PLAN (2001–2005)

This Five-Year Plan put China on a fast track to a free market economy. The FYP called for a number of economic initiatives. For example

- accelerating the pace of technological and scientific development,

- creating a better means of income distribution,

- promoting rural development and water conservation.

To help slow the rapid economic growth seen in 2004, Beijing reduced its spending on infrastructure in 2005, while continuing to focus on poverty relief through rural tax reform. Entry into the World Trade Organisation helped to strengthen China's ability to maintain strong growth rates but at the same time put additional pressure on strong political controls and growing market influences. China has benefited from a huge expansion in computer Internet use, with 94 million users at the end of 2004. Foreign investment remains a strong element in China's remarkable economic growth. Shortages of electrical power and raw materials might affect industrial output in 2005. More power generating capacity is scheduled to come on line in 2006.

ELEVENTH FIVE-YEAR PLAN

In 2005, China started to compile its eleventh Five-year Plan (2006–2010) for social and economic development. The Plan should address development problems, especially in the rural and western areas as well as tackling the major issues: economic growth pattern, industrial structure, balanced development between urban and rural areas and different regions, resources and eco-environment protection, talents and sci-tech education, opening up society. The aim is to enhance economic strength, change growth patterns, optimise industrial structure, improve the public service system, strengthen the capability for sustainable development, and accelerate reform and opening up so as to bring about sustained, fast and sound development of the national economy and the overall progress of society.

Adapted from *People's Daily Online*

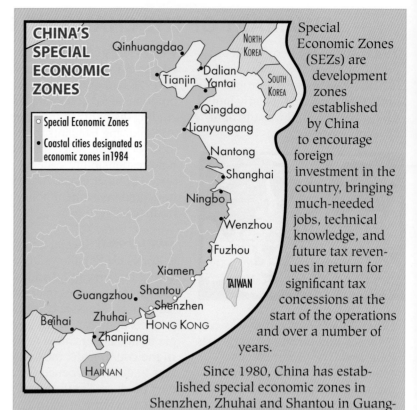

Special Economic Zones (SEZs) are development zones established by China to encourage foreign investment in the country, bringing much-needed jobs, technical knowledge, and future tax revenues in return for significant tax concessions at the start of the operations and over a number of years.

Since 1980, China has established special economic zones in Shenzhen, Zhuhai and Shantou in Guangdong Province and Xiamen in Fujian Province, and has designated the entire province of Hainan a special economic zone.

In 1984, China further opened fourteen coastal cities—Dalian, Qinhuangdao, Tianjin, Yantai, Qingdao, Lianyungang, Nantong, Shanghai, Ningbo, Wenzhou, Fuzhou, Guangzhou, Zhanjiang and Beihai—to overseas investment.

By 2000 the SEZs had achieved what they had set out to do, namely to pilot the market-oriented reform and to open China up to the outside world. They have therefore accumulated a wealth of experience and built up a good investment environment which will be useful for their future development.

Instead of turning to special policies and aid from central government as before, Yu Youjun, Mayor of Shenzhen, said that the SEZs should look into how to create more reforms and to open up further. He added that "it constitutes a new mission for the SEZs."

After more than two decades of growth, in 2005 Shenzhen recorded 16% of China's total imports and exports and generated more than 80 billion yuan (about US $9.63 billion) in taxes. It also returned some 50 billion yuan (about US $6.02 billion) to the State.

Nevertheless, the development of SEZs is not balanced. A few SEZs, such as Hainan island province, have lagged behind other open cities in the Zhujiang (Pearl) River Delta and Yangtze River Delta areas, because of various factors. The reality has prompted Hainan to readjust its plan and define a new objective for future development.

"The Hainan SEZ is an agricultural province, a province for farmers," said Wang Qishan, secretary of the Hainan Provincial Committee of the Communist Party of China (CPC). "It will be turned into an all-season lush green garden as well as a scenic tourist resort in China."

GROWTH OF THE PRIVATE SECTOR

Private sector grows

September 2005

China is not a member of the OECD—a group of the world's richest developed nations—but last week the Paris-based organisation published its first report on a country which has been transformed within a quarter of a century from having a struggling peasant economy to being an industrial giant.

It already accounts for 6% of world exports and its potential to supply the globe with low cost manufactured goods has caused tensions in the global trading system, for example by the recent 'bra wars' row. The OECD said that China's share was on course to rise to 10% by 2010, by which time it would overtake the US.

The centre of Shanghai is dominated by skyscrapers housing much of the private industry driving the Chinese economy

Despite twenty five years of gross domestic product (GDP) growth at an annual rate of more than 9%, China is not expected to slow in the near future. The OECD predicted that the world's most populous nation would overtake Britain, France and Italy to become the world's fourth largest economy within five years.

Nevertheless, the OECD also identified areas which will have to be reformed if Beijing is to complete the transition from a centrally planned economy. These include strengthening the financial system, further steps to allow the currency to float freely and measures to reduce inequality.

Agreeing with a recent report from the United Nations, the OECD said there was evidence of a growing gulf between urban and rural China and between rich and poor on the eastern seaboard. "Although economic dynamism has helped reduce the number living in absolute poverty, income levels are still low and inequality is on the rise, not only between the cities and rural regions, but also within the more prosperous coastal provinces," the OECD said.

Some of the biggest problems have been in the environment and health. According to the UN and the OECD, China's ability to meet the Millennium Development Goal of cutting infant mortality by two-thirds is being hampered by unequal access to health care.

However, the state is no longer the main force for change. The OECD noted that as a result of "profound shifts in government policies, the private sector is now driving China's remarkable economic growth". Well over half of China's GDP was produced by privately controlled enterprises, it added, but more needed to be done to improve the business environment.

Adapted from *Guardian Newspapers 2005*

MADE IN CHINA
China's exports ($billion)
Source: World Bank

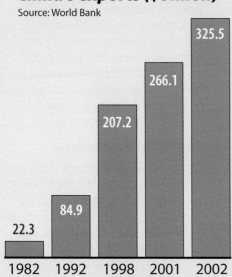

1982	22.3
1992	84.9
1998	207.2
2001	266.1
2002	325.5

Figure 15.5

Chinese exports surged more than 50% to $325 billion (£171 billion) in the five years up to 2002. Furthermore, they are accelerating, currently growing 20% year-on-year.

monday tuesday wednesday thursday friday saturday sunday

In seven days in 2004:

■ Korea's INI Steel Company launched a $500 million steel project in the Dalian development zone;

■ France's Saint Gobain invested another $70 million in one of its existing glass production lines;

■ Germany's Siemens opened its fortieth office in China to develop high-end software applications in Nanjing, and warned that it could shift thousands of jobs from Europe and America to China;

■ Finnish paper giant Stora Enso invested $1.6 billion in a pulp-paper project in South China.

monday tuesday wednesday thursday friday saturday sunday

WHAT MAKES CHINA SPECIAL ?

The obvious answer is that it is big, with 1.3 billion people and a $1.2 trillion economy. Its middle class is growing rapidly, domestic consumption is booming and the growth of its manufacturing sector is nothing if not spectacular.

"We set up our factories in China to export, but it is all consumed in the country itself," reported Swedish engineering group ABB's President Dinesh Paliwal.

Trouble ahead?

However, China's cost advantages are slowly eroding. On the eastern seaboard, the cost of people, property and other assets is rising fast. "In Shanghai the price of a good engineer is the same as in Slovakia," says Mr Paliwal. This means that if investors hope to compete on cost, they have to move inland, well away from the coast, according to Victor Chu, who runs Hong Kong-based First Eastern Investment Group.

There are other long-term worries, such as the stability of China's banking system, and whether the country can generate enough energy to sustain its economic boom.

Today, though, the biggest headache for investors is China's currency. For decades, the yuan has been pegged at a low rate to the US dollar. This has created stability, but has also acted as an export subsidy, creating huge trade imbalances. Washington is urging Beijing to float the yuan. Some Chinese manufacturers, who depend on cheap imports of components and raw materials, agree. Already "we see a massive inflow of foreign currency into China in anticipation of a floating exchange rate policy," says Professor Fu Jun of Beijing University, who is considered to be close to the Chinese leadership.

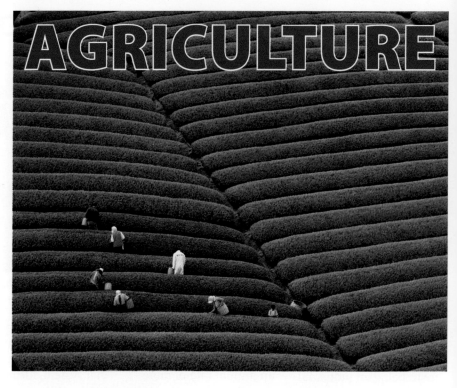

AGRICULTURE

Summary of the past

In 1949, agriculture was struggling. Between 1950 and 1953, the Chinese government carried out a wide-ranging programme of land reform in the rural areas. Peasants with little or no land were given land of their own, giving them great enthusiasm for producing crops etc. The period of the First Five-Year Plan (1953–57) was the first 'golden time' for China's agricultural development.

From 1958 to 1978, China's agriculture developed slowly. During this period agriculture was controlled from the centre—collective or commune agriculture. It was effective but inefficient. As a result, there was little enthusiasm from the farmers.

In 1978, China introduced the household responsibility system, linking income to what was grown. Contracting land out to peasants gave them increased enthusiasm to farm. In 1985, a second reform was carried out—basically the introduction of the market economy in agriculture. The farmers now had control over the land and what they grew, which in turn controlled the price they could get for the goods—supply and demand.

The responsibility system led to many smaller farmers losing their land and becoming poorer. Within the rural areas there is a noticeable divide between the comparatively few successful farmers and the remainder. Overall the rural areas remain poorer than the urban areas. (See Table 15.1.)

Per capita disposable income for urban and rural residents ($)		
	Urban	**Rural**
1997	620	250
2002	964	290

Table 15.1 Source: Official Statistics 2003

In 1999, China's agricultural production continued to develop and, as a result, the chronic shortage of major agricultural products was finally overcome. The problem of shortages of food which had troubled Chinese peasants for hundreds of years had been solved at last.

Township Enterprises

China's town and village enterprises have developed on the basis of the handicrafts industry and the processing of agricultural products and by-products. They have flourished since 1978, becoming the mainstays of the rural economy. Now there are more than 20 million township enterprises in China with 125 million employees. Township enterprises are involved in industry, agriculture, and transportation, along with the building, commerce, and catering trades. They produce a variety of goods, including products needed in agriculture, daily necessities, foodstuffs, sideline products and light industrial materials. Many of these products are exported.

Living standards in the countryside are improving for many. The story below shows how the opening up of markets has led to opportunities for farmers to diversify.

AMERICAN FARMER FULFILS HIS DREAM IN CHINA

Jesse Long, a 62-year-old American farmer who has been growing vegetables in China for thirteen years, usually says 'no' to any interviews with journalists. Since the horticultural farm was built in 1992, Jesse Long has moved it three times to keep pace with the economic and social development in Shanghai, an economic powerhouse in eastern China. The Pudong New Area in Shanghai has grown from being a tract of farmland into one of the most dynamic regions in China. Nevertheless, the municipal government has pledged to boost modern agriculture, which is characterised by environmental protection and recreation.

Among hundreds of vegetables on Jesse Long's farm, is lettuce which is popular with foreigners. "In the eyes of the Chinese, lettuce is only another type of vegetable, yet in the eyes of westerners, it is a big variety," Tang, Long's wife, said, adding, "Even though I have lived with an American for so many years, I still fail to have a thorough understanding lettuce." All of the 300–400 tons of vegetables on Long's farm are ordered by high-class hotels across China every year for cooking western-style food.

Adapted from: www.chinaview.cn 2005

FOREIGN INVESTMENT IN CHINA

The World Trade Organisation (WTO) is the policeman of global trade. Every member must abide by its rulings, so when the USA and the European Union are in dispute over GM foods, it is the WTO which acts as judge and jury. China was officially admitted to the World Trade Organisation in 2001 after a fifteen-year battle.

Impact on China

China hopes that WTO membership will help its commitment to economic reform which has led to a rapid economic expansion in the past twenty years and an explosion of foreign investment. It has been suggested that opening up China's markets will benefit the whole world.

However, some other countries, particularly in Asia, fear that China may take away export markets as it expands its trade. Also, developing countries fear that China's increased access to important global markets will have disastrous consequences. They are concerned that Chinese goods will capture Western markets from them, especially in areas such as textiles and footwear.

In the next few years, as China lowers its import tariffs and opens up once highly protected sectors such as banking and telecommunications, Chinese consumers are likely to see many more products entering their market and at lower prices.

However, giving greater access to foreign business will also have some serious knock-on effects for China's state-run heavy industries and family-run farms, which are unlikely to be able to stand up against faster, more efficient foreign competitors. One immediate outcome of entry to the WTO has been the rapid increase in the number of Chinese citizens travelling abroad.

Some argue that in the long term, foreign investment and a more direct link with the international community can only bring more opportunities for China. Other economists, though, warn of millions of job losses as state firms and agricultural enterprises face up to foreign competition. The result could be widespread protests and social unrest.

Joint ventures occur when two or more companies join together to form a new company in which they share all expenses. Below is an example of one such joint venture in China in 2005.

GM TO OPEN TWO NEW CHINESE PLANTS

General Motors' Chinese joint venture involves taking over a disused car factory in the city of Qingdao to help meet rising demand for small-sized vehicles. GM said that SAIC-GM-Wuling Automobile would be able to make up to 70,000 cars and trucks a year at the plant on the eastern coast north of Shanghai.

GM also announced that it is going to spend $387 million (£213 million) building a new engine plant in China. The engine facility is being constructed at GM's main Chinese base at Liuzhou, in the Guangxi region in the south-west of the country. When it opens in 2007, it will be able to make 300,000 engines a year.

SAIC-GM-Wuling Automobile, in which GM has a 34% stake, specialises in small-sized cars, trucks and minivans. It currently has a car making capacity of 300,000 vehicles a year and is said to be struggling to keep up with demand. Its sales rose 30.5% in 2004. Its minitrucks and minivans are badged up as Wuling, while its small car is called the Chevrolet Swift, better known in some overseas markets as the Matiz.

"Mini-vehicles account for more than 25% of all vehicles sold in China and remain one of the fastest growing market segments," said Kevin Wale, President and Managing Director of the GM China Group.

CHAPTER 16

Social and economic issues in China

China's economic reforms have improved the lives of millions of people. However, corruption, migration, crime, inequalities, housing and health issues, and unemployment have also become part of the lives of just as many. These economic and social problems are often interlinked.

ENVIRONMENTAL ISSUES

China's Big, Dirty Secret

China's economic growth is taking a heavy toll on the environment and public health. The country is fast becoming an ecological wasteland, home to some of the world's smoggiest cities as well as experiencing rampant water shortages, soil erosion, and acid rain. China's economic growth is also taking a toll on public health with a dramatic rise in respiratory diseases in recent years.

Chinese officials have acknowledged a problem in the past, but quickly termed it a necessary side effect of rapid industrialisation and catch-up economic growth, not unlike what Japan experienced in the 1960s. What's more, China is now a net importer of oil and relies heavily on coal, much of it dirty and high in sulphur, for about 70% of its domestic energy needs. Unless China can secure significantly more oil supplies from abroad and increase cleaner domestic energy sources such as nuclear power and hydroelectric plants, Chinese President Hu Jintao and his Communist colleagues will face a policy dilemma.

The Vice Director of China's State Environmental Protection Admin-

Hong Kong is partially obscured by smog which comes mainly from factories on the Chinese mainland.

istration (SEPA), Pan Yue, has announced the suspension of thirty large projects which have failed to meet environmental standards. The list includes twenty six hydroelectric power stations. However, SEPA has little authority and must be given some soon—but that is not likely to happen.

China leads the world in sulphur dioxide emissions, has a massive acid rain problem, and contains more than a dozen of the most polluted cities on earth. Smog is a public health risk in many Chinese cities with Beijing, Shenyang and Xian ranking among the world's top ten polluted cities. One World Bank study estimated that environmental damage costs China some $170 billion a year in lost productivity and associated health care.

It is not unusual to see Beijing covered in smog as shown in this photo

Pollution in Beijing

Along with Mexico City, Beijing shares the distinction of being the world's most polluted capital. Part of the problem for Beijing is its geographical situation. It is in a basin surrounded by hills, over a hundred kilometres from the coast and at the mercy of dust-filled winds from the Mongolian planes. Yet the city is also a microcosm of the environmental challenges facing China.

In Beijing's streets the sources of pollution are not hard to spot. Every day, 35-year-old Mr Wang pedals his cycle cart through the narrow lanes of Beijing's old residential districts. Behind him is a pitch black cargo—briquettes of coal for the area's old courtyard houses. This is the traditional fuel for heating and cooking in many Chinese cities. It is low grade and high in sulphur. When burned, it coats surrounding surfaces with a noxious grey dust. China's national dependence on coal, which is still the source of some 75% of its energy, is seen as a key cause of the country's environmental problems.

However, Beijing has plans to phase out coal use, making people like Mr Wang a thing of the past. "We're changing the energy structure of the whole city," says environment official Li Tiejun adamantly. "First we tackled the small food stoves; now, in just two years, almost the whole catering industry has gone over to natural gas or electricity, and all small and medium sized industrial boilers are using clean fuels." Thousands of homes are also being converted to natural gas, for which the World Bank is providing assistance.

New measures

One source of hope may, ironically, be the sheer scale of China's problems. After twenty years of uncontrolled economic development, officials and citizens alike are finding it hard to ignore the chronic air pollution. Respiratory diseases have become one of the country's biggest health risks. Furthermore, there are billions of dollars of crop losses each year. Clean-up measures are now being announced thick and fast. In Beijing, after years of apparent inaction, a total ban on leaded petrol for cars was implemented within the space of just six months. The authorities are also taking action against polluting factories. Some have been closed, and others were under threat if they did not cut pollution by the end of 2005.

Jobs at risk

Many environmentalists agree that China now has some of the toughest environmental laws seen in any country, but putting them into practice nationwide is a major challenge. Even in Beijing, officials admit it would be difficult to close down the massive Capital Iron and Steelworks which belches out smoke in the city's western suburbs. This one-time icon of China's socialist industrialisation has been told to cut back on production. However, it retains significant political backing, and, perhaps crucially, it provides employment for about 40,000 people.

"The environmental protection bureaux know what they should do—the problem for them is the social issues," says Patrik Lund, North China Director for the environmental consultancy ERM. "Basically they have the choice of putting all the people on the street or letting the pollution continue."

Motor industry

There are other economic pressures on environmental policy. Despite all the measures to tackle car pollution in cities like Beijing, the government has made it quite clear that it sees the expansion of the motor industry as a pillar of China's economic development. Furthermore, the environmental officials cannot hold back the ambition of more and more Chinese people to own a car. Beijing environmental official Li Teijun believes the solution is to prevent excessive car use. He is establishing bus-only pedestrian zones and putting up parking fees. He hopes to persuade people to leave their cars in the suburbs and take the bus into town.

Consumerism or clean air?

Developments in public transport cannot compete with an explosion in car ownership. In Beijing alone, an extra 100,000 vehicles come onto the streets each year. China's entry into the World Trade Organisation is expected to boost demand further by bringing cheaper car prices. It is this tension between environmental concerns and the desire of China's vast population for Western-style consumer comfort which may ultimately determine whether blue skies really do return to the nation's cities.

China's Health in Figures

Total population		1,311,709,000
GDP per capita ($) (2002)		4,460
Total health expenditure per capita ($) (2002)		261
Total health expenditure as % of GDP (2002)		5.8

	Male	Female
Life expectancy at birth (years)	70.0	73.0
Healthy life expectancy at birth (years) (2002)	63.1	65.2
Child mortality (per 1000)	32	43
Adult mortality (per 1000)	164	103

Table 16.1 Figures are for 2003 unless indicated. Source: *The World Health Report 2005*

CHINA'S AILING HEALTH CARE

The results of a survey released by China's Health Ministry in 2004 underlined the problems facing the country's health care system and what many see as a pressing need for reform. The investigation found that 36% of patients in cities and 39% in the countryside did not go to see the doctor because they were unable to afford medical treatment. Nearly 28% of those admitted to hospital left because of economic difficulties.

One commentator noted that before the reforms "the government gave people low incomes but it looked after them from the cradle to the grave". However, more than a decade down the road of market reform, "the rich aren't satisfied with the medical care offered by the government because it's too inefficient, while the poor can't even afford it".

Chinese state media said that the study was conducted in late 2003 among more than 190,000 urban and rural residents. It found that the cost of medical treatment had increased by 14% annually between 1993 and 2003, a rate far faster than the rise in people's incomes.

Health officials quoted in the media said a major factor was the practice by doctors of unnecessarily prescribing expensive medicines in order to increase hospital revenues. "I think it's true that doctors take 'red envelopes' (bribes) or they prescribe expensive medicines because

their incomes are so low," admitted Yu Qiusheng, a doctor at a Shanghai hospital which combines Chinese and Western medicine. She said a doctor's average basic salary was about $360 a month.

All this adds up to the fact that even among urban Chinese, who benefit from government-run medical insurance schemes, the cost of medical care is a critical issue.

Pilot reforms

These problems mean that China is being forced to experiment with various reform schemes. One such scheme is in Shanghai, where two hospitals are being established with foreign ventures taking a majority shareholding. Also, 200 out of the city's 600 hospitals are reported to

have entered into cooperation arrangements with foreign hospitals or foreign investment capital.

Faced with what they call an increasingly 'bipolar society,' economists such as Wang Liang advocate a course of health care reform. This would include concentrating government spending on fewer hospitals, which would be run as public services rather than for profit. It would further invole contracting out the administration of hospitals, while retaining the government's supervisory role.

However, the biggest problem is that most rural Chinese have no access to medical facilities or health insurance. State media reports say that in the countryside the cost of an average in-patient hospital treatment is about $270, compared with the average rural income of $315. In poorer inland areas of central and north-western China, that ratio is even more extreme. Many families are plunged into poverty by illness.

China is currently experimenting with pilot rural health insurance schemes under which farmers pay an annual $1.20, which is then matched by local and central governments. In one pilot area in eastern China's Anhui province, health officials told the BBC that more than 90% of local farmers had signed up to the scheme. The government says it plans to extend the scheme nationwide by 2010.

China needs more nurses

China needs at least 2.2 million well-trained nurses to care for its 11 million bedridden elderly, but it presently has only 1 million carers, the majority of whom are laid-off workers or rural women who have never been trained properly.

China presently has 130 million people aged over 60, including 94 million over 65. It is estimated that by the middle of this century, there will be more than 400 million people aged over 65 and at least 100 million aged 80 or older. Moreover, most nurses are working in big cities; the rural and western regions are in desperate need of nurses.

Adapted from www.chinaview.cn (2005)

The People's Republic of China

URBAN AND RURAL INEQUALITIES

Economic reforms have led to a widening gap between rich and poor, and urban and rural in China.

The wealth gap between China's urban and rural citizens is now one of the largest in the world. A new survey by the Chinese Academy of Social Sciences found that in 2002 urban residents earned three times more than their rural counterparts. The man in charge of the study, Li Shi, says that even the new figures do not paint a true picture of the disparity, which he claims is even wider.

Farmers pay their own health care and education costs, which means that their real incomes are one-sixth of those of China's urban residents. An academic quoted by the official Xinhua news agency also blamed policies which are biased against heavy taxation.

China's leaders are conscious of the potential for discontent in the countryside. They recently announced that they will spend $18 billion raising farmers' incomes.

China targets rural reform

One of the crucial tasks faced by China's new leadership is to try to narrow this gap as they push ahead with rural reforms. Large numbers of China's 900 million-strong rural population have an average annual income of 2,200 yuan ($267) and more than 30 million farmers live below the official poverty line.

China's Prime Minister, Wen Jiabao, made it clear in 2004 that he regarded closing the gap as a key priority.

"If we set the benchmark of the poverty line with an increase of 200 yuan then the total poor population would be 90 million".

While living standards have risen in absolute terms in China's overcrowded countryside, disposable incomes are going up half as fast as in urban areas. Nevertheless, improvements are taking place.

Rose Acock is a British woman who runs the Development Organisation of Rural Sichuan, a small development charity in an impoverished mountainous area of south-western China. In the last seven years, she said, many villages which previously were without electricity, have been connected. One of the most important effects is to give rural dwellers a window, through television, on what is happening in other areas of China.

"They do see it on television and they know that a lot of people are doing a lot better and they would like to improve their lot, but they have not got the opportunities. Another important advance is that many villages in the area are now accessible by road, making it much easier for farmers to get their crops to market. However, in the remote villages, some of the children have to walk for over an hour to get to school and many are not in school."

The Chinese media has raised a whole raft of serious issues surrounding rural reform. These include the question of who pays for rural education, how to trim local bureaucracies, the problem of credit for non-agricultural businesses, and the difficulty that rural residents face trying to survive economically when they migrate to the cities for work.

Economic migrants

More than 100 million people have abandoned the poor countryside, with 30 million alone heading to the urban area along the Pearl River Delta, mostly to find low level factory jobs. They do so illegally. China uses a residential permit system (the hukou) to keep people in their place of residence.

Encouraging farmers to work in cities, increasing farmers' incomes, and improving farmers' living conditions are policies adopted by central government to solve farmers' problems. Time has proved that these policies are effective. How-

A Chinese migrant family share a happy moment in Beijing in 2003. China is taking steps to speed up the relaxing of the official 'hukou', or household registration system. In the past decade, an estimated 100 million rural residents have sought jobs in the cities, but because of their rural 'hukou' they are denied equal access to jobs, welfare and legal protection.

ever, these migrant workers are not treated well in the cities because of the hukou.

What is the hukou?

The hukou is a system of permits devised in the late 1950s as China adopted Communist central planning. The permits link every Chinese citizen to a home district, outside which they have few rights to welfare benefits, medical care or schooling.

Wang Hailong sells newspapers on the streets of Chongqing. He is an illegal migrant worker who moved to the industrial city seven years ago to escape the poverty of the countryside and share in China's economic boom.

"The police do hassle us rather than the city newspaper sellers, making us move on from our pitches," says Mr Wang, who has held temporary jobs on construction sites and in factories. He is one of a 'floating population' of migrants, whom the Chinese authorities have estimated number at least 100 million.

In November 2005 the Chinese state media announced that the residency permit Hukou system would be abolished in eleven of China's twenty three provinces. This would be the first step in ending the discrimination against rural residents. Significantly, the provinces chosen are mainly along the developed eastern coast which needs an influx of labour from poor western regions. Neither of China's two biggest cities, Beijing and Shanghai, are included and therefore there has been a cautious reaction to the proposed reforms. The intention is that local government, would retain administrative control over their populations.

China's entry to the World Trade Organisation and its present economic growth are important factors in convincing the Chinese government that it should eventually scrap the Hukou system.

The Hukou: a Case Study

Workers at Shenzhen's Zhufeng Electronics Factory—some of them in their early teens—work 90-hour weeks, more than twice the legal limit, making telephones for export to South Korea. They live in a company dorm: a ten-square-metre room sleeping nine people in eight beds. The only decoration is a tiny wall calendar suspended by telephone wire. When a group launched a strike, a worker from Hubei described what happened: "The boss said, 'If you're not going to work, then get out of here.' We said we'd leave as soon as we got our backpay, and he replied, 'And if I don't pay you, what are you going to do about it?' " Going ahead with the strike, they were denied meals, were rebuffed by the local labour bureau, and eventually were evicted from the dormitory. The worker from Hubei says, "We haven't got our money. Now we have nothing to eat, nowhere to live."

China's migrant workers will have no future and no rights until the government revises the residence permit system to give migrants access to social services.

UNEMPLOYMENT ISSUES

China's soaring economic growth will not stop hundreds of thousands of staff at state-owned firms from losing their jobs in the next few years, the country's state media has reported. According to *China Daily*, the main English-language paper, more than 2,000 state-owned enterprises (SOEs) will go. That, the paper warns, will worsen China's already serious unemployment problem. Almost 8,000 SOEs have already gone bust—although another 159,000 remain in business, the paper said.

China's government is keen to see the back of many more, since their inefficiency often means the goods they make are worth less than the cost of making them. Following the country's entry into the World Trade Organisation—and the resulting increase in imports—the mismatch is likely to get worse.

State benefits for the unemployed are limited in China, remaining little changed from the pre-market economy days when everyone had a job in a state enterprise. That means those forced out of work may end up swelling the numbers flocking from the provinces to China's big cities and often ending up sleeping rough.

The modernisation of China's economy and the opening of its markets have brought wealth, but at the cost of unemployment for many. Over the past decade more than a million people have lost their jobs in Shanghai, as an increasingly competitive market place and government-planned economic restructuring have sounded the death knell for many of the city's old core industries.

The textile industry, once Shanghai's pride, has shrunk most dramatically, with many of its old plants being transferred to inland areas of China, and others closing completely. Many people have lost their jobs. According to Professor Liang Hong of Shanghai's Fudan University, these people, who grew up during China's political turmoil of the 1960s, are a lost generation. "They were assigned jobs in the factories so they didn't have a chance to study more. There are new jobs in Shanghai now, but they're usually for technically skilled workers, and the competition is very intense."

Professor Liang is an adviser to the 40–50 Project, a new employment scheme set up by the Shanghai government which seeks to tackle the problem. As part of the scheme the city government provides tax breaks, financial rewards and loan guarantees to new, labour-intensive private businesses, as long as they hire laid-off workers. The scheme is the first of its kind in China and reflects a growing conviction among Chinese officials that the private sector—and in particular the service sector—has become the main source of job creation.

Early retirement

Mr and Mrs Li tend to their pet birds in the courtyard of their single-room home in a soon-to-be-demolished 1920s Shanghai lane. They have plenty of time to spare. Mr Li, who is in his 60s, was forced to take early retirement from his job as a high school teacher to make way for younger staff when student numbers went down. His wife, who is in her early 50s, was asked to retire from her state-run timber factory at 47 when its business started going badly. Hundreds of thousands of people like Mr and Mrs Li have been pushed into early retirement in an attempt to streamline the workforce. Many are women. Female factory workers are now routinely retired at 50.

Even Shanghai's job creation scheme is only targeted at those under 50. Yet by many standards the Lis are lucky. They receive a basic but adequate pension and medical insurance. Some unemployed workers in Shanghai receive only what is known as the Minimum Living Allowance—currently set at around 280 yuan (£24) a month. In less wealthy parts of China, even this would be a luxury. In many towns,

local governments have struggled to pay pensions, sometimes for months or years at a time.

Protests

The contradictory system of struggling state firms being responsible for paying unemployment benefits to the same workers they have just laid off is clearly breaking down in some parts of the country. Such problems have provoked a series of protests. Up to 50,000 laid-off workers demonstrated in Daqing in north-eastern China, demanding unpaid benefits and pensions. 30,000 workers in another north-eastern town, Liaoyang, staged two weeks of protests against non-payment of wages and official corruption. Young people hope that joining the Communist Party will improve their prospects.

URBAN OVERCROWDING:

A 2005 International Population Conference stated that China's massive wave of urban immigrants represents the greatest danger in the country's struggle to contain the spread of HIV/AIDS. "The growing migrant population in China may be the 'tipping point' in China's battle with the AIDS epidemic," they said.

The growth of urban migration in China since the early 1980s has been phenomenal with census data showing a rise from 11 million in 1982 to more than 79 million in 2000 and an estimated 120 million by 2006.

Research by Yang and his colleagues found that the risk of HIV infection among temporary urban migrants was much higher than for non-migrants. They were four times more likely to have unprotected sex and twice as likely to have used illicit drugs in their lifetime. Urban migrants, mostly males in their late teens, live together either in living quarters provided by employers at their place of work such as construction sites and restaurants, or in camps on the city fringes. These are characterised by poverty, overcrowding and lack of health services.

The number of HIV infected people in China is 840,000 or 0.1% of the population. UNAIDS estimates that if the current trend continues, up to 10 million people could be infected by the end of the decade, creating serious problems for public health, social stability and economic development.

CHINA REVALUES THE YUAN

China has abandoned its currency's relationship to the dollar and revalued the yuan by 2.2%. It now buys more US dollars than before.

Why has China revalued its currency?

China's currency was been fixed at 8.28 yuan to the US dollar for ten years. However, since China joined the World Trade Organisation it has come under increasing pressure to break that link. The US, in particular, has been worried that China's cheap currency gives it an unfair advantage as it sells its goods to Western consumers. Already China has built up a huge trade surplus with the rest of the world, and appears to be able to make things more cheaply than its developing country rivals.

What difference will it make to China?

China's exports will become more expensive as a result of the increased value of its currency. This might slow the rate of growth of its exports, which are the main reason for China's impressive economic growth. A slowdown in economic growth could have serious social consequences in China if it led to higher unemployment. Nevertheless, the relatively small size of the revaluation means it is unlikely to have a huge, immediate economic effect.

EDUCATION

China's public education system, once hailed by the Beijing regime as one of the greatest achievements of the 1949 Revolution, is facing a crisis.

The national government's education budget is mainly spent on urban universities and colleges, rather than on the 204.7 million students attending the country's primary and secondary schools. Since the mid-1990s, the lower tiers of government have been expected to shoulder the lion's share of these education costs using their own locally-raised taxes.

Many areas of regional and rural China, however, have been unable to attract investment and have been hit by the closure of state-owned industries, rising unemployment and falling farmers' incomes. Local governments are crippled by debt and are on the verge of bankruptcy.

According to Zhou Yuxian, an education expert at Beijing Normal University, "The funding gap [on education] between city and country is huge. In some rural areas the average annual spending per child is less than a dollar." In poor counties, education can use up to half of the annual budget, most of it going to pay teachers' salaries. Authorities have responded by neglecting maintenance, employing unqualified teachers on lower rates of pay, increasing class sizes and levying an array of fees. Although education is supposed to be free, parents say they are expected to pay for everything from their children's paper and report cards through to the electricity bill.

The central government's strategy for overcoming the chronic underfunding of education has been in line with its drive to restore the capitalist market in every area of Chinese society. It has encouraged schools to go into business. In 1999, school-run businesses raked in US $15 billion, nearly equal to the state's entire education budget.

Besides assembling toys and producing small handicrafts, schools in rural areas have been known to put children to work in mines, on pig farms and into other forms of intensive and dangerous labour. The results of this policy were exposed to the world when fifty children and four adults were killed in a catastrophic explosion in Fanglin village, Jiangxi province. The children were assembling fireworks in their classroom for a local business, in order to raise money for the school.

In the cities, schools are renting out space. In a case reported by state television, a classroom was let out as a gambling den. Other enterprises operating out of schools include restaurants, taxi fleets and markets.

CHINESE CLOTHES EXPORTS TO THE EU—THE BRA WARS

Millions of textile goods and clothing from China were held in European warehouses, because of a dispute over import quotas. The quotas were introduced in June 2005 after a sharp rise in import volumes, which the EU feared would harm European producers. A deal to unblock the goods was reached on 5 September, during talks between the European Commission and the Chinese government. However, the agreement still needed the approval of the twenty five EU member states.

What was the situation in the warehouses?

In November 2005 about 75 million items of Chinese textile goods were waiting to be let in to the EU. They represented orders which had been fulfilled—but they were not allowed in because China had already exceeded the annual quotas agreed in June.

The global textile industry had been in flux since the beginning of 2005 after a quota system, which had limited worldwide clothing sales for thirty years, was scrapped. The move, part of a global drive towards trade liberalisation, resulted in a huge increase in Chinese clothing exports, with sales of certain items to the EU rising by up to 500%. China's huge manpower and industrial capacity mean it is able to produce large volumes of cheap clothing at much lower prices than producers in Europe.

Some developing countries also found themselves at a disadvantage. However, as part of the rules governing China's entry to the World Trade Organisation, Europe had the right to place temporary limits on textile imports to give European manufacturers time to adapt to the new trading environment.

"Sparrow schools"

Even as schools are hiring out their buildings to businesses, many are plagued by massive overcrowding. A report in the *South China Morning Post* detailed the emergence of 'sparrow' schools, where students are crammed into buildings and play areas far too small for their safety and health.

At the Peoples Road primary school in Guangzhou, the capital of Guangdong province, 820 children are squeezed into two small buildings with a total area of just 1,700 square metres. The only playground is a small basketball court. The students take turns using it to do morning exercises, while the rest of the students stand behind their desks and are instructed to wiggle to disco music. Seven nearby primary schools are even worse off. Children at the Minxingli primary school, for example, do their morning exercises on the pavement.

Of the 323 primary and secondary schools in Guangzhou, 96 are classified as 'sparrow schools', meaning they have an area of less than 2,000 square metres for primary schools and 4,000 square metres for secondary schools. An area of 2,000 square metres is equivalent to a strip of land just 100 metres long and 20 metres wide.

The authorities blame overcrowding in schools on the massive growth of China's urban population. In one of the largest migrations in history, an estimated 120 million people have moved in the last twenty years from China's rural towns and villages to find work in the cities.

Furthermore, China's residency system, which strictly limits the ability of people to move from their place of birth, has meant that many of

The Chinese government allocates most of its education spending to universities and colleges (top photo) while overcrowding is a feature of many primary schools (bottom photo)

those who have moved to the cities have no permanent residency status. With only temporary residence permits, they are not entitled to the services provided by the municipal government, which includes education.

Although Beijing is home to at least 100,000 migrant children ranging in age from seven to fifteen years, the city government has refused to grant legal status to any migrant school. They are at the mercy of officials, who have the power to close schools if their buildings are needed for other purposes—or on any other grounds.

For China's new class of businessmen and managers, the solution to the decline of public education has been to enrol their children in elite private schools or send them overseas to be educated. For the mass of the country's workers and peasants, there are no such options.

ORGANISED CRIME

During Mao's rule China was organised into communes, township units and neighbourhood 'committees.' Such social controls kept organised crime to a minimum. The market reforms introduced in the late 1970s, however, changed China's social structure, allowing new and old forms of organised crime to flourish. The relaxation of governmental controls, the boom atmosphere of the new Special Economic Zones and growing incidents of official corruption have all contributed to rising crime rates.

Chinese authorities are attempting to cope with organised crime groups which have a hand in such activities as illegal gambling, extortion, drug trafficking, gunrunning, smuggling, prostitution, illegal immigration, fraud and the manufacture and sale of pirated goods.

According to official statistics, crimes registered by police for investigation in 1998 rose by 50% during 1999. Gang crimes with Mafia features handled by courts across the country went up seven times, with many involving high-ranking Party and government officials.

This led to the Chinese government introducing a 'strike hard' campaign which focused on three kinds of crimes: gang crimes with Mafia features; violent crimes involving explosives, manslaughter, robbery and kidnapping; and thefts. Theft of motor vehicles and other property accounted for 65% of all the reported criminal offences in 2000.

A government campaign in 2002 to 'wipe out gangs and hooligans' led to the detention of over a dozen gang leaders and their members. The police department has also drafted new regulations on the control of explosives for civilian use.

Greater attention has been given to preventing theft. In this regard, anti-crime specialist Wang Dawei said that prevention is of prime importance. He suggests that more effort should be made to educate the public on safety measures. The dramatic social changes (income inequalities for example) taking place in China are producing a growing disadvantaged population, he said, noting that this is likely to give rise to underground violent gangs engaging in illegal activities.

Many measures have also been introduced to try to prevent crime:

- The Supreme Court is changing the rules to set up juvenile courts across the country to better protect, educate and reform children, as children are becoming an ever-growing number of the country's offenders.

- Central and local governments are investing more in remote mountainous areas to prevent farmers there from growing opium.

CRIME AND LAW

Computer crime

China already has the second biggest Internet-using population in the world, even though only 8% of its people go online. Internet use is growing fast and by 2007 the number of people using broadband in China will probably be greater than the number in the USA. However, China is also a world leader in computer crime. Spam, viruses and the like have recently started to cause big problems in China.

The Chinese government controls where people can access the Net, which sites they can look at, the news they get and the topics for discussion in chat rooms. This rigid control helps to limit the effect of viruses and spam but problems have started to emerge now that some controls are being relaxed.

The only types of e-mail scam that Chinese Internet users do not fall victim to are those that ask for credit card details. Hardly anyone in China has a credit card!

Chinese residents view thirty one criminals being paraded for stealing motorbikes and bicycles in Hangzhou, Zhejiang, south-east China, in 2005. More than a thousand motorbikes and bicycles were recovered by the police from those arrested.

Wealthy crimes

The Chinese government has warned its wealthy citizens about the danger of being kidnapped for ransom. The Ministry for Public Security said that nearly 4,000 people had been kidnapped in the previous year. It added that entrepreneurs, celebrities and students from rich families are the most likely targets.

China's economic and social reforms have created a wealthy new middle class. At the same time crime rates have gone up, a result of growing unemployment and new policies which have enabled people to move around the country freely, making it easier to evade the authorities.

Drugs

China has reported a worsening drugs problem which is said to be costing the country billions of dollars a year. Police officials have reported that 72% of China's 1.05 million registered drug addicts are under the age of 35. Many of the addicts are unemployed, migrant workers or farmers, they said.

According to the Deputy Director of the National Narcotics Control Commission, Luo Feng, the drugs crisis is contributing to the spread of AIDS and social instability in the country. The Xinhua news agency reported that 80% of male addicts are involved in other crime and 80% of female addicts are engaged in prostitution.

Corrupt police

China has fired more than 30,000 police officers not having proper qualifications, according to the state media. Nearly 11,000 others were removed for 'sub-standard work', Xinhua news agency said. The majority of those sacked were public security officials who had been improperly wearing police uniform and collecting fines and fees from the public. Xinhua said some had even committed crimes.

The news agency suggested that many problems stemmed from under-staffing. It said that one police station in north China's Hebei Province had only ten officers to cover 126,000 people. In addition, police in rural areas are often expected to take on more than their official duties, including raising taxes and promoting family planning, Xinhua said.

Last year China fired more than 250 police officers for gambling, drinking on duty, drunk driving and carrying guns off duty. More than 500 police officers were also disciplined for corruption in 2004.

CHAPTER 17

Politics and protest

China functions as a one-party state in which all aspects of social, economic and political life are dominated by the Communist Party of China (CPC). The CPC provides ideas and leadership and oversees the work of the government. The structure of the government is laid out in the Constitution.

THE CONSTITUTION

Since the establishment of the People's Republic of China in 1949 the country has seen four different Constitutions—1954, 1975, 1978 and 1982. The 1982 version of the Constitution was revised in 1993. Apart from outlining the government structure it also "guarantees the fundamental rights of every citizen, including the right to vote and stand for election, the freedoms of speech, of the press, of assembly, of association, of demonstration and of religious belief." It also states that "the People's Republic of China is a socialist state under the people's democratic dictatorship led by the working class and based on the alliance of workers and peasants."

These two extracts appear to contradict each other. The first extract describes "freedoms" and "fundamental rights" guaranteed to every citizen in China, but the second extract uses the phrase "dictatorship led by the working class." The official Chinese interpretation of this is that democracy is practised within the ranks of the people while dictatorship is exercised over the enemies of the people who are the masters of the country. In effect, the people of China can enjoy their wide-ranging "freedoms" and "fundamental rights" within the limits laid down by the CPC. These limits may vary from time to time.

THE PEOPLE'S LIBERATION ARMY (PLA)

The PLA played an important role in the victory of the CPC between 1934 and 1949. It has retained its political significance ever since. It was 4 million strong in the 1970s and is still the largest army in the world with 3 million soldiers. A programme of modernisation has turned it from an ill-equipped peasant force into a well-equipped professional organisation.

However, the PLA is more than a fighting force. It has developed a wide network of businesses. There are 10,000 registered military enterprises producing everything from tanks to toothbrushes. Although originally intended to make the army self-reliant, 70% of the output of PLA-owned enterprises are consumer goods for the civilian market and for export. One PLA division enterprise trades as China North Industries Corporation (Norinco) and makes such diverse products as window glass, contact lenses, motor cycles and buses.

It is reported that the PLA made US $5 billion from its civilian enterprises in 1993. The process of restructuring the Chinese economy has enabled the PLA to become involved in a wide variety of joint venture operations with foreign investors and, it is reported, in several illegal enterprises. In Guangdong, the army owns many hotels, bars, discos etc. as well as illegal brothels and gambling dens.

The vast incomes generated by these enterprises are encouraging corruption on a grand scale. They are also creating a huge divide between the officer corps who are making large fortunes and the low paid ranks. Officers who are involved in business are diverted from studying the art of war. This, along with growing dissatisfaction in the ranks means that the PLA is not as efficient a force as it might be. Public respect for the PLA, which was once held in high regard, is rapidly diminishing.

FORMAL ORGANISATIONAL STRUCTURE IN CHINA

The Chinese political system largely duplicates itself at each level. Each level, on both the Party and the government sides, has a basic organisational structure. Each has a large congress that meets infrequently but is, in theory, the most powerful body; a smaller committee that brings together important people and meets more frequently; and a still smaller committee that brings together the top few people. Theoretically, the larger the body, the more powerful it is. In reality, the opposite is true—the smallest committee is the most important structure. Under these committees, administrative departments actually run the day-to-day affairs of the various Party and government organs.

Organisation at the centre

At the centre, the main CPC organs are, in ascending order of importance, the Party Congress, the Central Committee, the Politburo, and the Politburo Standing Committee.

National Party Congress

Every five years, the Communist Party of China holds a National Congress which has about 1,500 members. These meetings are major Party events. They are like American political Party conventions where members hear speeches, pass resolutions and adopt rules of procedure. In theory, the Party Congress is the highest organ of authority but its large size and the infrequency of its meetings mean that it announces some major decisions and makes them legal rather than deciding important policies. Formally, the Congress serves two functions: to approve changes to the Party Constitution and to elect a Central Committee, which is about 300 strong. The Central Committee in turn elects the Politburo. In practice, positions within the Central Committee and the Politburo are determined before a Party Congress, and the main purpose of the Congress is to announce the Party's policies and vision for the direction of China in the following few years.

Central committee

This is a smaller body which convenes infrequently (recently, once or twice a year). Its members all hold other important positions.

STRUCTURE OF THE CPC (founded 1921)

- Standing Committee of the Politbureau
- Politbureau
- Secretariat
- Central Committee
- National Congress of the CPC
- County & Provincial Organisations
- Primary Party Organisations

They receive special privileges and have access to inside information on Party affairs. Normally the Central Committee meetings discuss and announce policy and appointments rather than deciding them.

The Politiburo

This also functions as a committee—a small and powerful one. This is considered to be the command headquarters of the Party. It normally has fourteen to twenty four members. Membership of the Politburo is not a full-time job and often some members will be leaders in distant provinces such as Guangdong.

The Party's centre of power is the Politburo Standing Committee. The process for selecting Standing Committee members, as well as Politburo members, occurs behind the scenes at the time of the National Congress. The new power structure is not announced directly, but through the positioning of portraits in the *People's Daily*, the official newspaper of the Party. The number of Standing Committee members varies and has tended to increase over time. The Committee was expanded to nine at the 16th Party National Congress in 2002. The Standing Committee meets weekly. The General Secretary has the right to convene and preside over meetings of the Politburo and its Standing Committee.

Secretariat

The General Secretary is the formal head of the Secretariat. Mostly, this body provides the staff support for the Politburo and the Central Committee. Its members oversee the preparation of documents for the Politburo. The Military Affairs commission is in charge of the People's Liberation Army. Party Leader, Hu Jintao, controls the military through his post of Supreme Commander of China's Armed Forces. He replaced former Party Leader, Jiang Zemin, as Chairman of the Central Military commission in September 2004.

STRUCTURE OF THE GOVERNMENT

On the government side, the basic current structure was adopted in 1954, although many changes in specific structures have occurred since then.

A new National People's Congress (NPC), the legislature and government equivalent of the Party Congress, is chosen every four years. The NPC convenes annually and each meeting is attended by about 3,000 delegates. The NPC has a Standing Committee that meets more frequently. More importantly, during the 1980s it developed its own permanent committees which began to operate regularly. It is thought that the role of the NPC in debating policy should be strengthened. Over the years since Mao Zedong it has brought China from a country in which virtually no laws existed to a state with laws which have helped the country to grow in political and economic power. The move to a market economy has meant that many laws are needed, for example, and contracts, relating to property rights.

The State Council is, in theory, chosen by the NPC. It is headed by the Premier (Wen Jiabao since March 2003) and serves as a Cabinet in the Chinese political system. The State Council's membership consists of Premier, Vice Premier, state councillors and nearly all heads of commissions and ministries.

To a far greater extent than the Party, the government has changed its organisation over the years. Relatively few government organs below the level of the Premier have avoided organisational changes since 1954. For example, the number of ministries has varied from about a dozen to over sixty. Presently the ministries are streamlined. The aim has been to create a more efficient government which would regulate rather than administer an increasingly market-driven economy.

Jiang Zemin, left, confers with Hu Jintao at the 10th National People's Congress of China in Beijing in March 2003. Hu was elected the President of China to succeed Jiang at the meeting.

Provinces

The country is divided into thirty one provinces. Provinces are a very important part of the political system. The political structure at provincial level largely mirrors that of the centre. This is because most provincial bodies must deal with their counterparts at the centre. The centre has essentially replicated itself in the provinces.

In theory all provinces are ranked equally with each other, but in practice, some provinces such as Shanghai which contribute a great deal of money to central government, are actually more important than others. Their leaders are therefore accorded more respect than other government ministers. Unlike states in the USA, provinces do not have powers that belong to them by law. The powers they have are delegated to them from the centre. Nevertheless, the provinces are very important in the political system. They lobby the centre for resources and greater freedoms. It has to be remembered that the provinces are very varied and that Beijing cannot manage the whole of China without assistance from the provinces. The centre, then, is generally happy to negotiate more power for the provinces. (Many provinces are the size of European countries. Beijing cannot manage a country the size of China without important tasks

being performed at lower levels of the political system.) The reforms in China have meant that power has, to a great extent, shifted to the provinces. This approach is to ensure that the provinces do their utmost to develop the local economy fast enough to maintain social and political stability. Each province largely controls the appointment of all but its highest officials. The provincial Party committee has a powerful role in the running of the province.

Cities

Cities can fit into the national political hierarchy at any level depending on their size and importance. For example, Beijing, as a metropolis, has the rank of province. According to a 2001 handbook, China has 660 cities at the rank of county or higher. Each city has a full set of Party and government organs which mirror those of the centre. Headed by mayors, city governments are normally organised into departments. The reforms have in-

creasingly made cities the key level of organisation for the economy. National level regulations on many important issues, such as health insurance and pensions, are implemented in a different way in each city. The city makes the decisions on how national principles are dealt with in that city. At the provincial level a Party committee is in charge of each city and that committee is the most powerful in each metropolis.

Counties

Counties (about 2,461 of them) play a strong role in the political administration of China. Orders from above normally mean that counties can exercise considerable discretion when it comes to implementing the order in their county. The counties can follow their own strategies of economic development. Counties also contain almost the full range of Party and government organs so they can deal effectively with their counterparts at the level of city or province.

Townships

Townships were part of communes during the Great Leap Forward. They emerged as separate units after the reforms. They became key localities for establishing local enterprises staffed by peasants. Indeed, during the late 1990s about 50% of peasant migrants to cities went no further than their own township to find work. Changes in residence rules (see page 132) mean that peasants can move to townships without needing special permission to do so. Township governments are not elected. Given their small size township governments are structured more simply than their higher level counterparts but they still retain the basic major structures on both Party and government sides. In 2000, China had 44,867 townships.

Units

For most Chinese the unit (danwei) refers to the place of work—factory, research institute, ministry etc. Units in the state and collective sectors are the lowest level of the political system and are not wholly independent organisations.

Danweis used to be a major source of many things for their employees—schools, housing, healthcare etc. The danwei provided ration coupons for food, clothing and furniture. It administered the birth control programme and provided pensions. The danwei's permission was needed to get married and to change jobs. The danwei also participated in political tasks and campaigns were carried out by it. Mao used the danwei to manipulate and create tensions between units. The key to the strength of the danwei was that very few individuals ever got permission to transfer from one to another. This meant that peasants could not move about freely. Each of the appropriate higher level political units had close links with the danwei. The head of the danwei rarely controlled it.

The reforms have significantly affected the danweis. In summary, the danwei level of the Chinese system is changing fundamentally and in the near future will cease to be an important part of the political structure. Few Chinese still work in danweis as they existed before the reforms.

Community committees

One of the important tasks of the coming years is to create alternatives to the danwei. In cities a shift is being made to a more residence-based unit of organisation, the community committee. the following example is one type of community committee which exists in Beijing. It has a staff of five or six people and also employs some migrant workers. The director is elected but there was only one candidate—was the CPC secretary of the local Party branch. All staff live locally and get about 500 yuan per month plus health care. The committee is responsible for day care, teenage community activities, security, care of the elderly, birth control, a clinic (primary care), legal aid, newspaper delivery, rubbish removal, barber service, mail de-

livery, laundry, weekend entertainment, and a small shopping centre. Many of these are money-making activities to support the running of the community committee.

The CPC retains control over these new arrangements. These developments reflect a change in the structure of the economy—less public ownership and an increase in personal mobility. This means that state services must be delivered on the basis of residence and not work. Many social services such as pension plans and health insurance are now provided through city-wide programmes. The overall ability of the state to send out political messages to the people has diminished considerably. Also, there are no rural equivalents of the community committee. The economic and social reforms have meant that major adjustments have to be made to the functions and structures of the political system itself.

The political system is very bureaucratic which does not help China to progress economically.

CORRUPTION IN THE POLITICAL SYSTEM

China set up a system whereby every official is vulnerable to those above. This means that every official is able to act like a petty dictator to the person below. Under the danwei system officials could strongly influence a person's career, for instance holding the person in a meaningless position for years. They also controlled available housing and so on. This power is weakening with the decline of the danwei system.

The economic reforms have meant that such power breeds corruption. Previously, ideological beliefs meant that most people did not turn their power to their personal advantage. The reforms mean that it is all right to amass money and material goods and so officials are demanding these things in return for favourable decisions. Corruption has spread to the point that if officials refuse 'on the side' payments they are viewed with suspicion. Approvals and licences are often granted only on payment of illegal fees. Some officials embezzle funds and put them in private bank accounts or send them abroad. It is estimated that corruption involves sums of money that equal nearly 15% of China's GDP.

CORRUPTION

Cheng Kejie, former Vice Chairman of the Standing Committee of the National People's Congress, was sentenced to death for accepting bribes. Cheng, 66, was found guilty, in collaboration with his mistress Li Ping, of having taken 41 million yuan in bribes when he served as Deputy Secretary of the Party Committee of Guangxi Zhuang Autonomous Region and Chairman of the People's Government of Guangxi.

The court ruled that Cheng, as a government official, had been found guilty of taking bribes as he sought illicit gains for others by abusing his power.

"The amount of bribes Cheng took was extremely huge," said the verdict, adding that "the crimes he committed in the capacity of a senior leading official have seriously violated the normal working order of government institutions, tarnished the clean and honest image of government functionaries, discredited the fine reputation of government officials, and thus should be harshly dealt with in accordance with the law."

Adapted from *People's Daily* 2000

Anti-corruption banners are displayed on the exterior of an apartment building in Shanghai, April 2005. The banners read: "God, don't you see the officials are so corrupt?" Shanghai has been hit by a number of corruption scandals involving property, with many residents claiming they were not compensated adequately for homes that were demolished in redevelopment projects.

STATE CONTROL OVER SOCIETY

The principles of Chinese society demanded that the state should dominate the people. All non-official organisations existed only if tolerated by the Party. The CPC permitted very few of these to exist. Today, however, relations between state and society are changing rapidly. Few hard and fast rules now apply. Officially, all citizens are obliged to register with the government any organisation which they form. The government retains the right to oppose groups it finds threatening. However, tens of thousands of groups have been formed to bring together people with shared interests. In theory, the highest level of government controls all groups, but in reality organisations are flourishing.

For instance, religious organisations are obliged to register with the government, but some local authorities tolerate underground churches. Thousands of voluntary groups have formed throughout China with no real government interference. Citizens have access to public media. Shanghai has a call-in radio show with an audience of 10 million. Many callers complain about problems with local government.

Satellite TV and the Internet have seriously breached state control over information. (See page 150.)

Military—The People's Liberation Army (PLA)

After 1949 the military retained a very special place in the political system. The PLA does not answer to the government, though there is a Ministry of Defence and a government military affairs commission. The real leadership of the PLA is through the CPC which the PLA is sworn to defend. The PLA also runs a huge network of military industries and transport links. More than in any other Communist country, the military has played an important role in domestic politics, notably Tiananmen Square in 1989. However, this role is diminishing. The PLA is becoming a more professional military force. The PLA may be playing an increasingly influential role in China's foreign policy, especially in Asia. In summary, a fundamental principle of the Chinese system is that the Party controls the gun, and the military then protects Party rule.

The CPC and its challenges

The total membership of the Party is huge (66.4 million in 2002). This was always an exclusive club representing less than 5% of the total population. The CPC no longer retains a sense of discipline and commitment among its members. Today, many Party members look upon the Party as a way to get career promotion and higher living standards. New members do not have to face ideological education and tough political demands. Capitalists can now join the Party. The

A poster glamourising the unity of the Chinese people within the CPC. Today the Party is used by individuals to promote their own careers rather than as a vehicle to promote Communist ideology.

Party continues to exist because of its total control of political power. The Party decides China's foreign and security policies. However, the CPC's monopoly of political power also means that problems within the CPC become substantial problems for China's overall political system.

These problems include the following:

● Corruption and lack of commitment are widespread within the Party.

● Changes to China's society and economy are happening faster than adjustments to Party organisation.

● The private sector, the most rapidly growing part of the economy, has little participation in the CPC.

● Many of China's now well-informed and sophisticated people question why a country of this wealth and complexity should be governed by a possibly corrupt political party.

CHINESE DEMOCRACY MOVEMENT

The Chinese democracy movement is a loosely organised movement in the People's Republic of China

against the Communist Party of China. The movement began during Beijing Spring in 1978 and was important in the Tiananmen Square protests of 1989. The origin of the movement can be seen in the brief liberalisation which occurred after the Cultural Revolution. The founding document of the movement is probably a magazine article written in the late 1970s called *The Fifth Modernisation*. Its author, Wei Jingshen, was sentenced to fifteen years in prison for writing the article. In it, Wei argued that the holding of power by the people was essential for modernisation, that the Communist Party was controlled by reactionaries, and that the people must struggle to overthrow these reactionaries through a long and possibly bloody fight.

Throughout the1980s, the idea of trying to overthrow the government increased in popularity among college-educated Chinese. In response to the growing corruption, the economic changes, and the sense that reforms in the Soviet Union and Eastern Europe were leaving China behind, the Tiananmen Square protests erupted in 1989. These protests were put down by government troops on 4 June 1989. It is estimated that 2,000 people were killed and 10,000 injured in the massacre.

In the 1990s, the democracy movement underwent a sharp decline, both within and outside China. Part of this decline was due to repressive measures taken by the Chinese government against the movement with strict controls to prevent any mention of democracy on the Internet or in the media. In addition, after the September 11, 2001 attacks in the US, China passed a series of anti-terrorist laws which many believed were merely an excuse for increased powers to curb any suspected potential dissent.

China Democracy Party

In 1998, Xu Wenli, Wang Youcai and other dissidents formed the first opposition political party in China, the China Democracy Party. In 1981, Mr Wenli had been sentenced to fourteen years in prison for "illegally organising a clique to overthrow the government". He was released in 1993 and continued his demand for an end to one-party rule. The new party demanded freedom of speech, a new constitution and free elections. The actions of the party were short-lived. It was declared illegal by the Communist government and its leaders were arrested. Xu Wenli was sentenced to thirteen years in prison and Wang Youcai to eleven years. In 2002 Xu Wenli was releasesd on medical parole and now lives in the USA. The China Democracy Party exists in exile in America. Mr Wenli admits that the party has made little impact in China and that "many people do not know of its existence".

Within China today, most protest activity is now expressed in single issue demonstrations which are tolerated to a degree by the government.

POLITICAL PARTICIPATION IN CHINA

The People's Republic of China is a single-party state. This means that only one political party, the Communist Party of China, is legally allowed to hold effective power at the national level. Eight minor parties are allowed, but they are legally re-

quired to accept the leadership of the dominant Party.

Eight registered minor parties:

▲ Revolutionary Committee of the Chinese Guomindang (53,000 members)

▲ China Democratic League: The League is mainly made up of middle-level and senior intellectuals in the fields of culture, education, science and technology. It has a membership of 144,000 and its chairman is Ding Shisun.

▲ China Democratic National Construction Association

▲ China Association for Promoting Democracy

▲ Chinese Peasants' and Workers' Democratic Party

▲ China Party for Public Interest

▲ September 3 Society

▲ Taiwan Democratic Self-Government League

The CPC sees these political parties as providing a useful link to the intellectuals whom it cannot attract itself. It seems that a plan was drafted by the CPC in 1989 to expand the role of these parties. The proposals included a greater role for the parties in the state structures and the suggestion that they might be consulted on the choice of state leaders. Many people see these parties as merely doing what the CPC wants. However, all eight parties have kept their distance from setting up an opposition party like the China Democracy Party. The CPC sees the involvement of the eight parties as multi-party politics.

TRADE UNION PARTICIPATION

To head off mass political opposition, the CPC has traditionally tried to extend its control over as much of the population as possible. The Party has relied on mass organisations such as trade unions to do this. In recent years the number of labour disputes and protests involving massive numbers of work-

Illegal parties/ parties in exile

✗ China Democracy Party

✗ Chinese Workers/Labour Party

✗ Green Party of China

✗ Party for Freedom and Democracy in China

✗ Inner Mongolian People's Party

✗ National Democratic Party of Tibet

✗ Southern Mongolian Freedom Federation

✗ East Turkistan (Uighuristan) National Congress

ers has risen dramatically in China. Workers have been protesting about conditions of employment, low or missing wages, corrupt management and other issues. Such protests are generally illegal as are independent trade unions. Workers, activists and labour leaders have been detained, harassed or imprisoned for taking part in such protests or for publicising them. The rights to freedom of expression and association are routinely denied to many groups and individuals in China when the authorities perceive this as a 'threat'.

Independent trade unions are not permitted in China. The All China Federation of Trade Unions is the national body which governs trade union activity. It is meant to look after and control the interests of 'primary' trade unions throughout China. These are either regional official unions or one of sixteen official national industrial trade unions.

According to the constitution of the ACFTU;

"Guided by Marxism–Leninism, Mao Zedong Thought and Deng Xiaoping's theory, the Chinese trade unions implement the Party's basic line of centring on the economic construction, upholding the

(continued on page 145)

DISSIDENTS

The term is used to refer to political dissidents, usually people who are against authoritarian regimes. Political dissidents usually use non-violent means of political dissent, including voicing criticism of the government. There are a number of active dissidents in China but there are also many who have been imprisoned or exiled. Below are two case studies.

Wang Bingzhang

In 1982, Dr Wang established *China Spring*, the first pro-democracy Chinese magazine overseas. In the next year, he launched the Union of Chinese Democracy Movement. He also co-founded the Chinese Freedom Democracy Party and Chinese Democracy Justice Party in 1989 and 1998, respectively.

In June 2002, Dr Wang went to Vietnam with Yue Wu and Zhang Qi where they were abducted by Chinese secret agents. In December 2002, the Chinese government announced his arrest after six months of secret custody.

In February 2003, Dr Wang was sentenced to life in prison. He has been imprisoned in Shaoguan, Guangdong Province, China.

Jiang Yanyong

Jiang Yanyong is a Chinese physician from Beijing who publicised a cover-up of the Severe Acute Respiratory Syndrome (SARS) epidemic in China. He is a senior member of the Communist Party of China, and as a military doctor holds a rank within the People's Liberation Army which is equivalent to Major General.

When the SARS virus began spreading in China in late 2002 and early 2003, the number of cases being reported in mainland China was drastically understated by the government. In the first week of April 2003, Jiang faxed a letter to Chinese Central Television (CCTV) reporting

A woman and child wear masks to protect against the SARS virus as they wait in a queue to enter Beijing's West Railway Station. Faced with back-to-back outbreaks of SARS and avian flu in the past year, China has been forced to examine and reshape its shaky health care system and the way it handles—and appears to handle—public health emergencies.

that fact. Although CCTV did not publish the letter, it was leaked to Western news organisations which did publish it. This letter forced the resignation of the Mayor of Beijing and the Minister of Public Health, and the Chinese government began to deal actively with the growing epidemic. Most public health experts believe that this act prevented the disease from reaching pandemic proportions.

In February 2004, Dr Jiang wrote an open letter to the Premier Wen Jiabao, several Deputy Premiers, the Politburo and many other members of the Chinese government. The letter asked for a re-examination of the responsibility borne by the Chinese government for the Tiananmen Square Massacre. A number of media sources indicated that because of Jiang Yanyong's senior rank the topic of what to do with him was discussed by the Politburo.

On 2 June, 2004, two days before the fifteenth anniversary of the

massacre, Dr Jiang Yanyong's family in California reported that he and his elderly wife were missing from their house in Beijing after being arrested and placed in military custody. Many sources have indicated that, while a number of high level members believed that Jiang should have been ignored, his arrest was the result of personal intervention of Jiang Zemin (no relation) who,- as Chairman of the Central Military Commission, ordered the arrest of Jiang Yanyong on the grounds of violating military discipline.

On 15 June, 2004, a source close to the Jiang family reported that Hua Zhongwei, the elderly wife of Dr Jiang Yanyong, had been freed two weeks after being detained in secret. In early July 2004 it was reported that Dr Jiang was being subjected to strenuous indoctrination efforts by the Chinese military, described by one source as "brainwashing". His wife was said to be safe in her Beijing home. The doctor himself was released from Chinese custody on 19 July, 2004.

Four Cardinal Principles and adhering to the reform and opening-up ... The Chinese trade unions shall safeguard the socialist state power of the People's democratic dictatorship led by the working class and based on the worker-peasant alliance, assist the People's Government to carry out its work and play the role of democratic participation and social supervision when the government exercises the administrative powers of the state."

The extract above shows the lack of independence of the ACFTU and the fundamental principle that the ACFTU and the trade unions in China are guided by the Communist Party of China. Although the ACFTU does play a role in representing workers' interests and does have officials at the workplace level who are employed to solve disputes as they occur, it is when disputes begin to push the barriers of what is acceptable to the state that the ACFTU has difficulty supporting workers. When protests which are not officially sanctioned by the ACFTU occur, workers have no access to legitimate union support and are forced to create their own 'illegal' unions or attempt to lead protests without organisation.

While the right to strike is not expressly forbidden in Chinese law, this right was removed from the Constitution in 1982 as it was reported that the political system had "eradicated problems between the proletariat and enterprise owners".

Since the late 1980s there have been several attempts to create independent trade unions to give an independent voice to the needs and grievances of workers. None of these lasted long and were quickly repressed, with their leaders being imprisoned.

In May 1989, during the pro-democracy movement, groups of workers in various cities formed Workers Autonomous Federations (WAFs) as an alternative to the ACFTU. The WAFs were short-

lived. They were banned by the authorities following the 4 June 1989 crackdown and their organisers were arrested and prosecuted on 'counter-revolutionary' charges.

Recent Industrial Action

In 1999 Yue Tianxiang and Guo Xinmin established the China Workers Monitor in Gansu province, exposing corruption among officials and mismanagement of the company which had laid them off. Yue was sentenced to ten years imprisonment and, along with another activist Guo Xinmin, was sentenced to two years.

On 13 March 2001, some 5,000 taxi drivers surrounded the government offices in Lanzhou city, Gansu province, to protest against the increase in taxi fines and road tax and over regulations requiring taxis to be fitted with metal bars. They also presented a petition to local government officials. According to reports, the demonstration was stopped by the intervention of 300 armed police who allegedly beat the protesters. Several were injured and some were taken away by the police.

In Heilongjiang province, workers from the Daqing Oilfield, one of China's largest state-owned oil fields, began staging massive demonstrations on 1 March 2002 in front of the Daqing Petroleum Administration Bureau (PAB). They were protesting over insufficient compensation for lost jobs, inadequate welfare benefits and increased premiums on their pension insurance. Up to 50,000 workers reportedly joined the protests. Several injuries were reported on 19 March when paramilitary police clashed with the demonstrators. The workers' demands included setting up

an independent trade union. It is reported that the Daqing Laid-Off Workers Trade Union Committee was set up during the protests and is operating underground.

In Beijing, on 27 March 2002, hundreds of pensioners converged outside the gates of the Beijing Automobile and Motorcycle Works to protest against the lack of medical, housing and other benefits. They continued their protests the following day in an attempt to obtain a meeting to discuss the issue with the management of the company. Many of the pensioners were elderly and infirm.

Interaction between China and the rest of the world is increasing and contacts between foreign trade unions and the ACFTU have also increased. Official visits and exchange trips to China are common. However, the issue of independent trade unions and the detention of labour activists is rarely discussed openly.

PARTICIPATION AT THE GRASS ROOTS

The most meaningful form of participation for most people is doing something which affects their immediate life. Participation at the workplace has been taking place but the signs are that there is not enough. The main forum for workers' participation is the Workers Representative Congress that operates mainly in state-owned enterprises (SOEs). In reality the workers do not have much power to run the factories. The powers of the congresses are limited to factors such as the level of direct interference by the Party Committee.

There are also urban residents' committees. They play an important role, but more in terms of monitoring behaviour and ensuring compliance with policies such as family planning.

The use of direct elections would represent a major change in the relationship between the state and society. The most noteworthy step in this direction is the introduction of elections for villager committees since 1987. However, the process has been complex and the motivation to set up the committees came as a result of needing some governing structure for the 930,000 villages in China. Under the 1987 Organic Law of the Village Committees, all villages are expected to hold competitive, direct elections for village committees. Both the government and foreign observers estimate that more than 90% of villages have participated in elections for local leaders. Foreign observers who have monitored local village committee elections, e.g. the Carter Centre, have judged the elections they observed to be fair on the whole. Successful village committee elections have included secret ballots to select candidates, active campaigns by multiple candidates, and the use of secret ballots in the election itself.

In general, the Party maintains a control over the electoral process thanks to the government screening of candidates. Candidates favoured by local authorities have been defeated in some elections. Approximately 60% of the members elected to the village committees are Party members. This limits the effectiveness of the village election system.

NATIONALIST GROUPS

There are many nationalist groups in China and working in exile. For example:

- International Tibet Independence Movement
- Government of Tibet in Exile
- Free Tibet
- National Democratic Party of Tibet.
- Taiwan Independence Movement
- Several groups in Mongolia

VIEWS OF THE MIDDLE CLASS

"The Communist Party still allows no opposition. Nevertheless, its new ideology embraces private enterprise, private property and almost anything else that will help make China richer and stronger—and keep the Party in power."

"After one of the fastest periods of economic growth in history, China is set to reclaim its place as one of the world's great powers. Furthermore, the Communist government, which once despised such displays of wealth, is counting on a new middle class to help it succeed."

"I used to want to move to the US and have a beautiful house with green grass in front of it, but now I think this kind of thing can be achieved in China."
David Zhang, student

Tina Yang, a 23-year-old trainee in a foreign company's Beijing office, said she was more than happy to face the challenges—and reap the rewards—of China's new, competitive environment. "In the past people obeyed the rules and the government. Now we can have our own ideas and our own say ... even if it may not have much effect," she said.

Case study:
The National Democratic Party of Tibet

The National Democratic Party of Tibet (NDPT) is the first ever democratic political party to be formed in the history of Tibet. It was founded on 4 September 1994 on the initiative of the Tibetan Youth Congress (TYC), the largest Tibetan non-governmental organisation. Its objective is to safeguard and strengthen the democratic process begun by the Dalai Lama in 1960. It also aims to ensure that the Tibetan people's commitment to democracy remains firm and resolute while they remain tolerant. It also aimed to provide the Tibetan public with a clear direction in the struggle for the restoration of Tibetan independence.

Inner Mongolian People's Party

Supporters of IMPP demonstrate in Times Square, New York

In 1949, China completely destroyed the religious and political system of Mongolia. The Communists have suppressed any resistance by introducing great numbers of Chinese immigrants and military forces into the region and by their heavy-handed efforts to change the traditional customs of the Mongolian people. The Mongols were conquered but they have not given up resistance.

"In order to force this rich land to satisfy your greedy needs in military, economic and population spheres, your government, for a long time, has been suppressing the human rights of the entire native Mongolian nationality in the most barbarous and cruel manner. According to your government's official records, during the fifty two years, your government has directly or indirectly slaughtered a total of 150,000 Mongolians. You have destroyed the Mongolian culture and religion of Tibet. The continuous migration of Chinese people into the grasslands of Mongolian territory has produced severe damage to the ecology system. This has resulted in the expansion of desert lands. Now the Mongols have become a 'minority' in their own land."

Extract from a speech by Mr Backe, Vice Chairman of the Inner Mongolia People's Party in 1999.

THE MEDIA IN CHINA

Within the People's Republic of China, there is heavy government involvement in the media, with many of the largest media organisations (namely CCTV, the People's

Uighur ethnic minority group

The young and the old

Among the various foreign fighters who have been captured in Afghanistan by anti-Taliban forces are a number of Chinese Muslims. China has a short border with Afghanistan, and now Beijing wants the captured Chinese prisoners returned to face trial in China. Most are members of the Uighur ethnic minority and the government says they are members of a violent separatist movement in western China. However, human rights groups fear that the authorities intend to take advantage of the international campaign against terrorism to suppress legitimate dissent.

Activists campaigning for the Uighur people of Xinjiang province say that increasingly ruthless tactics are being used to crush local culture in what they call China's "other Tibet". Uighurs are ethnically different from the Han Chinese and speak a Turkic language. They were once the majority in Xinjiang, but now they make up less than half of the population.

The government has published a list of bombings, shootings and riots in the province. According to this account, Uighur separatists have killed forty people and injured 330 over the past ten years. China accuses the Muslim Uighurs of connections with Bin Laden.

Uighurs fear their language and culture are disappearing, while their leaders are either co-opted or suppressed.

Daily, and Xinhua) being agencies of the Chinese government. There are certain taboos and red lines within the Chinese media, such as a taboo against questioning the legitimacy of the Communist Party of China. Yet within those restrictions, there is a fairly open discussion of social issues and policy options within the boundaries set by the Party.

Much of the surprising diversity in the Chinese media is attributable to the fact that most state media outlets no longer receive sizable government subsidies and are largely expected to pay for themselves through commercial advertising. As a result, they can no longer serve solely as mouthpieces for the government but must also produce programmes that people find attractive and interesting so that money can be generated through advertising revenue. In addition, while the government does issue directives defining what can and cannot be

(continued on page 149)

HONG KONG

Hong Kong became a Special Administrative Region of the People's Republic of China in July 1997. It is located on the south-eastern coast of China. The former British colony is now administered by the PRC under the policy of 'one country, two systems.' In the Joint Declaration, the PRC promised that under the 'One Country, Two Systems' policy proposed by Deng Xiaoping, the socialist economic system in mainland China would not be practised in Hong Kong, and Hong Kong's previous capitalist system and life-style would remain unchanged for fifty years, or until 2047. Hong Kong would enjoy a high degree of autonomy in all matters except foreign affairs and defence. Hong Kong is constitutionally entitled to a relatively high degree of autonomy; for example, it retains its own legal system, currency, customs, negotiating rights, such as air traffic and aircraft landing rights, and immigration laws. Hong Kong even maintains its own road rules, with traffic continuing to drive on the left.

On 1 July 2003, half a million people marched in the largest protest rally ever aimed at the government of Hong Kong. They were voicing their concerns about a proposed anti-subversion bill that would have eroded freedom of the press, of religion and of association, arising from Article 23 of the Hong Kong Basic Law. In addition they were expressing dissatisfaction with the poor state of the economy. Regina Ip, then Secretary for Security, and Anthony Leung, then Financial Secretary, were forced to leave office in 2004 under public pressure.

Another protest on 13 July drew 20,000 people. Like the protest on 1 July, the relatively large turnout indicated deep-rooted hostility among the population to the assaults on democratic rights. The legislation, which was to be enacted under Article 23 of Hong Kong's Basic Law, would effectively have extended China's police state methods to the former British colony. It would have enabled the prosecution of groups

HONG KONG DEMOCRACY PROTEST
Hong Kong's former No. 2 official, Anson Chan, front left, who remains highly popular and influential despite quitting as head of the civil service in 2001, attends a pro-democracy demonstration on a downtown Hong Kong street in December 2005. Tens of thousands of people marched in Hong Kong to pressure the government to speed up political reforms which would allow voters to pick the city's leader and entire legislature. At front right is her bodyguard.

such as Falun Gong and the China Democracy Movement, which are outlawed in China but are currently given sanctuary in Hong Kong.

Acutely aware that the protests in Hong Kong had the potential to trigger political unrest elsewhere in China, Beijing played down their significance, claiming that only a "minority" had been involved. The *People's Daily* on 10 July, for instance, accused the Democratic Party and the Catholic Church of instigating the demonstrations. "The vast majority of them (Hong Kong residents) did not want to see their expression of opinion turned into a political storm that would paralyse the government and throw it into a ruling crisis," it declared.

Again in 2004, 10,000 people took to the streets of Hong Kong to protest against Beijing's ruling that it alone will determine the shape and timing of elections in the city.

"The one country, two systems is a complete washout, but the Communist Party is just forcing its will," said Leung Keung, 58, who brought his two grandsons to the march.

Beijing, which already has the power to veto any political reform, now has the added power to decide if changes are even needed, meaning it can delay any change for as long as it likes.

China fears that full democracy would yield a leader who can challenge the authority of the central leadership.

These events in Hong Kong have shown that the claims of the new Chinese leadership of Hu Jintao and Wen Jiabao to represent a move toward a more open, democratic political system in China are false. Their attitude to the protests has been fairly autocratic.

published, it does not prevent, and in fact actively encourages, state media outlets to compete with each other for viewers and commercial advertising.

Government control of information can also be ineffective in other ways. Despite government restrictions, much information is gathered either at the local level or from foreign sources and passed on through personal conversations and text messaging. The withdrawal of government media subsidies has caused many newspapers (including some owned by the Communist Party) to take bold editorial stands critical of the government, as the need to attract readers and avoid bankruptcy has been more pressing than fear of government repression.

In addition, the traditional means of media control have proved to be extremely ineffective against newer forms of communication, most notably text messaging.

Contact with the West

Closer and more varied contact with the West appears to be having an increasing influence on educated urban opinion in China on concepts such as a free press, freedom of speech, and the idea of having more than one political party.

Virtually all foreign reporters in China operate under restrictions which are considerably more severe than in most Asian countries. One result is that Western media influence on Chinese media organisations as a whole is generally limited.

Advertising

Television revenues are growing dramatically: they totalled about $2 billion in 1995 and were expected to rise above $6 billion by the end of 2005. In 1995, China Central Television earned nearly $150 million in advertising revenue, covering almost 90% of its total costs. In the past, Chinese radio and television tended to run well behind the print

media in their news coverage. More recently, television has come under market pressure to be as timely, informative, and responsive as the newspapers.

Competition from outside mainland China has also forced domestic media organisations to become more varied, assertive, and sceptical of official authority. For example, in order to compete against higher quality Hong Kong radio stations that could be heard in Guangdong Province, Guangdong radio managers created Pearl River Economic Radio (PRER) in 1986. PRER, copying Hong Kong radio's approach, began to emphasise daily life, entertainment, 'celebrity' DJs, and caller phone-in segments, while eliminating ideological, preachy formats which include little information beyond what was provided by government sources. Local groups of Party activists in southern China reportedly are unhappy about PRER, mainly because some of the station's commentators, as well as its talk radio programmes, highlight Party failures and the misdeeds of individual Party members in the region.

Cable Television

Residents on the Chinese mainland now receive more than twenty outside television channels by satellite, including Chinese-language services of CNN, Star TV, and the United States Information Agency. In the southern province of Guangdong, 97% of the households have television sets, and all—except those in a few parts of the city of Guangzhou, where reception is poor—have access to Hong Kong television through cable networks. Some local stations even intercept the signals and insert their own commercials. Beijing is unable to monitor effectively, let alone control, the illicit cable operators who have sprung up since the early 1990s. As of 1995, about 1,000 of the 3,000 cable stations in China, which are linked to perhaps 50 million homes, were unlicensed.

Weakening of Party controls

Over the last decade, the ways in which the Communist Party of China has operated—especially the introduction of reforms aimed at decentralising power—have spurred greater media independence in several ways. The growth of 'peripheral'—local and some regional—media has taken away some control by the Party. In general, the further reporters and media organisations are from Beijing and important provincial capitals, the greater their leeway.

As state resources have become stretched more thinly, the media has found it far easier than before to print and broadcast material that falls within vaguely defined grey areas. Officials are too few, too busy, and often too incompetent to be able to manage the media as they did in the past. Prior to the 1990s, it was common for Party and government officials to participate in the actual drafting of newspaper editorials. Now, for the most part, these officials merely discuss editorial policies with newspaper managers.

In the past, prime-time news on Chinese Central Television was routinely examined, prior to airing, by the Ministry of Radio, Film, and Television. Since 1994, however, the Ministry has ceased to watch CCTV news programmes before they are screened. The diversity and quantity of material, moreover, has compelled officials to prioritise their reviews of broadcasts. The 7.00 p.m. news broadcasts, for instance, receive far more attention from the authorities than does the midnight news. Another indication that government controls are weakening is that new programmes are examined after they have been aired. Recently launched news programmes, such as CCTV's Focal Report and Beijing Television's Express News, include moderate criticisms of the Party and government and explore some controversial public topics in an effort to make the programmes more relevant and topical.

CHAPTER 18

Human rights

The state of human rights in the People's Republic of China has been criticised by various sources as being poor in many respects. Critics include other nations—particularly Western democracies—as well as international organisations. While acknowledging major deficiencies, the Chinese government has asserted that the human rights situation is improving and is better than ever. Many contentious events have been seen as abuses by groups or nations outside mainland China, while the Chinese government tends to view them as necessary for public safety and social stability.

Abuses reported have included random and lengthy detention without any means of communication, including use of laogai (prisons where inmates are forced into hard labour) and re-education through labour (hard labour without trial). Other abuses of human rights include forced confessions, torture, and mistreatment of prisoners, as well as severe restrictions on freedom of speech, the press, assembly, association, religion, privacy, and workers' rights.

ISSUE 1: **ONE-CHILD POLICY**

The reforms in China have had a massive impact on social policy. One area that requires consideration is the difficult policy area of family planning. Over the years there have been conflicting policies including the 'one-child policy.' The introduction of the household responsibility system (late 1950s) set up incentives for households to increase family size rather than fol-

low the tightening family planning policy. There were two reasons for this. Firstly, when land was divided up it was allocated on the basis of household size so there was a benefit to having a larger family. Secondly, there was an understanding that if you wanted to get rich and be looked after in your old age you

needed more children, especially boys. The policy makers feared that the rapidly increasing population would undermine any economic gains.

The one-child policy introduced in 1979 has been one of the most unpopular policies in China, especially in the countryside. The government set up an elaborate system to monitor the programme. The State Family Planning Commission sets the national birth rate and the provincial quotas. It is then the responsibility of the local family planning officials to ensure that the targets are met in their areas. In each work unit a list is kept of whose turn it is to conceive.

The policy has not been kept across the country. Some Party members do not follow the policy. In one village with twenty five Party members, twenty one had three or more children. It does not apply to minority households and in most of the countryside the actual policy was for two, if not three, children. The Chinese government has a target for a population of 1.6 billion by 2050. The current census shows that the sex ratio of males to females is 106.74:100, resulting in 41.27 million more men than women. Given the long-standing preference for boys, it is suggested by some that the one-child policy has made female infanticide common. Baby girls are often abandoned at orphanages. One consequence of the policy is that around one million men per year will probably not find a marriage partner. This will drive up the bride prices in rural areas and will result in illegal trade in women and also in prostitution. There has been a relaxing of the policy since 2000. In some rural provinces it has been decided that if both parents are single children they may have a second child.

China needs to develop a pension scheme which would alleviate reliance on the family as the primary source of support in old age. There also needs to be a more educational approach to family planning than the quota-driven approach that exists just now in China.

Another potential issue arising from the one-child policy is that of obesity, especially among children. Some of the issues are:

- China will have at least 200 million obese people within ten years if current trends continue.

- High fat diets and less active lifestyles in a country with rising incomes has exacerbated the problem.

- 10% of children are considered obese.

- The number of obese children is increasing by 8% every year.

- China's one-child policy means that many families have just one boy or girl who receive all the attention he or she wants from parents and grandparents.

However, in Hong Kong the government is telling couples to have three children to stem the territory's falling birth rate. The government hinted that it is considering measures, including tax incentives, to try to encourage couples to have more children. Hong Kong has one of the lowest birth rates in the world and a rapidly ageing population. The average married couple has two children.

China halts baby trafficking ring

Chinese police say they have broken up a criminal ring which was trafficking dozens of babies. They said they were investigating ninety five people in the city of Hohhot, in China's Inner Mongolian region. The case is the latest in a series of high-profile police operations against child traffickers.

The oldest baby was five days old, while the youngest was two hours old when they were allegedly bought by a trafficking ring from doz-

ens of privately-run hospitals and clinics. Many of the mothers were unmarried women, including students, or were unemployed. A police source told the BBC that most of the babies were girls, but did not give details

of the final buyers.

Baby girls are traditionally less highly regarded by rural Chinese families than baby boys. But ironically this bias is fuelling a massive gender imbalance in favour of males, thanks to the illegal use of ultrasound scans. The technology is helping to drive up the commercial value of girls, at least in the eyes of the traffickers, as they become an increasingly scarce commodity.

Adapted from: *BBC News*

ISSUE 2: **FREEDOM OF INFORMATION**

The Chinese government thinks that ordinary Chinese people should not be exposed to the websites of many of the foreign media. BBC World cannot be seen in China, except in the more expensive Western-style hotels and under certain very specific circumstances.

Access to the Internet is also heavily restricted. Recently, a leading human rights agency accused Yahoo of helping the Chinese government to identify an investigative journalist through his emails. The journalist, who had uncovered some disturbing information about the ways of bureaucracy in China, has been jailed.

In 2005, the BBC correspondent in Beijing, Rupert Wingfield-Hayes, broadcast a television report about a local electricity authority in rural China which wanted to take over the land of some farmers, and hired a gang of thugs to do it. The farmers decided to resist and they used video cameras to record the violent tactics of the thugs. Rupert's BBC colleagues were arrested for going to the village, and were roughly treated before being released.

However, the report, complete with the farmers' extraordinary video footage, was seen around the world—though not in China itself, of course.

China Internet cafe culture crackdown

Chinese authorities shut 12,575 Internet cafes in the closing months of 2004, the country's government said. Chinese Internet cafes operate under a set of strict guidelines and many of those most recently closed broke rules that limit how close they can be to schools. The official Xinhua News Agency said the crackdown was carried out to create a "safer environment for young people in China". Rules introduced in 2002 demand that Internet cafes be at least 200 metres away from middle and elementary schools. The hours that children can use Internet cafes are also tightly regulated. China has long been worried that Net cafes are an unhealthy influence on young people. All of the 100,000 or so Internet cafes in the country are required to use software that controls what websites users can see. Logs are also kept of the websites that people visit.

ISSUE 3: **HUMAN RIGHTS AND THE 2008 OLYMPICS**

CHINA OLYMPICS PROTEST JUNE 2005

A Chinese protester waits near a barrier to 333 hectares of land where a venue for water sports is planned to be built for the 2008 Beijing Olympic Games on the outskirts of Beijing. A dozen protesters gathered near banners which read "support for Olympic Games that reasonably compensate farmers who lose land". Protest organisers claimed that as many as 1,000 farmers from four villages had gathered over the previous twenty days to protest against local authorities for using the land without proper compensation.

Beijing has been chosen to host the 2008 Summer Olympics, but some groups consider this inappropriate in the light of alleged violations of human rights. Indeed, modernisation, construction, and urban planning in Beijing, and specifically the process of preparing the city for visits and study by the International Olympic Committee, is reported to have involved authoritarian measures possibly in violation of the civil rights of some residents.

Below is a section from the Human Rights Watch website about the alleged forced evictions that have taken place in preparation for the Beijing Olympics.

Forced evictions

"In the middle of the night, while they were sleeping, people came in and broke up the courtyard wall. There were lots of people living there together in this building, they had a shop, it was really dangerous, there were still people living there."

'Zhang,' friend of a forcibly evicted Beijing family

China's rapid urban development, fuelled in Beijing by preparations for the 2008 Olympics, is leading to the eviction of homeowners and tenants in violation of Chinese law and international standards on the right to housing. In many cities, Chinese local authorities and developers are forcibly evicting hundreds of thousands of homeowners and tenants who have little legal recourse. Evicted residents, left with few avenues of redress have increasingly taken to the streets to protest, where they have met police repression.

Developers often work with local government officials to request and implement forced evictions. Widespread corruption can lead Communist Party officials to favour the interests of developers over those of residents. Courts often refuse to hear eviction cases because of pressure by local officials. As a result, people who challenge their eviction cannot properly pursue their claims through arbitration or in court. Where residents do receive compensation, it is often inadequate. Human Rights Watch said that national legal reforms have had minimal impact in reversing this situation.

ISSUE 4:
THE DEATH PENALTY

It is said that in China the death penalty targets poor and marginalised groups, including ethnic minorities, migrants, political dissidents, and so-called 'separatists'. Standards seem to vary in the application of the death penalty and sentences often depend on the political climate and timing. Executions tend to be clustered around national holidays such as the Chinese New Year. According to Amnesty International, they have even commemorated International Children's Day by holding grim rallies around the execution of prisoners.

'Strike Hard' campaigns are periodically launched by local leaders as a means of cracking down on crimes such as drug-related crimes or corruption. During the campaigns, prisoners may meet much harsher punishments than would be given under normal circumstances. Executions rocket during these campaigns. Many of those executed are sentenced at public 'execution rallies' where thousands of spectators witness the sentencing of criminals who are then led out of the arena and are taken directly to the execution ground.

Organ Trafficking

Amnesty International is very concerned about reports of the sale of organs taken from executed prisoners without permission. While officials deny the practice, accusations have been made that prisoners are given blood thinners and are executed in a way which would preserve the organs.

Reduction in executions?

In November 2004 China's official media said that the country was in the final stages of revising its law on the death penalty. Prominent lawyers believe that the number of executions carried out could be reduced by up to one-third. The number of people executed in China each year is regarded as a state secret. A figure which has recently been discussed among academics is 10,000, but some believe even that is understated.

ISSUE 5: **THE CHINESE LAOGAI**

The Laogai is the name given to the network of prisons, labour camps and 'hospitals' which exist in China. The system works on two principles: hard labour and political thought reform. In China all prisoners are forced to work. The idea is that through forced labour prisoners will reform their ideas and will embrace Communism and the socialist system. Human rights are ignored and torture, squalor and degradation are the norm.

In recent years the Chinese Communist Party has attempted to create the impression that the Laogai is simply a prison system for detaining, punishing and reforming convicted criminals. It was for this reason that the term Laogai (which means reform through labour) was officially changed to Jianyu (which means prison). A change of name has not impressed the International Community who regard the Laogai as a tool of political repression, used to silence all voices of political dissent throughout China.

The Chinese leaders no longer arrest individuals for 'counter revolutionary crimes': instead most political prisoners are arrested for crimes such as 'subverting state power', 'stealing state secrets', 'hooliganism' or 'protesting without a permit'. This has made it more difficult to estimate the number of political prisoners held in Chinese prisons.

Individuals can be held for up to three years in Re-education (Laojiao) Camps with no trial or sentencing procedures of any kind. All that is necessary is an order from the Chinese Public Security Bureau. This order can be extended if the authorities decide that the individual is not fully 'reformed'. All prisoners in the Laogai are forced to work, often in highly unsafe conditions

including working in mines and with toxic chemicals. The camps, therefore, contribute to the national economy.

Prisoner of Conscience Mao Hengfeng in China

Mao Hengfeng is currently held in a 'Re-education through Labour' (RTL) facility in Shanghai. She has petitioned the state authorities for many years over her coerced abortion, her right to work and other basic rights. In April 2004 she was sentenced to eighteen months RTL by the Shanghai Municipal Public Security Bureau. Mao Hengfeng has reportedly been subjected to torture and ill-treatment in the labour camp. In October 2004, she was suspended from a ceiling and severely beaten. In November 2004 her wrists and ankles were bound with leather straps and her limbs pulled in opposite directions. This continued for two days, during which time she was also denied food. She has also reportedly been held in solitary confinement for short periods and strapped down on her bed for hours on end. It is further reported that she has been force-fed with an unidentified substance that is turning her mouth black.

Amnesty International considers Mao Hengfeng a prisoner of conscience and calls for her immediate and unconditional release. It is also urging the Chinese authorities to abolish RTL altogether as the formal criminal justice system already provides a sufficient basis to punish a broad range of minor offences.

ISSUE 6: **RELIGIOUS CONTROL**

While the Chinese constitution guarantees freedom of religious belief, the government maintains close supervision over religion and religious activities within a complex system of legal mechanisms and enforcement actions. In March 2005 the government introduced new regulations which, it claimed, provide more legal protection for religious believers and safeguard religious freedom in China. However, this only applies to the recognised religions and those which belong to the Patriotic Religious Associations.

The government has created four categories of religious groups: officially sanctioned religions, unregistered groups, cults, and feudal superstitions. Of the more than 200 million religious believers in China, only about 140 million belong to registered religious groups.

The Chinese government officially recognises four religions—Buddhism, Islam, Christianity and Taoism. Authorities require the faithful to belong to 'patriotic' churches, mosques and temples. The Vatican does not recognise the 'patriotic' Catholic Church in China, choosing to support the six to ten million Roman Catholics who take part in underground services in 'house churches.'

China's record of religious tolerance in Tibet is also questionable. During the Cultural Revolution of the 1960s thousands of Buddhist temples and monasteries were destroyed and hundreds of Buddhist clerics were detained. The Dalai Lama, the spiritual head of Tibetan Buddhism, fled to exile in India in 1959 following a failed uprising. The Chinese government has also ignored protests by the Dalai Lama and others.

Falun Gong

Falun Gong is a controversial Chinese Qigong (chi kung) practice which is supposed to improve the mind, body and spirit. Its leaders claim that they are a peaceful law-abiding group.

Falun Gong has been persecuted in mainland China since July 1999. Some argue that this happened because the number of Falun Gong practitioners in China grew to a larger number than the membership of the Communist Party of China. However, others argue that groups similar to Falun Gong have suffered less persecution (in mainland China there are twelve Christian churches currently banned and labelled as 'evil sects').

The persecution of the group is currently the subject of complaints by many worldwide human rights groups. The PRC government claims that Falun Gong is an evil cult. Even before the crackdown, many scientists in China had warned that there was no scientific evidence to show that Falun Gong is beneficial for health.

Falun Gong's membership has fallen in China as it is classified as an illegal organisation. It now operates underground and its members are still being arrested. In January 2006, Liu Ruping, a lawyer in Shandong province, was sent to a labour camp for publishing a public statement supporting Falun Gong. He had been seized by the Public Security Bureau in October 2005 and sent to 'transformation' classes to force him to give up his beliefs. He refused to be reformed and was sentenced to the Wangan Labour camp for fifteen months of 'Labour Education'.

ISSUE 6: **HUMAN RIGHTS AND WOMEN**

Issues regarding women and human rights have already been considered when looking at family planning matters. However, family planning is not the only subject which merits consideration.

The Chinese Constitution and other laws provide equal rights for men and women in all spheres of life, including ownership of property, inheritance, and educational opportunities. Equality between the sexes has been a part of the agenda from the early days of the People's Republic of China.

Abduction and Trafficking of Women

Trafficking and sale of women as brides or into prostitution is a serious problem in certain parts of China, and Chinese women have been sold into brothels in South-east Asia. The Chinese government has introduced various laws to stop the sale of women.

Until recently, the authorities have not prosecuted men who purchased women as wives. Consequently, the trade has continued unabated. Official action to rescue victims of trafficking is generally initiated only if a complaint is made by the woman or her family. Local officials often turn a blind eye, even formally registering marriages into which the woman has been sold.

Discrimination in Employment and Education

Open discrimination against women in employment and education has continued to grow during the period of reform.

According to Chinese government surveys, women's salaries have been found to average 77% of men's, and most women employed in industry work in low skilled and low paying jobs. An estimated 70 to 80% of workers laid off as a result of downsizing in factories have been women and although women make up 38% of the workforce, they are 60% of the unemployed. At job fairs, employers openly advertise positions for men only, and university campus recruiters often state that they will not hire women. Employers justify such discrimination by saying that they cannot afford the benefits they are required to provide for pregnant women, nursing mothers and infants.

Although China has a law saying that primary education is compulsory, increasing numbers of rural girls are not being sent to school. Rural parents often do not want to 'waste' money on school fees for girls who will 'belong' to another family when they marry. According to official statistics, about 70% of illiterates in China are female.